A Smoldering Wick

A Vietnam Vet Chronicles His Life
from Hell to Redemption

Ron Brandon

*"A bruised reed he will not break,
and a smoldering wick he will not snuff out.
In faithfulness he will bring forth justice"*— (Isaiah 42:3 NIV)

ENDORSEMENTS

From the rice fields of Vietnam to prison to a ministry in prisons that has touched thousands of men, Ron Brandon's life exemplifies the true and authentic meaning of grace. Ron's life, much like the life of the Apostle Paul, is a life God has used to be a pattern of long suffering for others to follow. If God can take this Marine combat veteran who left the service of his country to a service of sin and crime, He can use anyone. Ron's raw honesty, his love for Jesus, his love for those in prison, and his years of dedicated service to the ministry to which God has called him makes this book not a trumped up story but a living testimony of the power of the gospel that is still working in the author today. *A Smoldering Wick* is a must read if one wants to know about the power of the Gospel.
Pastor Bob MacGregor
Lead Pastor
City Harvest Church
Vancouver, WA

As a former officer in the U.S. Navy, assigned to Vietnam during 1965, I know what Ron went through. This book is an open explanation of how PTSD has affected so many, including myself, and it was so refreshing to see how God set him free. It is an insightful read, and demonstrates how veterans and ex-offenders can escape the traps of an elusive enemy and, the past, no matter how traumatic they have been! Courageously raw and real!!
Michael G. Langsdorf, JD; MBA
University of Washington
Former Professor, Marylhurst University; Clark College, Vancouver, WA
Attorney at Law (ret.)
Vietnam Veteran
U.S. Navy

Ron's story is an example of overcoming the trappings of the world to lead a life of service to a forgiving God. As a Viet Nam Veteran, I understand how difficult life can be when you have experienced the horrors of combat. Ron overcame obstacles, over and over again, from a difficult childhood through an unpopular war, to the lure of the criminal life, to become the man of God that he is today. Each time the Lord picked him up and dusted him off, because our Lord was not through with him. I had the pleasure and some of the grief of knowing Ron through part of this amazing transformation. God knew the value of Ron's life experiences in assisting those who had also fallen.
Jerry Keen "Doc"
CMDCM, USN (ret)
Director, Point Man Ministries, Vancouver, WA chapter

I have partnered with Ron and Donna in doing events in prisons for nearly a decade and have seen close to one thousand prisoners come to Christ through our band's outreach. Their passion and heart for those in prison has been a shining example to me of what it truly means to walk beside the broken. Their faithful and steady presence is a constant reminder to those they minister to that they will never leave them nor forsake them. Reading Ron's story has given me a greater compassion for what he and other Veterans have walked through and continue to walk through in search of healing and peace from their PTSD. Having worked through years of my own childhood trauma and abuse, I can stand beside them and say with confidence that here is hope, healing and peace as we press into God and the resources of His people!
Kate White, Kate White Band
musicthatmattersnw@gmail.com

I have just finished reading "A Smoldering Wick", a perfect title to a heart wrenching story & life of my friend and brother in Christ, Ron Brandon. It is a MUST READ! It was emotionally searing! My heart agonized as I saw all he went through, from the horrors of Viet Nam to surviving the evils and violence of maximum security penitentiaries. These prisons are some of the worst in the country. This I know personally as I ministered in them. All that he so honestly expressed, the mental and emotional daily damage that he suffered, unforgettably impacted me. The difficulty of his family childhood...the generational curse of alcoholism...the nightmares of the war, were all triggers that led to Ron's choices of crime and prison. All of the pain & suffering--the remorse, guilt and shame that Ron carried-- affected me deeply. I love my brother...and his precious wife Donna, as I ministered with them for years. I only knew the Ron Brandon that God redeemed, set free, and healed of all those things that haunted him. I see the awesome grace of God, God's everlasting love. I have seen inmates that were led to Jesus who loved and respected Ron. Yes, he became a new creation as it tells us in 2 Corinthians 5:17. God sure used for good what the devil meant for evil. The Ron that I know is a gentle giant & I am blessed to know Ron & Donna. I am honored to be included in this awesome book and to be called their friend. Lord bless you two. Semper Fi my Brother. In His Love & Grip,
Mel Novak...Soul-dier for Christ
Former Professional Baseball Player
Actor
Prison Minister and skid row chaplain
Los Angeles, CA

Ron has given us a vivid description of the horrors of war. More importantly, he has given us myriad examples of God's steadfast love for us even when we have had no love for Him. A great read for anyone who wants to be lifted up to a higher place!
Woody Ennis
President
Asset Protection Professionals Inc.
Lt. Col. U.S. Army (ret.)

A Smoldering Wick details the life of an American born in the middle of the twentieth century. From sweet innocence to the horrors of war, from white middle class suburbs to homeless shelters, from depression and despair to redemption and transformation, the true stories touch the heart of our generation. " Cameo" celebrities appear in historical context. We get the impression that Ron was always where the action was! And Ron still is living the abundant life he found in Jesus Christ. You will find this book compelling and entertaining. It will touch you!
Dr Greg Romine
Called to Rescue
Vancouver, WA
(Dr Greg Romine has served as an International Evangelist, Pastor, Church Planter, Educator for the last 47 years. With innovative ministries addressing some of the most difficult issues of our times. "Called to Rescue" is a ministry in partnership with Dr Cyndi Romine, reaching children who are victims of sex traffickers. They locate the perpetrators and connect with law enforcement for assistance with the rescue and then help the children to recover.)

Ron's service to country and God has been present in ministry and military for many years. His book *A Smoldering Wick* is a testimony and outstanding example of life in both good and difficult times. This book is from the heart and will impact millions of readers.
Ron and his wife Donna, continue to minister to the unreached, leading them to Christ and simultaneously meeting humanitarian needs the new converts may have. His commitment to serving God and country is a total commitment just as in a marriage commitment, for better or for worse.
I met Ron after he was in the Marines and after he spent time in jail. Fast forwarding, he now is in prison ministry, church and for the last five years, has served as a fellow officer in Full Gospel Business Men's Fellowship in America. (FGBMFA) His strength and commitment continue as a marine and a warrior for Christ because, as Ron so succinctly put it, "God never left me nor did He forsake me."
Arnold Rekate
CPA
President, Vancouver, WA chapter of Full Gospel Business Men's Fellowship in America (FGBMFA)

This book is truly an amazing and powerful story of how God's Love and Redemption have flowed through Ron's life to give him the strength that he needed to overcome a difficult and tortuous past. A gripping first person account of his struggles with Post Traumatic Stress Disorder and substance abuse that resulted in numerous instances where he repeatedly hurt himself and those around him, Ron gives insight into the life of a soldier, a criminal often on the run and, ultimately, a man of God who stopped running and committed himself to helping others who were walking the same path he knew so well. His account of personal transformation is a grace-filled testimony that is a great example of how God never gives up on any of us and how hope and faith can always overcome whatever trial we endure. Thank you, Ron, for your service to our country, for sharing your story

and for your Ministry of reaching out to those imprisoned by their transgressions and working to help them break free to experience the saving power of our Lord.
Tom Iberle, Executive Director
Friends of the Carpenter
Vancouver, WA

This book contains a heart-wrenching story that plummets us along a journey down into the pitch black of sin and despicable acts in war and peace at their lowest point, and then sweeps us upward into the glorious light of the interventions of our Father in heaven, full of grace and truth. Powerful, dramatic and profound. If I were a vet or an inmate or ex-offender or just a lost soul, I would feel compelled to consider knowing the Lord of my life, and I think I would make a personal response to the message of hope and peace in Christ that resounds in this story.
Forrest Brandon
San Rafael Police Dept. Ca. (ret)
Crime Investigator (ret.)
Marine Corp Sgt.
Vietnam Combat Veteran
(Brother of Ron)

A SMOLDERING WICK

Copyright © 2015 by Ron Brandon

All rights reserved. No portion of this book may be reproduced in any form or by any means, except for brief quotations in reviews, without written permission from the publisher.

Published by Nancy Meacham-Cole
11407 NE 65th Avenue, Vancouver, WA 98686

Scripture quotations are from the following sources:

Holy Bible, New International Version®, NIV® Copyright ©1973, 1978, 1984, 2011 by Biblica, Inc.® All rights reserved worldwide.

Holy Bible, New King James Version, Copyright ©1982 by Thomas Nelson Publishers

A Smoldering Wick can be ordered through booksellers and at www.createspace.com.

Because of the dynamic nature of the internet, any web addresses or links contained in this book may have changed since publication and may no longer be valid.

ISBN-13:978-1519418395 International Market (CreateSpace-Assigned)
ISBN-10:1519418396 USA Market

Printed in the United States

A PRAYER AUTHORED BY THOMAS JEFFERSON; READ BY RON AT A CLARK COUNTY COMMISSIONER'S BUSINESS MEETING

Almighty God, who has given us this good land for our heritage, we humbly ask you that we may always prove ourselves a people mindful of your favor and glad to do your will. Bless our land with honorable ministry, sound learning, and pure manners. Save us from violence, discord and confusion, from pride and arrogance and from every evil way. Defend our liberties and fashion into one united people, the multitude brought here out of many nationalities and tongues.

Endow with your spirit of wisdom, those whom in your name we entrust the authority of government, that there may be justice and peace at home, and that through obedience to your law, we may show forth your praise among the nations of the earth. In time of prosperity fill our hearts with thankfulness, and in the day of trouble, suffer not our trust in you to fail; all of which we ask through Jesus Christ our Lord. Amen!

Thomas Jefferson; Washington D.C.; 1801

ACKNOWLEDGEMENTS

First of all, I want to thank the Lord God of the universe and my savior Jesus Christ, who gave me life in the first place, has sustained me, and who delivers me from death continually. I also want to thank God for all the wonderful people He has brought into my life.

This book would not be possible without the assistance of Ms. Julie M. Zander, Mr. Bob Goldsby, Mrs. Nancy Meacham-Cole, Mr. Forrest D. Brandon, and Donna Schafte-Brandon, who were invaluable in the process of bringing this book into existence. Thank you so much everyone for all your labor of love.

I want to thank each one of my children also for their encouragement and help in this project: Ronda my daughter, who talked to me many times on the phone, sent lovely greeting cards, and visited; Ron Jr. who has been a steady, strong support and offered his love and forgiveness as well as technical and web support; and my son Daniel, working hard to take care of his family, showing a great heart of fatherhood for his own children, overcoming high hurdles of the past, and becoming the fine young man that I am so proud of today!

My children are 'bright shining stars' in God's kingdom, greatly loved and very special, unique and destined for great things in the future! I am a blessed man to have such strong, persevering, determined, bright and thoughtful children. Thank you for forgiving me and allowing me to still be 'Pops.' I love you!

DEDICATION

This book is dedicated to three people who have been instrumental in my own growth and success over many years. Without them this story could not have been told. With all of my heart, I want to thank them for all their dedication and assistance, their faithfulness and compassion, during my journey toward freedom.

The first is my wife Donna Schafte-Brandon, a retired school teacher, my true helpmate and best friend. I would not be here without her loving kindness and steady belief in me.

The second is my brother Forrest, a retired police officer, who has also been a prayer warrior extraordinary. Forrest was a good Marine, a great cop, a leader, a shining example of a man of God, and is one of my heroes today.

The third is my former father-in-law Rev. James C. Walton, now deceased, who was an active minister for over fifty years. He never gave up on me and told me that one day he would see me in heaven.

All three are unique and special people, gifted, and highly esteemed by the God whom I serve. May God bless them all!

Ron

TABLE OF CONTENTS

Endorsements ii

A Prayer authored by Thomas Jefferson; read by Ron at A Clark county Commissioner's business meeting vii

Acknowledgements viii

Dedication ix

Table of Contents x

Preface xiii

About the Author xiv

1. 1

   Growing Up 1

2. 5

   The Brandon Family 5

3. 29

   The Marines 29

....37

Military Service is a Brandon Family Tradition: Photo Gallery 37

4. 40

   Vietnam: A Life Changed Forever 40

5. 56

   Casualties and Ambushes 56

6. 71

   Return to The World 71

7. 79

   Arrested 79

8. 84

   San Quentin-The Big House 84

9.	93
A Revolving Door	93
10.	102
Released Again	102
11.	108
Stevenson, Washington	108
12.	123
Last Time in Prison	123
13.	126
Introducing Donna, My Future Wife	126
14.	130
New Beginnings	130
15.	141
Together in Ministry	141
16.	153
Serving Others; Give to Grow	153
17.	159
Prophetic Words Bringing Confirmation of God's Call	159
18.	163
Worms and Redemption	163
19.	168
Miraculous Healings	168
Bibliography	**174**
Appendix I	**177**
Interesting Thoughts and Facts About Vietnam Vets	177
Appendix II	**179**
Post-Traumatic Stress Disorder	179

- Appendix III 180
  - More on PTSD with Audie Murphy 180
- APPENDIX IV 181
  - The Whole Armor of God 181
- APPENDIX V 182
  - Eutychus Housing Article from The Columbian 182
- APPENDIX VI 183
  - Newspaper Article on U.S. Rep. Brian Baird 184
  - regarding Eutychus Ministries. 184
- APPENDIX VII 185
  - Volunteer of the Year Nomination 185
- APPENDIX VIII 186
  - Prophetic Assembly 2015 186
- APPENDIX IX 189
  - Robert Lightfoot Smith's Testimony 189
  - Miraculously Healed of Hepatitis C 189
- APPENDIX X 190
  - Copy of Spoken Tribute to Ron and Donna by Larch Inmate 190
- APPENDIX XI 192
  - Ron's Essay on the "Three Strikes You're Out" Law 192

PREFACE

The story you are about to read is true. Although perhaps hard to believe in some parts, all of it actually took place, with slight bits of poetic license.

Truth is stranger than fiction sometimes. During my youth, during combat as a Marine in Vietnam, during the cops and robber days, and even during the redemption period of my life, one thing is very apparent; Someone provided divine protection and escape from certain death, repeatedly.

It's a chronicle of accidents, mistakes, and abject failure. It's the brutal truth of struggling to overcome adversity, to grow in maturity, and to become the person God intended all along. It's the good, bad, and the ugly.

This is the story of a Father who will not stop loving and caring for a son who is rebellious, willful, lawless, fractured, and self-destructive. It is about the One who never fails, who will not let go; whose mercy and grace are truly as high as the heavens themselves. It is a true story with a great ending. The Father's great heart of love wins out! The son is set free and returns to his Father's house! "Semper Fidelis!"

ABOUT THE AUTHOR

Ron Brandon had some rough bumps in life from the very start. Growing up in a dysfunctional household with an alcoholic father, he went into the world wholly unprepared for the catastrophic emotional impact and psychological horrors of a savage war in Southeast Asia

Ron graduated from a small town high school and attended a local junior college. He had above average grades and in many respects appeared to be an average young adult male venturing into the challenges and responsibilities of adulthood. At 19 marriage and family were on his mind.

He attended church for the first seventeen years of his life and seemed to be a well-adjusted maturing young man with solid moral values. Then he went into the Marine Corps.

The Marines did a great job turning Ron into a fighting man, with a warrior heart, teaching him many useful skills. They taught him the value of discipline, honor, courage, loyalty, and faithfulness, making him a Marine for life.

However, nothing in his life was enough. He came back from Vietnam feeling lost, numb, confused, and angry with severe PTSD which nearly destroyed him. The child in Ron was gone forever. It was as if something sinister had pierced his soul and taken him captive. Something was still missing. He felt like he had a hole in his heart. He felt lost until God came along and set him free.

After many years of suffering disappointment, imprisonment, and a failed marriage, Ron underwent a radical change in his life and he went on to earn his Master's Degree in Divinity, serving as an ordained Chaplain in Veteran organizations and prison systems of Oregon and Washington State. He was also invited to become an adjunct professor of Triune Bible University.

Today Ron is married and a past and current business owner, and counts himself greatly blessed of God. He loves to teach and preach in the prisons wherever God opens the doors.

Ron serves as Vice President of the local Vancouver chapter of Full Gospel Business Men's Fellowship in America and is available for speaking and teaching.

He is currently a member of: Veterans of Foreign Wars; Marine Corps League; 40 et 8; American Legion; Vietnam Veterans of America; Patriot Guard Riders, and Disabled American Veterans.

Ron as Two-Year-Old Ronnie

1
Growing Up

The front door burst open. Dad staggered in, mumbling, glaring at Mom who sat on the couch, mending another rip in my pants while she watched the black-and-white television. I stood in the kitchen, having just finished my eleventh grade homework.

"What're you still doing up, Ronnie?" he bellowed.

Stumbling toward the closet, he rifled inside as Mom and I glanced at each other, then to Dad's stooped back. I finished my glass of milk and set it beside the sink. Mom nodded toward my bedroom, so I walked down the hallway, glancing over my shoulder.

Dad yanked a hunting rifle out and pounded in ammo.

"I'm gonna blow your head off woman!" He lifted the gun, aiming it toward Mom.

I dropped my book to the floor and rushed forward.

"Dad!" I held up my hands. "Hey, Dad."

He whirled toward me, aiming the gun.

"Shut up Ronnie!"

I heard a bedroom door open behind me. Glancing over my shoulder, I saw two-year-old Ferral and seven-year-old Kelly. I whispered to them, "Stay in your room." My fifteen-year-old brother, Forrest, slept through the whole thing.

Dad cursed his wife, who would not stop talking, while he was waving the rifle in his upraised arm. Mom reached for the gun while standing beside him.

"Calm down, Bill," she said.

He whipped away from her, growling as he stumbled toward the couch and collapsed. The gun clattered to the floor. Mom crept toward his prone body, grabbed the gun, and hid it in the kitchen.

I stood there, helpless, leaning over the father I loved and hated, respected and feared.

***

Many years later…

I felt a hand on my shoulder. Startled, I jumped to my feet and whirled, fists clenched and upraised.

"Hey, man, whoa!" The bartender backed up, both hands lifted. "Calm down. Hey, it's time for you to go sleep it off. You didn't seem to hear me. You need to leave now."

I lowered my arms, rubbing my eyes with one hand, mumbling as I pulled a bill from my pocket with the other. I tossed a buck on the bar, swallowed the last bit of beer in the stein, and sauntered out the door.

I glanced around the parking lot, and then crawled behind the wheel of my souped-up emerald green '69 GTO Pontiac, known as the 'Judge'. I revved the engine and tore out of the parking lot, tires squealing. I sped onto Highway 101, pressing the gas pedal to the floor, zipping past cars.

The speedometer shot to 110. Wipers swished rain from the windshield. I cursed aloud as I spied a swirling kaleidoscope of flashing lights in the rearview mirror. Three, four, five cop cars on my tail: The Sausalito police, Mill Valley cops, Corte Madera sheriff's deputies, and California Highway Patrol.

"You stinking pigs!" I thought aloud.

Standing water shimmered ahead. As I plowed into it, the Pontiac's wheels lost traction. I heard water splashing the floorboard under my feet as the car spun, like an elephant sliding on ice.

"Whoa!" The car began to hydroplane.

I went into a left hand turn and spun 360 degrees full circle, before I felt the wheels grip the wet pavement. I sped forward. Wow! An unseen hand had to have been guiding the car to come out perfectly! Speeding up a hill, I saw the flashing red and blue lights in my mirror fade as the cops slowed at the standing water covering sixty yards of roadway.

"I lost them!" I said.

Dropping over a ridge, I took the San Rafael exit onto the winding road that led to the drive-in theater. Then I spotted flashing lights ahead. Cop cars blocked the road. Officers stood with guns aimed at me and my car. I stomped on the brakes, screeching to a halt. *I doubt this will end well.*

Stepping out of the car with my hands up, I squinted into the sunlight. I looked at all the officers, hoping to see a familiar face. Sure enough, there was someone I knew well.

Forrest Brandon, Policeman

"Hey, Forrest," I said, grinning toward my younger brother, dressed in his San Rafael police uniform.

"You know this guy?" One of the police officers tipped his head my direction.

Officer Forrest "Felony" Brandon nodded, "He's my brother. I got this."

He jerked me around to face my car, patted me down, and then pulled my arms behind my back, clamping handcuffs on my wrists. All the other cops got into their cars and peeled off. My brother got the nick name 'Felony Brandon' from making so many felony arrests over his career.

"C'mon, Ron." He led me toward his patrol car, opened the back door and bent me forward so I wouldn't hit my head as I climbed inside. He drove me to jail and booked me on a charge of reckless driving. He dropped a bunch of other charges that could have been filed.

I'd been drinking, but I wasn't drunk, so I didn't lose my license.

***

Perhaps my risk-taking started as a child. I remember another chase in my youth that left me on the losing end.

Growing up in northern California in the 1950s, my brother Forrest and I spent most of our time outside as kids. We shot marbles, explored the woods, roller-skated along sidewalks, and rode bicycles around Marin City, an unincorporated community of wooden houses built hastily for World War II servicemen and Navy shipyard workers. We climbed tall trees, pretending they were sailing ships jostled by wind and waves, and hiked the hillsides of the Marin Headlands. At the top, we sat on cardboard boxes, our make-shift sleds, and schussed down steep grassy slopes at more than twenty miles an hour, crashing at the bottom, only to repeat the adventure. We broke off stinkweed stocks to wield as swords, one day envisioning ourselves as daring knights and the next as jungle explorers spearing wild animals. We played cops and robbers, cowboys and Indians, Hide-and-seek.

When we stayed inside, we watched *Tarzan* and *Hopalong Cassidy* on television; Mom even dressed us like cowboys and gave us little *Lone Ranger* cap guns, red *Howdy Doody* kerchiefs, and a little toy pony. She also took us to rodeos. But most days we raced outside seeking yet another adventure. Life was all about worms and spiders and shoving dirt in our mouths. We let a tarantula as big as my hand crawl over us. Praying mantises fascinated us.

Forrest and I loved to play cat-and-mouse, after the cat and mouse cartoon characters *Tom and Jerry*. As the oldest by two years, I was always Tom, the old cat, while Forrest scampered quickly like the mouse, Jerry. I gave him a little head start and then ran as fast as I could, tackling him when I could, pounding him a bit as I did.

One day, I chased him through cypress trees on one of these hillsides. As I closed in, Forrest skidded, grabbed a sapling and swung midair to the right. I was running so fast I couldn't stop or grasp the tree to follow him. I flew right off a thirty-foot dirt and rock cliff! My feet spun in the air before I plunged down the hillside, toppling end over end, bashing my head on a rock outcrop as I tumbled. I landed feet first until my knees buckled and I splattered onto the asphalt of a paved road. Fortunately, no cars were coming.

Blood flowed from the gash on my head, from elbows, knees, and even my nose. Forrest thought he had killed me. He slid down the embankment created when workers built the road and found me sitting, clutching my hand to my head, bloodied and bawling. Forrest helped me get home. I didn't break any bones and never saw a doctor. Mom patched me up and chewed us out for carelessness.

That cat Tom was always getting into trouble. Just like me.

2
The Brandon Family

My dad, Forrest (Bill) Brandon, stood almost six feet tall with black hair and blue eyes and was as strong as Popeye. He grew up poor in Oklahoma and attended a small church with his mother and sisters until his father died at a young age. Thinking he needed male influences, his mother asked two uneducated hillbilly uncles in the back woods to raise him, but they were abusive alcoholics who chained him to a tree overnight in a region rife with wild animals. He learned to shoot game if he wanted to eat. He became a crack shot with a rifle. Once when he was running barefoot, since he had no shoes for many years, he stepped on a broken beer bottle. It sliced into his foot cutting him up badly. It took a lot stitches to close up that nasty wound.

Dad played sports in school, excelling in basketball. His senior year the six-man basketball team he played on from Sumner, Oklahoma won the state championship.

After he graduated from high school, he joined the Army at seventeen with his mother's permission. After training he shipped out for Europe in World War II. While stationed in England, his unit was staging for the Normandy invasion when he contracted rheumatic fever and nearly died. Recovering in a London hospital, he was blown from his bed on two separate occasions as German bombs pummeled the city. Shipped stateside, he received an honorable discharge at Fort Baker, north of the Presidio in San Francisco. He never talked about his military service.

At a military dance hosted by the United Service Organization, (USO) Dad met my mother, Comoretta (Rita) Johnson, who had joined her sister Bertina and brother-in-law, Sgt. Lee Madison, a decorated Army veteran, for the evening. Mom was working as a secretary in San Francisco at the time. Dad was twenty-one; she was nineteen. They fell in love and married.

Ron's Aunts Billie Jean and Willadean on left; his parents Rita (Topsy) and Bill on right at USO dinner 1945.

My dad's name was Forrest, but most of his friends called him "Wild Bill." My mom always called him Bill. He called her Topsy, but most of her friends referred to her as Rita.

Dad, a hardworking, hard-drinking man, was the nicest guy on the planet when he was sober. When he drank, he got mean. He could tear somebody's head off.

He left the Army in 1946, the year I was born, and moved from Fort Baker to Sausalito, where I lived in my early years. He drove a Greyhound bus for a dozen years and later a lumber delivery truck.

My mom was a knockout with auburn hair, blue eyes, and a good figure. When Dad was a Teamster, he entered her into a beauty contest where she won first place. With a crown on her head, she had her photo taken with Rocky Marciano, light heavyweight champion of the world. Mom worked as a waitress at the Alta Mira Hotel in Sausalito, and later as a car hop at the Circle Drive-In at Corte Madera and the King Cotton in San Rafael.

My mom's mother, Grandma Florence Nuss, owned Flo's Diner, a popular restaurant with a big soda fountain on Main Street across from the central city park in Sausalito, California. I think she was married three times. My mother's father was a devout Christian man who died at the young age of thirty-nine. Her second husband was an Army major and her last marriage was to a railroad engineer named Homer Taneyhill to whom she was married over forty years.

Grandma Florence J. N.Taneyhill

Mom used to take Forrest and me to Grandma's restaurant for lunch and afterward we played in the park.

One day when I was about six I wanted a milkshake. Since I knew the way to Grandma's soda shop, I ran down the street toward her restaurant. As I began to dart across Main Street, a big police officer in full uniform snatched me into his arms, just as a car swept past. He probably saved my life. Imagine that. I was saved by a cop.

Later, Mom and Dad had three more kids: my brother Forrest, who is just two years younger than me, my sister Kelly, who is ten years younger, and my brother Ferral, who is fifteen years younger.

***

My folks really did love and care about us, but they never said those words or hugged and cuddled us. My mom didn't go out of her way to say affectionate things. They never had good role models for parents, especially my dad, who was raised by two uncles who drank and beat him. Mom and Dad tried to show us their love by buying us presents on special holidays. As the oldest child, I was their guinea pig.

When we were little, Mom took us to the Sausalito Assembly of God, where Forrest and I both performed in Christmas plays. Later Mom and Dad visited church only on Christmas and Easter. Mom was always working Sundays, but she made us go to church. When my mom was a child, she and her sister Bertina sang in the church choir. Both of them had become Christians at a young age. After all, they had plenty of opportunities to know Jesus, as their father was very devout, always in church on Sunday.

Dad worked during the day and Mom at nights as a waitress at the Alta Mira Hotel. We didn't have a lot of money, although we never went hungry. Mom scraped together money from her tips to buy school clothes for us. We ate meals at the large wood dining room table. Mom kept an orderly house; it was never messy. She liked everything in its place.

We seldom visited the doctor and never the dentist. My teeth were rotten, which kept me from fully developing. I just stayed skinny as a bean pole. But we couldn't afford to pay for medical or dental care.

One time when Dad climbed onto the roof to fix the antenna and clear up our television picture, the antenna fell off the roof and even though I tried to duck, it hit me on the front of the head. The lump swelled as big as a goose egg. Mom simply put an ice pack on it. She never did take me to the doctor about my head injury. On another occasion, while riding with my Dad's father, my grandfather Ralph, he suddenly hit the brakes and threw me into the full metal dash. Hitting my head hard, the impact knocked my eyes crossed, and for about 10 minutes my eyes would not focus. It seemed like I gravitated toward head injuries of some kind as a kid.

Ron and Forrest

In the evenings, we would sit beside Dad and listen to radio programs like *The Whistler,* a murder-drama where a deep-voiced narrator described a guy walking along a cold windy pier, whistling with foghorns in the distance. We snuggled closer to Mom as she read books like *Moby Dick*, *The Adventures of Huckleberry Finn*, *The Adventures of Tom Sawyer*, *Treasure Island*, and *Girl of the Limberlost* to Forrest and me.

Mom drove Forrest and me on summer field trips all over the United States, especially to the South where she and Dad both grew up—Oklahoma, Arkansas, Mississippi, and Missouri. Dad was usually working, but he joined us a couple of times, such as during the trip to Reno, Nevada, where he hit the casinos while Mom took us to Virginia City and historic landmarks in the region.

We never visited the eastern seaboard, but we traveled to New Mexico, Arizona, Nevada, Colorado, and many other states. We stopped at state and national parks to see the sites and learn the history, enhancing what we learned in school. We visited the California missions, Sutter's Fort in Sacramento, and gold and silver mining towns.

I especially remember one trip to Placerville where we had a near-fatal car crash. Mom was obeying the speed limit like always as she drove down the freeway in our station wagon at approximately sixty-five miles an hour. She went down a long descent out of the Sierras into the Sacramento foothills as I reclined in the back seat, reading. Forrest sat in the front seat beside Mom.

All of a sudden, we heard a loud pop and the car swerved to the left, spinning across all four lanes, barreling over the grass dividing eastbound from westbound traffic, careening into oncoming traffic. Mom fought to control the car, pulling hard to the left to keep it from screeching to the right. Three or four times the car shot across those highway lanes, zigzagging right and left, heading for forty-foot sheer drop-offs on either side until Mom yanked the steering wheel hard, struggling to keep the car on the road and away from the cliffs.

She slammed on the brakes as she pulled hard to the right, aiming for a small bank. The car spun out, drove up the bank and stopped. Trembling, we scrambled out of the car to see a blown tire and a few dents and scratches in the grill and right fender. Nobody was hurt.

A dozen cars stopped and drivers checked to see if we were injured. They commended Mom on her excellent driving.

"I didn't control the car,' she told a friend, recounting the terrifying incident. 'It was like an invisible hand reached down from heaven and took the wheel."

It's amazing we didn't strike another car head-on, but each time we veered into the oncoming lane there was a gap in traffic. God was looking out for our family that day!

Closer to home, the folks drove us to San Bernardino to visit Dad's mom and step-father, Jay and Ina Mae Ralph, and their son, Loy. Other times we drove to Porterville and Fresno to visit Mom's relatives, including Uncles A.L. Johnson and Fate Johnson. We really liked our cousins the Johnson boys. They had some great looking Studebaker cars all fixed up, regular hot rods. They had a billy goat in the back yard and we used to try to ride him for a while before he threw us off. What fun we had with our cousins.

Mom also took us on shorter excursions—ferry boat rides between Sausalito and San Francisco to visit the zoo, Morrison Planetarium, Golden Gate Park, Fisherman's Wharf, and The Fun House Amusement Park on Highway 1 at the Cliff House. It featured a hall of mirrors, a large disk you tried to stay on as it spun, and a long high roller coaster we rode. We loved it! She always bought us cotton candy and other goodies.

Mom and Dad were good friends with an ex-Navy seaplane pilot named Don Holt, who worked for Don Law who operated an air taxi service in the San Francisco Bay area. Every three or four months, Mom would drive us to see Don and we'd fly above the bay and over Angel Island, Alcatraz, the Golden Gate Bridge and San Quentin Prison. It was an ominous looking fortress! Don, a very talented pilot, gave her a discount on the flights. It was a blast taking off and landing on the water.

Both Mom and Dad worked hard to provide for their family. We never faced homelessness or hunger. They bought us tons of presents at Christmas. We could scarcely sleep anticipating gifts under the tree in the morning. At Christmas I always felt loved.

When I was ten and Forrest eight, Dad started letting us go hunting with him and our uncles and his friends from work. Boy, we were playing outdoors with the big boys then!

Several times a year, we hunted near Cloverdale on weekends because Dad didn't have a lot of vacation days. We'd leave Friday night, set up camp, hunt all day Saturday and Sunday morning, and return home Sunday afternoon so Dad could be back at work Monday morning.

Dad taught us how to clean, carry, and shoot rifles. He bought me my first BB gun, and later a .22-caliber rifle. We hunted for deer, elk, bear—it didn't matter. If it had four legs and moved, we'd shoot, clean, and eat it. We camped in the woods and tracked the animals quietly. When we shot a buck or doe, we'd drain its blood in the woods, I'd haul the carcass to the pickup in a wheelbarrow, and dress the meat at home.

We loved these hunting and camping trips. Dad didn't usually drink much, at least not the hard liquor that turned him from nice Dr. Jekyll into violent Mr. Hyde. But if my uncles came along, they often started drinking beer long before we left. Drinking beer didn't make him too crazy, although he couldn't always drive well.

I remember the time on a dirt road when Dad clipped a corner too close at thirty-five miles an hour near the Truckee River in Nevada, slid sideways into a ditch, and stopped suddenly, throwing both Forrest and me out of the pickup's bed. Fortunately, we landed in a grassy cow pasture, neither of us hurt. Dad used a shovel to dig a path out of the ditch and we hopped back in the bed of the truck.

One time, sitting in the bed, Forrest and I struggled to breathe through the dust kicked up by the truck on logging roads. We pounded on the back window. Dad stopped and let us sit on the truck fenders, where we didn't have to eat the dirt. Forrest fell off the fender when Dad navigated one turn too quickly.

Another time when Dad and Uncle Lehman were drinking heavily, Dad ran off the road, crashing the truck sideways in a ditch, rolling until it leaned against a bank and stopped. Forrest and I had been lying in sleeping bags on the floor of the truck camper. The accident kicked up a lot of dust and dirt, left the truck with a few scratches, but nobody was hurt. Dad let Uncle Lehman drive while he, Forrest and I pushed the truck back onto the road.

At four-thirty in the morning during a hunting trip near Cloverdale, Dad, Forrest and I pulled off our socks and shoes, holding them high above us as we waded across the frigid Russian River in the dark to climb a hill on the other side. After dressing again, Dad led the way up the hill at a gait that could beat a billy goat. As the sun peeked over the horizon, Dad suddenly brought his rifle butt up and rammed Forrest in the chest, knocking him head over tea kettle halfway down the hill.

Frowning, I looked at Dad and then saw four little rattlesnakes slithering across the trail. I didn't see the mama snake, but Dad did. He shoved Forrest to prevent him from stepping on it, probably saving him from a deadly poisonous bite. The snakes crawled away as Forrest found his feet and climbed back up the hill.

Later that morning, we rested under a big oak tree on the hilltop and spotted a huge buck stop twenty yards in front of us. Dad was fast asleep, his rifle cradled in his arms. Forrest shook him and he sprang to life, but too late. The buck darted away at the sound of movement. Years later, Forrest wrote an article in high school about that hunting trip and a literary magazine published it.

Dad also fished for abalone with Red Burkell of Burkell Plumbing in Sausalito and other friends, hauling home a gunnysack full of the large edible shellfish from an area near Jenner and Fort Ross. Mom cooked the meat and used abalone shells to decorate the yard for years.

Once in a while, Dad's big heart ruined our hunting and fishing excursions. Driving down the road, he'd see someone with a car or truck disabled beside the road, so he always stopped to help. Eight or ten hours later, when we were ready to resume our trip, we realized it was almost time to head home.

***

When we hunted with Uncle Lehman, Dad took vacation and we spent a week in the woods of the Sierra Nevada range, crisscrossing mountains and streams to find the best fishing and hunting spots. Dad and Uncle Lehman drank a few beers while packing the ice chest, sleeping bags, and other gear. Sometimes they stopped along the route at a tavern, leaving Forrest and me waiting in the car.

One ninety-five-degree afternoon, Dad and Uncle Lehman stopped for a midday drink in a small town in north-central California, not far from Bucks Lake. As they stepped inside the little main street bar, Forrest scrambled into the front passenger seat. Killing time, we watched people and blamed each other for talking too much and spooking the deer. Time passed and patience waned.

Uncle Lehman had propped his 30-30 Winchester lever-action rifle against the front edge of his seat, butt on the floor with the barrel pointing up. Forrest decided to dust the gun and, as he did so, he cocked the rifle, which he didn't realize was loaded, and jacked a round into the chamber. I looked into the gun's barrel, checking to see how well my brother cleaned it.

"This is just too hot. It's miserable,' I exclaimed. 'I'm going into that bar and haul them out so we can get going."

As Forrest dusted the trigger assembly, I pushed the seat forward to climb out the passenger door. Kaboom! A bullet whizzed past my ear, blasting a hole in the car's roof.

The sound of the rifle blast reverberated in my right ear. I couldn't hear anything for days!

At the sound, Dad and Uncle Lehman flew from that bar. As Forrest stammered his explanation of what happened, they climbed into the car and skedaddled out of town. Dad, who had removed all the bullets from his gun and asked my uncle to do the same, gave us both a lecture about messing with guns, but he reserved his greatest wrath for Uncle Lehman.

I didn't want to be standing in his shoes that night. Years before, they had quit hunting together for several years after a previous dispute they had. After all, Dad had tossed my uncle over his head into a fish pond. I could only imagine what was going to happen now between Dad and my uncle.

It's incredible how often the good Lord saved my hide. Why had I moved my head just in the nick of time before Forrest pulled the trigger?

***

On a hot afternoon following one hunting trip, Dad pulled over near the fast-flowing Sacramento River to cool off in the water by swimming a bit. We took off our shirts, slipped off our socks and shoes, and plunged into the cold water. Forrest and I both decided to swim across the river.

However, swimming against the strong current wore out Forrest, who stumbled on rocks as he pulled himself onto the shore. Then Dad hollered at us.

"It's time to go."

I dove into the water and swam across, but Forrest was done in. He knew he couldn't make it back, so he yelled at me.

"Bring me a big piece of wood! I need something to help me swim across."

Dad told me to find something, so I grasped a two-inch-thick tree limb, about seven feet long, and rushed into the water. As I swam across the water, dragging that big old stick behind me, I remembered Dad saying, "If you ever get close to a drowning person, don't let them get a hold of you because you'll both drown."

I thrust the limb toward him. "Grab the stick!"

He gripped it tightly with both hands as I swam as hard and fast as I could toward shore.

"Don't let go!"

I towed him behind me, my muscles burning as they strained to pull the extra weight. Eventually I let go when his feet could touch bottom.

When he climbed ashore, Forrest straggled up toward us and lifted that limb as if to strike me.

"What were you thinking? I wanted a log, you dummy—not a tiny little twig that couldn't support a mouse!" He was mad at me instead of being thankful that I just saved his bacon.

***

Dad liked working in his backyard single-car garage with friends, tinkering with car engines, replacing brakes, and rebuilding a huge bicycle with thirty-inch wheels and crafting a go-cart of plywood powered by pedals. His friends, Art Self and Ralph Haywood, and Uncle Lehman often helped him, pounding down a few beers as they visited beneath engine hoods. As they worked at night, Forrest and I held drop lamps for the men, untangled cords, and retrieved requested tools. When our minds wandered, as they often did, Dad yelled at us to keep the light on his hands so he could see. The longer they worked (and drank), the less they accomplished. So they would call it a night and say, "Well, we'll finish this tomorrow."

***

We always had dogs as pets. We took our dogs hunting with us and they'd chase the deer or flush them out of the forests.

As a ten-year-old kid, I considered one canine my good buddy as we raced from one adventure to another. But sometimes Duke sought adventures on his own, disappearing for a few hours at a time, leaving me behind in our Mill Valley neighborhood as he crossed the road to explore the rolling hills and cow pasture.

Duke watching us play

He usually returned home by the end of the day. But one night he didn't come back until late, and he was worn out and dirty.

The next day, a cattleman knocked on our door. When Mom answered, he asked if we had a dog and proceeded to describe Duke.

"Yes,' Mom said. 'We do. That would be Duke."

"Well now, you need to put this dog on a chain or something,' he told her. 'He's chasing my cattle, making them run and burn off weight. That's going to cost us a lot of money."

I heard his words, but they didn't make any sense to me. *How dare he tell us we had to chain Duke!*

"If you don't keep your dog under control, I'm going to have to do something myself."

"Okay,' Mom said. 'We understand."

But a few days later, Duke disappeared again. But this time he didn't return home. The next day, I looked everywhere for him, exploring his usual haunts and our hiking trails, calling his name, whistling. Returning to the railroad tracks, I found Duke. He was lying between the tracks, a big bullet hole through the middle of him. I squatted beside him, petting his fur, feeling the shallow rise and fall of his chest as he struggled to breathe. I bit back tears, lifted him in my arms, and carried him two miles to our home. He died along the way.

I knew who killed Duke. After Forrest and I buried Duke in the back yard, I marched to my closet and pulled down the BB gun. Walking into the kitchen, I paused briefly.

"Mom, I'm going to go shoot the mean old man who shot my dog."

"No, Ronnie, you can't do that,' Mom said, crouching before me, reaching for my gun. 'You're not going anywhere."

She put my gun away as tears slipped from my eyes. I felt so angry. I wanted revenge.

Later my dad tried to explain why the cattleman shot our dog, but I never forgave him. Dad brought home another dog, one that stayed home, which helped a lot.

***

As I said before, Mom and Dad attended church only once or twice a year, on Christmas Day and Easter, but sometimes they came to watch a play.

When I was about ten, one of my neighborhood friends, Ronnie Adams, the son of a career Navy man who later drove a dump truck, invited Forrest and me to go with him to a little Assembly of God Church in Sausalito, a church of about a hundred members. The church offered a lot of fun activities for thirty or so young people. We kept attending the church to participate in the activities, including Vacation Bible School. We learned Bible stories, memorized Scripture verses, played games, and sang a lot of catchy songs. One time we made working lamps from wood, cloth and wiring in a kit and gave them as Mother's Day gifts. I loved playing Roman soldiers in the church plays, but I didn't really comprehend Christianity well and never understood the concept of grace.

I was sitting in the back row of the packed church one Sunday when Pastor James Walton preached a sermon and at the end gave an invitation.

"Now, is there anybody out there who feels the Lord speaking to you, asking you to accept Christ and follow Him? Does anyone want to be born again?" There was a long pause.

For some reason I felt compelled to respond. I'd heard his words and they had spoken to my heart. I lifted my hand and then jerked it back down, hoping nobody would notice, but he was a hawk-eyed preacher. He spotted my arm go up and down.

"I saw that arm back there,' he said. 'Now I want you to be brave and come on up here to the front." Bracing myself, I stood and sauntered to the front of the church, dropped to my knees, and repeated after him the words of the Sinner's Prayer:

"Heavenly Father, I confess that I am a sinner, I have broken your laws. I believe that Christ died for me on the cross, He paid for all of my sins, He died, was buried, and rose up from the dead and is alive forever more. Please forgive me Lord Jesus, and thank you for saving my soul."

I invited Christ into my heart and promised to follow him. I meant the words, even though I didn't understand it all. I didn't feel much at the time, but a few weeks later, I started to see life more optimistically. My athletic skills improved. I gained confidence. I studied harder, raising my grades. I obeyed my parents a bit more and lied a little less, but I was still ornery. Something had happened to me but I didn't understand just what it was. After all I was still a young boy of only ten years of age.

We grew to know and respect Rev. Walton and his wife, Gladys, and their family as they drove a bus around to pick up kids for Sunday school. Or they'd stop by in their station wagon and we'd hop inside with their children for the ride to church.

We loved going to church, sitting in the house of God, providing an anchor in the turbulent sea of a dysfunctional home life. The people there were different, really nice, loving and kind.

Mom even gave us money to put onto the offering plate, but it seldom landed there. We stopped at the store a block from church and bought candy bars. She and Dad both insisted we attend church on Sundays.

When I was in second grade, we moved from Sausalito to House 81 in Marin City, where the population was predominately African-American. As white kids we were definitely in the minority. When Dad drove the Greyhound bus on long trips, and Mom worked as a waitress, they hired black women to babysit us. We pretty much did what we wanted as long as we arrived home in time to eat dinner each night.

My dad didn't have a prejudiced bone in his body; neither did we. Dad, Forrest and I had a lot of black friends, but my mother didn't want blacks even on her doorstep. She wanted to move from Marin City. She was very racist.

I tended to land in a bunch of fights, even in grade school. I was continually defending my territory or my property. Forrest and I walked the mile and a half to Richardson Bay School along a trail from Marin City to north Sausalito. Sometimes kids hovered above the trail and pelted us with rocks as we passed. We'd get rocked, which never sat well with me. Sometimes we'd run, but I usually picked up rocks and threw them back. One time kids tried to steal my bicycle, but I fought back. They stopped trying.

Forrest had a more easygoing, happy-go-lucky temperament. He smiled all the time and seldom fought, knowing his big brother would protect him. He avoided troublemakers; I tended to look for them. Being ornery, I never took any lip from anyone, although I earned good grades. Mom made sure of that. My folks also instilled ethics and values in us, but I had a rebellious streak. I couldn't fight back when my dad whipped me, but I could whip a kid who crossed me. I would fight at the drop of a hat.

One day in fourth grade, while I was in the school bathroom, a big Mexican kid threw a wet roll of toilet paper, smacking me in the head. I didn't stop to think; I grabbed him by the front of the shirt and punched him in the face, breaking his nose. He went wailing home, screaming and crying. I was expelled, al-though at a teacher meeting, his parents admitted he shouldn't have thrown the toilet paper roll. I think my parents paid his doctor's bill. They weren't happy.

I also clobbered Pat Smith, a tall, lanky basketball player who later married our cousin Vicky Madison.

***

Mom and Dad fought a lot about his drinking. She turned into a tornado, railing at him to quit drinking and stop gambling away their hard-earned money on horses. In the wee hours of the morning, we'd often hear our parents screaming and yelling at each other, keeping us awake on school nights.

Despite drinking sometimes on week nights, Dad always got up and went to work. Friday and Saturday night, he often returned home totally loaded, falling down drunk, and often violent.

One night, Dad had been drinking with his buddies in Sausalito after working all day and left the bar after two in the morning. He drove toward our home, located right off the highway in his '52 pickup, but fell asleep with his foot on the accelerator. The truck slammed into the back of a parked car, shoving the engine into the cab, ramming the steering wheel into his chest.

He slid the seat back enough to slip out of the cab stumbling more than a mile home. He was one tough cookie. Whenever he exerted himself, Dad had a habit of biting his lower lip. By the time he reached our house, he had bitten clean through his lower lip, a flap of red flesh hanging onto his chin, exposing his clenched teeth. He was in absolute agony.

He'd left his keys in the truck's ignition, so he pounded on the door, waking Forrest who was sleeping in a bedroom next to the door. He rushed from his room, just as Mom walked into the front room and opened the door to find her husband, blood soaking through his white shirt, drenching his tie, flowing freely from his dangling lip, and leaving stains on his suit pants.

"My God!" she screamed. "Bill, what happened to you?"

She drew him into the kitchen. Mom ran warm water over cloths, pressing them to his mouth to staunch the bleeding. She examined him for other wounds.

"My chest hurts." He slurred the words a bit.

"We need to call an ambulance," she told him, turning toward the phone.

"No!" He grasped her arm, wincing as he did so. She begged him, but he refused to let her call.

"Don't call. I'll go to the doctor in the morning."

The next morning, she accompanied him to the doctor, who diagnosed a broken sternum; two busted ribs, and cuts on his legs. The doctor couldn't believe he walked into the office with those injuries. He stitched up the lip and wrapped his ribs tightly in a soft chest cast. He would have tried to return to work if not for the doctor ordering him to stay home and heal.

Despite the alcoholism, occasional threats of violence, and frequently wrecked cars, Mom stuck with Dad. They were old school, believing marriage was forever. She saw her mother marry and divorce; she didn't want to do the same. She deserved a medal.

***

As kids, we didn't get away with much. Mom was a strict disciplinarian who didn't allow us to do squat. She was a tyrant, a sergeant major ordering us to wash dishes, mop floors, weed the garden, and clean the house. She demanded perfection and organization. She left a list of chores for us to do, and as long as we did them, she was satisfied. I felt totally controlled, like a prisoner at home. That's probably why Forrest and I spent so much time outside, but only after doing our chores.

If we didn't do our chores, Mom's temper flared. She'd spank us, usually with her hand, sometimes with a brush and eventually with a switch. She grabbed anything close at hand. She handled the day-to-day disciplining, but from the time I was in fifth grade, whenever I misbehaved—probably once a month—she turned me over to my father, who was merciless. Without saying a word, he led me to a back room and beat me with a thick leather belt on my legs, back, and shoulders lash after lash, ripping across my buttocks, thighs, legs, and back, leaving my body on fire and me gasping for air, unable to utter a sound. Half the time I didn't have a clue why I was getting a beating.

Although Mom put him up to disciplining us, one time when he was whacking me she flew into the room, grabbed his arm and screamed at him. "Stop! Stop! You're going to kill him!"

I never fought back. I was just a skinny kid, my dad a powerfully strong man. Forrest considered the discipline as severe spankings; I called them beatings. The red welts eventually turned black and blue.

My father, a conscientious man who drove a Greyhound bus and a truck for many years, was the nicest guy in the world when he was sober. He had a lot of friends and was well liked by many. He drank heavily when he wasn't working to become a mean, violent drunk. I feared his wrath, but I respected him. We all did, even when he threatened Mom with a gun. The next day, my dad didn't remember any of it. He had been in a 'black out.'

We never knew whether Dad would be in a good mood, eager to work on fixing cars in the back shed, or stinking drunk and violent as he was at least once a month. Mom seldom drank alcohol, and never to excess.

***

Dad suffered several work injuries. Once, while driving his truck in the 1950s, he pulled to the shoulder and hefted a 300-pound manhole cover that had slipped from another rig into a lane of traffic. He hauled it to the side of the road, but strained his lower back. He was hospitalized and in traction for several weeks.

During the 1960s, he drove a delivery truck for Mill Valley Lumber Company. As he was picking up a load of lumber at a competitor's mill in Corte Madera, he parked his truck and began walking toward the office. A forklift, carrying a large load of lumber in the air over the vehicles toward the bed of Dad's truck, dipped into a pothole, shifting the load to the side, and toppled lumber onto the cab while my dad dove inside it. The lumber struck him in the head, neck and shoulders, driving him into the ground, fracturing vertebrae and crushing discs. An ambulance rushed him to Marin General Hospital, where he stayed a couple of weeks, returning home in a tight body cast from his hips to his upper chest. He suffered tremendous pain for weeks, and one day, lying on the couch in the living room of our Mill Valley house, a muscle spasm dropped him to his knees. He plunged onto his forearms, screaming. Nobody could do anything to alleviate his pain. Mom called an ambulance, which took him to the hospital where they removed the cast. He remained there for several weeks.

The States Labor and Industry attorneys and lumber company attorneys fought to avoid paying him a dime for the injuries. He hired an attorney and won the case, but he never received much compensation. The money covered his medical bills, and attorney fees, but that was about it. Forrest and I were angry, and of course my anger always sought ways to vent. I wanted to hurt somebody, especially this one attorney. I got talked out of doing anything to him. But my folks were denied justice, since Dad was injured so badly and was in so much pain he couldn't work to earn money from that time on. He finally quit drinking in his fifties.

***

When he was healthy, Mom and Dad liked to socialize with family and friends. They played cards with other couples, enjoyed drinks over dinner or at bars on the Fourth of July and New Year's Eve, and often invited people over for dinner, drinks, and music. They loved country-western music, probably since they grew up in the South. When my uncles and aunts visited, they often played musical instruments and sang until two, three, or four in the morning. My mom's brother, Uncle Lehman Johnson, was a gifted musician who could sing, strum guitar, and play piano, and probably would have become a professional singer if he hadn't been such a drinker. He was a Navy chief petty officer after World War II.

Mom could sing and play the piano. Dad sang too. Our Uncle Frank played a fiddle. Others played harmonica, banjo, and other instruments. Art Self, a good friend of Dad's, often joined in the music-making.

Sometimes Mom and Dad danced, demonstrating fancy flips and other moves. They were something to watch.

Most of them liked to drink, but Mom seldom did. She occasionally sipped a glass of wine while working her shift as a cocktail hostess.

***

Forrest and I also joined the Boy Scouts of America, with Scoutmaster Dan Terzich, a Mill Valley police detective who later became chief. He saw me develop from a Cub Scout to a Boy Scout, to a Sea Scout, and then to the Marines.

***

Dad, a talented carpenter, also built hope chests, cedar cabinets, and other beautiful wood furniture. He fixed car engines and repaired our bikes. What we liked best, though, were his boats.

Dad built fishing boats in the garage, pounding together the wood, sanding and varnishing it to watertight condition and then installing an outboard motor. I claimed the spot in the bow of the boat, facing forward as we crashed through choppy waves and sliced through billowing wind in San Francisco Bay. I loved the thrill and exhilaration, facing potential danger head-on. I never grew seasick, then or later.

Dad built this boat from scratch. Kelly is playing guitar just after Sunday School.

We often fished off the coast of Fort Baker and Fort Cronkite, Army forts built during World War II armed with cannons to ward off Japanese attacks on the United States mainland and defend the Golden Gate Bridge. We loved exploring the old forts and armament. We regularly picked our way down a steep rocky cliff to the water's edge. We never used ropes, trusting in our footing on the loose rocks. Fear never factored into the adventure equation.

Sometimes as the tide rolled in, huge waves hit those rocks and splashed us. One time a wave knocked Forrest off the rocks into the bay. Dad dove off a rock and pulled him out. My Dad was fearless and an excellent swimmer.

My brother Ferral also almost drowned on a fishing trip with Dad. My dad tried to scrounge old railroad ties discarded in the woods, floating them downriver so he could drag them from the water and haul them away in his truck. Ferral was trying to retrieve one of these oil-soaked railroad ties when it knocked him over backward, pinning him underwater. Dad saw Ferral go under and swam to his side, hefting the heavy tie and tossing it off his son, who was unconscious. Dad dragged him to the shore and started cardiopulmonary resuscitation. Slowly, gradually Ferral spit out a copious amount of water from his lungs and recovered.

We cast our lines seeking rock cod, flounder, sea bass and all kinds of fish we could cook for dinner. Sometimes we pulled in stingrays, which we didn't eat. Dad could gut, clean, and fry up fish in a skillet over an open fire in no time. We always took fish home to feed the family. We grew up eating wild game—fish from the bay, venison, and bear.

During one fishing excursion on the bay, Dad hauled in a shark. As he pulled it into the boat, he hollered at me.

"Ronnie! Grab the knife and stab it!" He tried to angle it away from Forrest and me. "We don't want it biting anyone."

With the knife in hand, I plunged it over and over into the shark until we all knew it had died, no longer posing any threat to us.

***

When I was in eighth grade, my folks moved to a small older three-bedroom rental home at 63 Lomita Drive in Mill Valley, a more upscale neighborhood with nicer homes where we were no longer minorities.

Forrest and I spent a lot of time working in the yard, which was 200 feet long and probably seventy-five feet wide filled with fruit trees—twenty-two altogether—fig, tangerine, almond, English walnut, plum, apple, avocado, apricot and orange. A small grape arbor bordered the yard of our neighbor, John Baker. Rumor had it that John had served in World War II also, but as a German soldier. John and his wife Trudy were the nicest people and they got along great with our folks. We picked the fruit, planted two vegetable gardens, mowed the lawn, trimmed hedges, and watered. Mom expected the yardwork and housework—vacuuming, dishwashing, sweeping, mopping, and waxing—to be completed when she returned home from work.

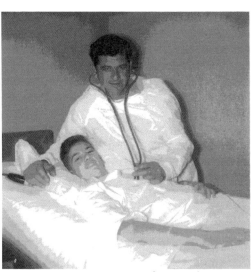

Forrest recovering from polio with Dad playing doctor

Despite our chores, we managed to play a lot of Little League baseball. In fact, my brother Forrest set a record pitching for the Mill Valley Merchants going five-and-a-half innings with seventeen consecutive strikeouts. Forrest played for the Mill Valley Anchors and later the MV Lions.

Rev. Walton and his family also moved from Sausalito to Mill Valley, where they set up their church in a large old building, anticipating growth that never materialized. The church membership hovered near two hundred. There had been a church split, a nasty affair that really hurt the church badly.

I attended the Edna Maguire Junior High; Forrest was at Alto Elementary. Dad drove a truck for Nielsen Freight Lines and later for Merchant's Express. Occasionally during the summer, Forrest and I helped Dad with his deliveries, stopping at a hamburger joint in Kentfield for burgers, fries, and a Coke or shake.

Relatives occasionally stopped to see us at our new home in Mill Valley. My mom's sister, Bertina, visited from Petaluma with her husband, Lee Madison and their two girls, Ginger and Vicky. Dad's sisters—Willadean Pinkerton-Reardon and her husband, C.B. Pinkerton, a pediatrician, stopped with their two children, Theresa and Benny. Aunt Billie Jean came with her husband, Bob Collins, an eye doctor, and their kids, Jeff and Renee from Oklahoma. Dad and his siblings all grew up poor, and both uncles served in the military during World War II. Both of my uncles had taken advantage of the GI Bill, returned to school while their wives worked, and both had become successful doctors. One time when they visited, my uncles noticed my rotting teeth and scrawny size, and told my folks that the diseased teeth could be stunting my growth, keeping me thin. I was tall at six-foot-one, but skinny at 165 pounds. Dr. Pinkerton told my dad, "Take him to the dentist. I'll pay the whole bill."

My cousins Ginger and Vicky, ages 11 and 10

So they did. We didn't have insurance, but with my uncle's help, a local dentist fixed my teeth, replacing one with an artificial tooth. The work took quite a while, but afterward, I gained sixty-five pounds within two years and inched up to 6' 3".

***

Later, when we were older, Forrest and I walked to church. After we moved from Sausalito to Mill Valley, the church was two miles away, or a four-mile round-trip, but we still walked it, weather permitting.

We joined in activities with two dozen or more other young people, gathering together on Friday nights and playing in the choir and orchestra on Sundays. Forrest was voted in as president and I as treasurer, of our youth group *Christ's Ambassadors*.

When Forrest fell ill after taking the polio vaccine in 1962, he was treated at Marin General Hospital in Kentfield for about two weeks for a life-threatening infection in his spinal fluid and paralysis starting in his legs. He very nearly died. Pastor Walton stopped to see him at the hospital and prayed for him.

Amazingly, Forrest began to make a full recovery but only after Pastor Walton prayed for him!

We both admired Pastor Walton, who worked at Mare Island Naval Shipyard in Vallejo as a civilian nuclear submarine troubleshooter. He baptized us and served as a spiritual father figure and mentor to us and many other young people. We loved him dearly.

A few years later, the church moved to Mill Valley too, locating in a former Wesleyan Methodist Church building on East Blithedale Avenue. The dark brown wooden structure had a large upstairs sanctuary, big downstairs basement with classrooms, and a social hall with classrooms and a kitchen at one end.

***

We were raised on country music, but by the time I reached high school, I despised the melodramatic storylines about heartache, loss, and death. Instead, I started listening to jazz and soft rock. I played the clarinet, attained the first B flat clarinet chair, and enjoyed playing classical greats from composers Mozart, Handel, Chopin, and Beethoven.

My music teacher, Mabel Pittenger, a violinist, often organized concert performances of her students in the gymnasium at Tamalpais High School. We also provided background music for plays. Sometimes we sang at school or during youth group activities at church.

It was in the orchestra class that I grew better acquainted with Bonnie Walton, the daughter of Rev. James and Gladys Walton, who pastored the church I attended. Bonnie started violin lessons in sixth grade and joined the orchestra at Tamalpais High School, where I played the clarinet. I was a year ahead of Bonnie, but she caught my eye. I caught her attention too.

During one high school band and orchestra outing, she saw me at the front of the bus smoking cigarettes with friends and later she told me how disappointed she felt. Since our names rhymed—Ronnie and Bonnie—we were teased at church functions. We started dating when in high school.

***

One time in high school, I picked a fight with Doug Goff. I accused him of stealing my wallet in the gymnasium locker room. Somebody stole it (I never found out who), but it wasn't Doug. When he left school, I confronted and falsely accused him in front of his girlfriend. We started fighting. It didn't last long. He beat me up pretty good and I deserved it. Later on, Doug became a deputy sheriff. I really felt bad about falsely accusing him.

I staggered home bloodied and bruised. But when my father saw me, he put his foot down.

"That's it,' Dad exclaimed. 'You're not losing any more fights. Don't come home if you lose another fight. If you get in a fight, you better win it."

That's when Dad taught Forrest and me how to defend ourselves. He bought boxing gloves, a punching bag, and other gear. We both learned to jab, use a left hook, the upper cut and right cross, and punch hard to injure others. He taught us how to fight and win.

"Now, I want you to punch me right in the nose," Dad told me one day. I couldn't do it.

"No, I don't want to hurt you, Dad."

"You are not going to hurt me. I want you to give me a good, hard punch,' he said, adding, 'If you don't hit me, I'm going to take you in the back room and light you on fire."

As a high school sophomore, I was six-foot-one and 160 pounds, dripping wet. I looked like a skinny overgrown rat. Now I had a choice: Punch him in the face or he'll take me to the woodshed. I hauled off and let him have it.

He just shook it off, although blood poured from his nose. He hadn't even budged an inch.

"That was good,' he said. 'That was a good one. That's where you aim when you're fighting. You go for the nose. You knock them out. Hit 'em in the jaw."

Dad liked boxing, and he was good at it. My uncle Lee told me he liked to start fights in bars, knowing Dad would finish them. At a Sausalito bar in the early 1950s, Lee started harassing a former world heavyweight champion, Max Baer, an American boxer of German descent. When Baer had enough, he turned to fight and Uncle Lee got out of the way. My dad had no idea who it was, but defending Lee, he knocked the guy flat onto the floor.

I fought in high school, but not as often as I had earlier. I was more into sports by then. Forrest said he only fought three times before graduating from high school. He was more of a peacemaker. When a couple of guys picked a battle on a basketball court, threatening to take our court and keep our ball, I was ready to fight, but Forrest kept walking away, calling my name. Finally, we left without fisticuffs.

I said, "That's fine with me. I don't need this fight."

Forrest and I fought each other, but it was more brotherly wrestling than real fist-fighting. Forrest would tease me, sneak up behind me as I watched television from a rocker recliner and flip my ear just to annoy me. I would jump up and race after him and we'd wrestle if I caught him before he locked himself in the bathroom. Forrest and I were very close and have remained that way all of our lives.

Mom didn't like us to fight. But Dad looked at it from a practical standpoint, knowing what happens among boys and the need to stand up against bullying. We also learned we needed to stand up for one another. But he didn't tolerate us starting fights without provocation. He made it very clear that we should never hurt anyone for no reason. My folks had a few spats about our sparring lessons.

***

While I was attending Tamalpais High School, Mom changed. Something terrible must have happened. She grew mean, hard, and cold, waking up angry every morning. We couldn't please her. She erected a wall, perhaps to keep her emotions inside and all of us outside.

Forrest thinks it's because she realized that she'd never achieve her dreams of owning a home, living with a sober husband and a happy family. She was a sharp, organized woman with a good head for business, a high I.Q. and she always encouraged Dad to start a business. He wouldn't do it, probably out of fear of failure. Her spirit was crushed.

She lashed out, verbally and physically, slapping or throwing items at us, screaming at the top of her lungs. She switched us with thin branches from the crabapple tree, leaving us bloody with raised welts and a twig only half the size of what it was when she started.

What set her off was usually something simple, like putting too much cream in her coffee…or not enough.

Dad liked to gamble on horse races, and all through high school, he took my brother Forrest and me with him to Tanforan, Golden Gate, or Bay Meadows racetracks. We picked up tickets tossed on the ground by losers, but sometimes found good tickets, which we gave to our dad. He always bought us plenty of hot dogs.

Since both Mom and Dad worked, Forrest and I, but primarily my brother, had to watch the younger kids. It prevented us from participating in a lot of extracurricular sports. I played football. So did Forrest for one year. And he participated for a year in track. But most afternoons, we had to arrive home right away to watch the younger kids. Mom left for work before four.

One time when Forrest was late arriving home, Mom stormed to the Edna McGuire Junior High and found him talking with other students. She grabbed his arm and started whaling on him with a belt, right in front of other students boarding buses, dragging him toward home. Humiliated, Forrest felt like he could've killed her.

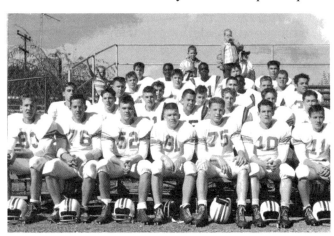

Ron, 2nd row, 3rd from left
Tamalpais Junior Varsity
1962-1963

"I was so angry. That changed me. From that day forward my mother and I never had the same relationship," Forrest lamented. That is, at least not until years later, when Forrest turned his life over to Christ and forgave her. As soon as he turned eighteen, Forrest left the house and enlisted in the Marines. He couldn't get out of there fast enough.

After Dad pointed a gun at Mom's head, she finally put her foot down.

"Look, you're either going to go get treatment and stop drinking or we're going to get a divorce,' she told him. 'We're through."

Dad was taken to a psychiatric unit after neighbors called the police. Later he agreed to go to an alcohol treatment center in Martinez. After a couple of months, he returned home a changed man. He had stopped drinking entirely, but he had deteriorated mentally. Mom said they had put him on a mental ward even though he was there for treatment of alcoholism. She insisted they let him go home to prevent further damage. Dad finally made a full recovery.

Later, after Dad quit drinking, they moved to Rohnert Park and bought their first home. Mom's angry attitude changed. She mellowed, returning to the woman we had known in our younger years. They started attending church regularly, returning to their Christian roots. They had been backslidden for many years and there had been nasty consequences for that.

Mom persuaded Dad to buy property for a home, which he did, even though commitments like that terrified him. They never built on that property though. When she died, Forrest sold the land for the same $5,000 price they had paid for it.

With such dysfunction at home, I felt anger simmering just below the surface all through junior high and high school. I kept a reign on it, for the most part. But I felt like someday I would explode.

***

During high school, I continued participating in church activities. I wanted to be there because I had given my life to Christ and everything changed. My basketball game improved and I earned my letterman's jacket. I played on the Junior Varsity football team. However, I never went out for Varsity; instead, I was their manager. Warren Domino, and Elmer Collett, two of the best players who ever came to Tamalpais High School, became my good friends. Those guys had some real class as well as talent. They were an inspiration to me. I also became an Honor "T" Society member and participated in student government my last two years of high school. Forrest was watching my younger siblings most of the time while I was playing sports.

Ron in High School Junior Varsity Football

I performed in the outdoor play at the amphitheater on Mount Tamalpais as one of Robin Hood's merry men, a production put on and directed by Mr. Dan Totherow. In this play, I was carrying a huge sixty-pound Bushmaster breakdown bow and shooting arrows. Perhaps running up and down Mount Tamalpais for physical training during high school made me look like the part for the play.

My dad gave me my first car when I was a high school senior, but then he turned around and sold it to a cousin. It was an old Rambler so I didn't much mind. But he bought me another car and fixed it whenever the engine needed work.

Mom bought me a LeBlanc clarinet for my birthday. I played in the school orchestra for years with George Duke, who became a world renowned jazz pianist and collaborated with Frank Zappa. Our music teacher, Mable Pittinger, offered me a scholarship in music because I was her first clarinet. But we had a tough time in her class because Pete Rossi, Dan Kelley, George Duke, and I would always start jamming, creating all types of music, while the only thing she ever let us play in

Ron with his first car

class was Mozart, Beethoven, Handel, Chopin, and other classical works. She was trying to teach us to be really professional, but we were playing hip hop music while she tried to start class. She'd be beating that baton shouting, "George, Ron, Dan, Pete." Nevertheless, I won a prestigious music award, the Arion Award for outstanding ability.

I also earned better grades in high school—all As and Bs—and graduated in 1964 in the top third of my class. I was offered a scholarship to attend college.

I dated three girls in high school—Linda Cruise, Lorraine Deluke, and Bonnie Walton, the preacher's daughter. Mom tried to squash my relationship with Bonnie.

She didn't think Bonnie was good enough for me, so she told me, "I don't want you seeing that girl. I don't want you stopping by her house."

Like that stopped me. Her parents sometimes hired me to work in their yard, but when I did, my mother would call hers and ask her to make sure I didn't see Bonnie. That didn't work, especially when I paid Forrest to do the work so I could slip away to the store, buy goodies for Bonnie, and sneak into her room.

Recalling my mother's wrath, Bonnie reported, "Sometimes I did not know he was on restriction, and when his mom found out, she would beat him with a garden hose."

Forrest and I also helped paint their house.

I quit fighting as much during my last few years of high school, although I did have one or two altercations. Forrest and I went our own different ways the last two years of school. He mingled with the upper crust kids, I with the average middle class kids. He was also more cerebral than I, although I did earn high grades my last two years. My high school years were a pretty good time of growing and learning. Tamalpais High was a beautiful school, laid out like a college campus. I enjoyed my time there from 1960 to 1964. The people who served on staff were just fantastic in my opinion. They were dedicated, passionate, and competent in their work as coaches, and mentors. I remember many of them so well. My coaches in football and basketball were Hank Marshall (formerly with the Los Angeles Rams), Marion Belden, Gus Gustafson and Mike Davilon. Some teachers that stood out were Peter Klain (English), Mabel Pittinger (music), William Wallace (English), George Pullman (social studies), and Robert Sherman (English). I believe I learned more from these wonderful teachers at Tam than most students do today with a college education.

During my last three years in school I usually had a part time job. Max Staley, owner of Staley's Delicatessen on E. Blithdale Avenue in Mill Valley, hired me to do all kinds of typical restaurant duties like washing dishes, preparing orders, and delivering hot food to such celebrities such as Sterling Hayden. He had been a Marine, a sailor and finally a Hollywood actor, starring in a lot of movies over the years, and in particular *The Godfather*, as a corrupt police lieutenant (he gets it in the end by the mob!). He lived over in Tiburon, Ca. I liked driving my boss's VW bus used to deliver food. I also worked in the school snack bar which was staffed by three wonderful ladies. They all treated me really great and often gave me donuts after work. I used to make points with lots of students by giving them free donuts.

Some of the classmates that I had are unforgettable. George Duke became a world renowned jazz pianist; Warren Domino played for Arizona State and happened to be shipped to Vietnam on the same vessel as me when he was in the Merchant Marines; Tami Bell, Doug Golf, Ellis Williams, Robin Prosch, Ron Pederson, and Bill Hall were fellow football players and friends. I also have to mention Paul Abbott who was a fellow manager of the varsity team; Freddy Mack who lived near my house and was a great baseball player; Bob Hope, a great runner, especially long distance; and Elmer and Cedric Collett, brothers that I sincerely liked and who were great football players. Elmer went on to make the NFL. I have run into him several times over the years.

There were some girls that I will never forget either. I thought I was in love with Barbara Breeze. Terry Brazell, Linda Cruiz, Jane Huffman, Audrey Richardson and Frances Stuart were also 'knockouts' as far as I was concerned. Stephanie was gorgeous too! Lorraine Deluke was my first real girlfriend. We went together for two years before I broke it off. Then a really fine-looking girl that I fell in love with came into view one day: Bonnie Walton. Wow! She drove me mad with desire. During my last year in high school I fell head over heels for her.

Some other guys that I cannot forget are Ron Adams, who became a life time friend and would go on to become a Command Master Chief in the Coast Guard; Dave Albright who went into the Army (a Vietnam Veteran); Mike Teague; Bernie Faustino (whose entire family were friends with our family and our mothers worked together for many years); Ron Williams, Pat Smith and John Wooley. Pat Smith married one of my cousins, Vicky Madison. I have to mention Creighton Wyatt, Rich Miller and Joe O'Brien (and all his brothers).

A dear friend, Chuck Locati, stands out in my memory also. We have kept in touch over the years but it's now been about ten years or more since I last saw Chuck. We ran into each other in his office a time or two in Mill Valley. He was a great quarterback in football and I always thought he would have made another Joe Montana. He was that good. Chuck had a terrible accident that ended his chances of a football career in the future. During a hard workout in the gym and lacking spotters to catch him, he broke his neck, becoming a quadriplegic. Chuck had a great attitude later on in life however. When I came down from Washington to visit relatives over the years, I would always stop by to try to see him.

Ernie Bergman and Vince Adcock remain friends today. Ernie, who served in Vietnam as part of the 'brown water' Navy, and saw a lot of combat, works with many Veterans and veteran causes today. Vince, who was also Navy, is today a very wealthy, successful man, who lives down near Palm Springs, last I heard. I'm looking forward to seeing these guys again someday soon. Hopefully at the next reunion of old Tam High we can hook up again.

Growing up was challenging for me. Growing up in dysfunction-junction, where I was told one thing and shown something else altogether was very confusing and frustrating for me as a young child. My folks would tell me not to drink or smoke and yet they both did the same. They did not permit me to use curse words but they cursed all the time. They didn't want me to fight with my brother or anyone else for that matter, but they fought all the time. They insisted I go to church, learn about God and act like Him, but they didn't do the same.

I had no grandfathers who lived less than 600 miles away or more and my own father was always gone, working or out on the town. Even when he was home he never talked to us boys, never told us about life, or explained anything to us. He never talked about his military experiences or his youth. He never talked about anything to us. It was as if he was ashamed of his background. Who knows? Maybe he was. I learned very little about life growing up. My mom was very much like my dad in this respect. She was a very secretive person, sharing very little with others. She was a proud woman.

After graduating from high school, I enrolled in College of Marin in Kentfield, California. But I was interested in only three things: football, cars, and girls. I played college football, but I didn't want to study. My grades slipped to Cs and Ds, so I figured after six months that I should do something different with my life. I was living at home and didn't like it. Mom seldom talked to us, except to give us chores to do, and I came to dislike her arrogant attitude and total lack of intimacy.

However, I looked up to my adopted father, James Walton. He was a great mentor to me when I was around him but that was not enough. Manuel Saenz was another important father figure to me growing up. He was a legal Mexican immigrant. He and his wife Cora were ministers in my church. Manuel taught Sunday school classes and occasionally preached for my future father-in-law. We came to be really close friends. He was such a Godly man and set such a high standard of conduct for me to follow. He always encouraged me and it was in one of his classes that I thought I would someday go into the ministry, perhaps becoming a preacher. Our lives would eventually intertwine and he would much later be used of God to save my life in a very dangerous setting.

Bonnie, Ron and Manuel (Manny)

In the local state prison, San Quentin, Manuel was the vocational baking instructor and supervisor. He once even took a bunch of us to his work place on a special visit as tourists.

When Bonnie and I were married, Manny baked our wedding cake and what a cake it was! He was a talented baker and very creative! He was a great help with many other facets of our wedding. I would not see Manuel for five or so years after I returned from the Marine Corp. It truly is a small world indeed.

After high school and a short stint at college, I decided to check out the military recruiting offices. I had always loved watching World War II movies such as John Wayne in *Sands of Iwo Jima,* and *The Flying Tiger,* or Tyrone Power in *American Guerilla in the* Philippines and thought the military might be my next step. So I found myself gazing at the posters outside before I talked to the military guys inside. I saw posters for the Army, Navy, and Air Force—and then saw a picture of a Marine in dress blues with a white cap and belt. Man, he looked sharp! That's what I wanted. *They definitely have the best-looking uniform.*

Then a guy walked out of the Marine recruiting office looking just as sharp as the man on the poster.

"I've seen you looking at that Navy Recruiting Office over there," he said as he shook my hand.

"Yes, but I'm also looking at the Marine Corps."

"Well, you don't want anything to do with that Navy," the Marine said.

"But the Marine Corps is a department of the Navy, isn't it?"

"Yes,' he responded. 'It's the men's department."

We laughed as I walked inside. He was friendly, a combat Marine. As a high school graduate without any criminal record, I met the basic requirements. I signed the papers, but when I took the physical examination in Oakland, I flunked. It turned out I had a varicocele in my groin, a swelling of veins inside the scrotum. I couldn't join the military without correcting the problem, so I told my folks about it when I returned home.

Mom and Dad Brandon

They scheduled an appointment with the doctor, who said he could repair the varicocele. My folks paid his bill as well as Marin General Hospital's, which is where he performed the procedure. He did a great job, and as soon as I recovered, I started working out, running several miles a day, and then I returned to Oakland a few months later to take the physical again. This time I passed. So many men were burning their draft cards during this time frame; men were moving to Canada and elsewhere out of America. They were using every excuse possible to avoid serving their country. I had an easy way out. The medical problem would have worked for me. But I was not that type of individual. At least I didn't think like that. Perhaps I should have, as things turned out later on.

I knew nothing about Vietnam and never anticipated going to war. I just wanted to be a Marine. In San Francisco in May 1965, I raised my right hand and swore the oath of enlistment, promising to support and defend the Constitution of the United States against all enemies, foreign and domestic, so help me God. My mom had kind of prepared me for the Corps with all its discipline stuff, but I sure had a great deal to learn about life in general. That would come slowly for me and painfully, as I would find out in years to come.

Hardly ready to join the military, I was escaping from home and running from further college education which was not a good reason to go in the Marines. I was so naïve and immature. I'd been so sheltered, so controlled at home, and I was never allowed to make my own decisions. I was a pathetic candidate for the Marine Corps or any other branch of the military. Life was going to be hell for me for many years.

I enlisted at the age of nineteen and left for boot camp in San Diego a few weeks later.

3
The Marines

I stepped off that airplane in San Diego and boarded a bus with other guys wearing all kinds of crazy hairdos—long, short, purple, brown, black, bald, you name it. At the Marine Corps Recruit Depot, we left the bus and landed in an entirely new world with a big, ugly-looking human being snarling at us. Our drill instructor, whose twenty-inch-round neck bulged, looked more like a bulldog than a man, with rippling muscles and fangs in his mouth as he barked orders, referring to each of us as "maggot."

Ron in uniform 1965

"Get over here, maggot! Line up those big Howdy-Doody feet of yours on the yellow lines and don't move. Look straight again. Don't turn those eyeballs; nobody told you to look sideways. Attention, you maggots! That means keep those eyes at attention also."

What a rude awakening! He ordered us to the barber, where we thought we'd all receive a nice haircut. Instead, we all wore a "chrome dome" after they shaved every hair off our heads. We donned green recruit uniforms with pant legs outside of our boots. We looked like a bunch of rag-tag hobos in green uniforms for about a month before we were allowed to blouse our trousers and start looking like something resembling a Marine.

I was assigned to Platoon 230, the 2nd Battalion Marines. Staff Sergeant Chase, our top drill instructor, was a devil dog if ever there was one. Military lore says German soldiers in World War I nicknamed the Marines who fought ferociously in the 1918 Battle of Belleau Wood "devil dogs" or "dogs from hell." They got this name because they just would not stop, ever. Attack is all they knew and attack they did! The Marines carry the moniker as a badge of honor to this day.

We learned to work together as a team, lifting telephone poles and moving them in unison, doing 500 push-ups a day or more, running five miles in the sand wearing combat boots and carrying a rifle, ammo, canteens full of water and other gear weighing sixty pounds. We trained in martial arts (judo primarily), bayonet fighting, and hand-to-hand combat. Drill, drill, drill was also part of the daily regimen. In addition to Staff Sergeant Chase, we had other drill instructors—Sergeant J.R. Volner and Corporals Wright and Thorpe. They were combat-tested, rough, tough drill instructors. During the three months of boot camp, I could have killed them a time or two. I hated and cursed them, especially when I was designated the house mouse.

The house mouse is a Marine selected to do stupid chores for them: carry notes and messages from one place to another, move cleaning supplies, and clean the Drill Instructor's office. I stood at attention straightening my six-foot-three frame and looking down at Sergeant Volner, who stood five-foot-eight and looked like a miniature Rottweiler.

"Who do you think you are, maggot?" He glared at me, a smirk on his face. "I asked you a question. You think you're pretty tough, don't you, maggot?"

And I said, "Sir, aye, aye, sir."

As the last "sir" left my mouth, he punched me with a right cross to my solar plexus. I doubled over, almost dropping to the ground, but pulled my body upright again to attention.

"Did that hurt maggot?"

"Sir, no, sir, it didn't hurt."

A big smile spread over his face. "Get out of my house, maggot. You're fired!"

I left his quarters, realizing I had passed his test. I was promoted to platoon guide and carried the pennant for Platoon 230. One day, carrying the flag and strutting ahead of the platoon while practicing rifle drills, Sergeant Volner ordered: "Port arms. Present arms. Right shoulder arms."

I made a mistake, hefting the rifle to my left shoulder. He stormed up, an ugly smirk on his face, then stomped the side of his boot hard along my right shinbone, scraping off about an inch of flesh.

"Did that hurt maggot?"

"Sir, no sir, it did not hurt."

"Would you like me to do it again?"

"Sir, no sir."

"Do you think you can remember your right from your left, maggot?"

"Sir, yes, sir, this Marine will remember next time."

I never made another mistake again with that rifle, believe me. But I did lose my lofty position. Later I became a squad leader, so it wasn't all bad.

Meanwhile, I failed another test. Corporal Wright, who was a big African American, assembled us and began, "Alright, now maggots, listen up. I'm going to honor you with one of my special jokes."

Interrupting himself, he asks a recruit, "Hey maggot, where you from anyway?" "Sir, I'm from Texas, Sir"

"Oh you're from Texas huh? Well the only thing I know of from Texas is steers and queers, and I don't see any horns on you, maggot! Are you a queer?"

"Sir, no Sir, I am not…."

"Good! Now here is my joke."

After telling the joke, with a big old grin on his face, no one laughed--except me. I thought it was hilarious! I laughed hard and loud…and then noticed it was silent. All hell broke loose then. He jumped on me for laughing without permission and made the entire squad bay get down and do fifty push-ups. He then chastised me for my insolence and audacity to laugh aloud at one his jokes until ordered to laugh. Corporal Wright was one more person I had to watch out for.

One day in about 100° temperatures, Sergeant Volner ordered us to fall in on the 'company street.' This so-called street was a large sidewalk, bordered by ice plants located between the rounded looking metal Quonset huts.

"How many of you maggots want to go see a movie?" he shouted.

Everyone shouted back, "Yes Sir, aye aye, sir!"

He then stated it would cost each one of us a dollar each. So, after he collected sixty bucks, he marched us out into the hot sand. He ordered us to get down in the push-up position.

Then he shouted, "Welcome to the movie called *The Sands of San Diego*. Enjoy it, maggots. You paid for it. Now give me fifty good ones!"

Meaning fifty push-ups. We hated him for real then.

Those drill instructors turned what they called "civilian pukes" and "maggots" into Marines, all in three months. When I graduated, standing tall in my uniform, I loved and respected every one of those drill instructors.

We weren't finished. After a half day of base liberty, we boarded buses to Camp Pendleton for advanced infantry training. It was just as bad. Part of our training required crawling under barbwire about a hundred yards while M60 machine guns fired live ammo right above our heads. We were in full battle gear with rifles. One of the Marines ran into a rattlesnake and without thinking, stood up. The machine gunner stopped firing too late and the recruit was killed.

Ron Training at Camp Pendleton

Training was extremely tough, especially with temperatures hovering around one-hundred degrees. One day on a company size outing, I made some kind of minor mistake and my drill instructor (D.I.), all hot and bothered, ordered me to shout "I'm a dumb ass" over and over, while crawling down the side of a mountain, on my elbows and boot toes only, carrying an M14 rifle in my arms. This continued for over one-hundred yards. My elbows were a bloody mess at the end. This was one D.I. I seriously wanted to kill someday. He was one mean S.O.B.

We learned how to use all kinds of weapons—throwing grenades, setting explosives, shooting a bazooka, and operating a machine gun. I qualified as a marksman while in boot camp, but afterward I always ranked as a high expert with a rifle, and sharpshooter with a .45 pistol.

When we finished training, we received thirty days leave. I traveled north to see my girlfriend, Bonnie, and my folks.

I joined the Marine Corps at six-foot-one weighing 165 pounds. A year later, I had grown two inches and gained sixty-five pounds of muscle. That's also when I started smoking.

I wrote letters home once in a while. When I returned home from boot camp, Forrest pestered me with questions. I was proud to be a Marine, but I didn't want to encourage him. "Forrest, Marine boot camp is tough. You might want to try another branch of service,' I told him. 'Men are dying in Vietnam, and the Marines are dying faster than they can send them over there." Of course, he didn't listen to his big brother.

***

MP in Bremerton

After leave I reported to my first full-time duty station as a military police officer at the Marine barracks at the Puget Sound Naval Shipyard in Bremerton, Washington. The base had about 200 Marines and 10,000 squids, anchor clankers, aka Navy guys. When we guarded the gates, we carried authority. Those Navy guys didn't come in or go out without our permission. We didn't let anyone through without proper identification. After all, we were now in a war!

Bonnie, Ron, Ron's Mom Rita

We also wore our dress blues and participated in parades, rifle handling and team excrcises. We greeted ambassadors and served at military funerals. We broke up riots, like the time several hundred Navy sailors brawled with Australian counterparts in a large nightclub. We'd go in there with nightsticks, knock them over the heads, and end the fighting.

My military occupational specialty was 0311, which basically means an infantryman, or grunt, even though I played first clarinet, attended college, and earned good grades in high school. I didn't understand why I wasn't assigned to play in the military band, but eventually I accepted that the Corps assigns people according to its needs. Besides, the grunts served as military police at overseas embassies, which sounded good to me.

I had taken Spanish in high school but, in the Marine Barracks, I was studying French, judo, and combat and squad tactics. Our judo instructor was a salty five-foot-nine Corporal busted from gunnery sergeant after he left six guys unconscious in a bar fight.

One of the Marines, Ted Shindelus, stood six-foot-six, while I was six-three and Roy Appel was about six-two. We each weighed more than 200 pounds. When we joined Corporal Dobson's judo class, the instructor's face split into a huge grin. He threw us all over that floor, even though I had played high school football and basketball and lifted weights.

One day while I was at the main gate, a car drove up and proceeded through. The man showed no identification and his car bore no stickers identifying it as belonging to a military officer. I immediately arrested him at the guard house. It didn't take long for him to gain his release given that he was the Navy base's admiral. I didn't know who he was; I just followed orders. Rather than a reprimand, I was meritoriously promoted to Private First Class, complete with a stripe and a letter of commendation from the colonel. I also received a letter of apology from the admiral. Here a military police private, the lowest-ranking maggot, busted an admiral and made it stick. I took my job seriously.

One night in the dead of winter, I was standing outside the gate, armed with a nightstick, .45-caliber pistol, handcuffs, and other gear when a car filled with a half dozen liquored-up college students screeched to a halt. The other guard, Lance Corporal Waddel, a combat veteran, was inside the guard shack.

The doors opened and these college kids poured out, screaming and cursing. "We're going to get us a Marine. We're going to kick some ass."

They tried to intimidate me, so I pulled out my .45, popped a clip into the receiver, and stood watching them as they approached the gate. I figured they were planning to go inside where the Lance Corporal was sitting. They kicked open the door of the inside gate and the unflappable Lance Corporal, who had his feet resting on the desk, pulled up a double-barrel shotgun and pointed it in their faces.

"You got something to say to me, maggots?"

Then he stood.

"Back off, you sniveling little punks! Get out of this office and off my base!" he barked.

"And furthermore,' I piped up, chambering a round loudly, 'if he misses, I won't."

We both growled at them. They almost started crying and whimpering. I thought they would pee their pants as they ran back to the car and burned rubber tearing off into the night.

Ted Shindelus drove a '57 Chevy convertible so we'd drive around Bremerton, Tacoma or Seattle, partying and enjoying a great time. We'd chase girls, flirt a bit, and live the wild life on our liberty time.

In the spring of 1966, a bunch of us Marines had ridden a ferry to Seattle to put on one of our precision drill team routines in our dress blues. Afterward, we stopped at a nightclub for drinks. We proceeded to get soused. We climbed four flights of stairs to reach the club. Either I tripped or somebody tripped me when we left, but I tumbled head over heels down those stairs, crashing into the door at the bottom. Liquored up, I felt no pain. But I was mad. I tore up those stairs, determined to kill whoever tripped me. I never figured out who it was, or how I stumbled. By then, most of the Marines had left, except for six or seven. We piled into a cab. The driver yelled at us for almost tearing off his door, but quickly quieted down as we jostled each other, swearing and angry. He drove us to the ferry.

On board we were in a bad mood. We found some Navy guys and started knocking heads, smashing benches, and tearing apart the boat. Blood flowed from noses, heads, and hands. Crew members tried to stop us, so we fought them too. Then I felt someone push me, so I turned and punched one of my good brother Marines, John Zamecnic, in the nose.

"What'd you do that for?" he asked with blood pouring from his nose through his fingers.

"Oh, I'm sorry."

I didn't realize I had smacked him. I handed him a handkerchief.

About then, the ferry boat captain climbed down the stairs dressed in uniform with braids on his cap. I was so drunk I thought he was a general or admiral. We snapped to attention, saluting him.

"Shut up and sit down!" he said. "Don't move."

He ordered us to sit on a bench and stay put until we reached port.

"Aye, aye, sir."

We clicked our heels, saluted him again, and sat down.

"I don't want to hear a peep out of you either."

"No, sir."

When we arrived at Bremerton, the shore patrol of Navy and Marine servicemen slapped handcuffs on us, threw us into a paddy wagon, and hauled us back to base.

"You will not leave this base under any circumstances,' the Sgt. Major said. 'Get out of those bloody uniforms. Clean yourselves up and then go to your quarters."

We each received Office Hours. I was demoted from PFC to puke private, my meritorious stripe stripped away.

Despite my infraction, my sergeant major recommended me and a few other guys for embassy duty, but he noted one condition: you cannot be married. Bonnie and I had just made plans to marry so I had a choice: embassy duty or marriage. I didn't realize then that I'd be sent to Vietnam rather than a cushy embassy post in France, Spain, Hong Kong, or even South America.

"Well, I'm sorry, but I'm getting married," I told him.

***

Marrying Bonnie

Bonnie and I started dating at the end of my senior year in high school. She was a junior at the time and my third girlfriend, after Linda Cruise and Lorraine DeLuke, an Italian girl I met at church. Bonnie wrote to me and I saw her when I returned home on leave.

She knew me as an all-American clean-cut straight laced kid at church, but during a combined orchestra-band event, she saw me experimenting with a cigarette at the front of the bus with some other boys. She said it made her so angry that she realized right then and there that she cared about me.

Bonnie lived in California with her parents, the Rev. James C. and Gladys Walton. They thought we were too young to marry. My mother opposed the wedding. Nobody liked the idea, except us. It turned out they were right: I was too unstable for any steady relationship, especially marriage. I liked to drink and often wound up in fights, as I did after our ferry trip. I fought way too many times.

But we announced our engagement in early May, with an article published May 4 in the *Independent-Journal*. Bonnie, after graduating from high school, worked at Bank of America in Sausalito.

I mailed Bonnie a wedding ring and we set the wedding date for June 4, 1966, at the First Baptist Church of Mill Valley. Bonnie and her mom decided to visit me to discuss the wedding. They drove north to Bremerton together, leaving Pastor Walton at home. I admired him, even wanted him for my father-in-law, since he didn't drink and never beat me. I admired him as a friend and mentor.

I hopped on my motorcycle, which I used as transportation in Bremerton, and drove to their hotel, looking for them. I'd been drinking. When they arrived at the hotel, Bonnie's mom asked the manager, "Do you know where Ron Brandon is?"

"You mean that crazy drunk Marine? He ran around here with his motorcycle looking for you."

Bonnie said she felt embarrassed; her mom prayed a lot. We talked about the wedding a bit before they returned home. She still thought of me as a clean-cut young man, not an untamed Marine with a wild side.

Rev. and Mrs. Walton

Then I tore up that ferry with the other Marines. After that incident, Mom called Bonnie and told her what happened, noting that I had lost my stripe. She told Bonnie that I was worried she'd never talk to me again. Bonnie later said her father called her into his bedroom, asking if she was sure she still wanted to marry me. She did, especially since the wedding was only a few weeks away. She couldn't imagine telling everyone it was off.

I quit drinking for a while, earned back my stripe, and left for my wedding. Bonnie's brother, the Rev. James C. Walton Jr., conducted the first part of the ceremony, until her father gave her away. Then Bonnie's father stepped up to finish the ceremony. Her younger sister Callie was maid of honor. My brother Forrest stood as my best man. After a reception in the church hall, we left for our honeymoon, which was simply a trip back to Bremerton.

Bonnie and I had a real love relationship when we got married. However, I didn't know the first thing about being a husband or a father. Our furniture that first year in Bremerton was old used stuff that we purchased cheaply or had been given to us. One night, Bonnie went to bed and I was soon to follow. As I leaned over and fell onto the bed, it suddenly collapsed, hitting the floor hard with a big bang. What a surprise that was. We both laughed it off and soon went to sleep.

We set up house together, reveling at first in life as newlyweds. But then I started drinking again, spending nights at bars with friends. One of my friends from church stopped by and asked Bonnie if she had prayed before marrying me.

"It was such a knock on my head,' Bonnie recalled. 'Here I am, a preacher's kid, and I didn't even know enough to pray about getting married. It was such an innocent question. It shook me up and I have thought about that many times."

Bonnie stated that she did in fact love me with all of her heart but she had made a grave mistake. Now she was stuck with it and a child was now on the way. Well, thirteen months in Vietnam was a long time. A lot could happen during that tour of duty. She went about life and, along with her father, prayed a lot for me while I was gone. Prayer was probably what kept me alive and well those long months.

My father-in-law had given us a nice 1956 Buick for a wedding present. All I had at the time was an old motorcycle, a Honda. I had owned and ridden motorcycles most of my life. Harley-Davidson bikes were all I was ever really interested in, although I had a Triumph, a Yamaha and a Honda at one time or the other. I came home from guard duty one night with a cigarette hanging out of my mouth. I had never smoked cigarettes regularly until I joined the Marines.

Bonnie saw that smoke hanging from my lips and hauled off and slapped it out of my mouth sending it flying across the room. I was kind of shocked not only by her audacity but her courage.

Laughing, I asked her "What did you do that for?"

All she could say was, "You are not going to smoke in my house, now or ever."

I laughed again and agreed not to smoke again in her presence. Our marriage was rocky to say the least. Somehow we managed to make it through the next four months in spite of my immaturity, lack of responsibility, and indecent behavior for that matter. Leaving for Vietnam did not hurt our marriage nor did it help it. Being separated was probably both good and bad in many ways. She waited for me and wrote to me faithfully. I ended up missing her a great deal too.

Then I received orders to report to Camp Pendleton, California for a month or so of jungle warfare school and preparation for deployment to Vietnam. I lived on base and Bonnie moved in with her older married sister, Geneen Langen, who lived not too far from the base. We saw each other twice, I think, during that month and we never knew when I would be ordered to board ship. I finally left on a troop ship December 6th, 1966, stopping in Hawaii for about an hour, long enough to unload a sick Marine. Bonnie then moved back in with her parents in Mill Valley, Ca. I didn't know then that she was expecting our first child by July 1967. We had been married less than five months, during which I followed orders including Camp Pendleton and Vietnam.

MILITARY SERVICE IS A BRANDON FAMILY TRADITION

Forrest (Bill) Brandon, Ron's Dad, U.S. Army

Ron Brandon, U.S. Marines

*Forrest Brandon
U.S. Marines*

*Ron Brandon Jr. U.S. Marines
on right*

*Ferral Brandon,
U.S. Air Force*

Veldon Johnson, Cousin, U.S. Army

*Forrest (Bill) Brandon's funeral;
Ron is visible in the middle*

4
Vietnam: A Life Changed Forever

As the rust-bucket World War II troop ship USS *General LeRoy Eltinge* churned across the Pacific Ocean in December 1966, many Marines became seasick. Not me. I had gained my sea legs years earlier on my father's boat, so I just savored the adventure. However, looking in every direction and seeing only water and gray sky gave me an eerie feeling.

In the dining hall, a bunch of guys were playing instruments and they asked if anyone could play the clarinet. So we put together a band, and as I was playing, in walked a familiar face wearing a white Merchant Marine uniform. It was an old high school buddy, Warren Domino, who graduated a year ahead of me. What a total surprise. It was a pleasant one at that. We talked awhile before parting company. I would not see Warren Domino again but I would hear good things about him!

After arriving at Okinawa, I left for eight hours of liberty with a buddy I met on the ship, Clarence Bursaw. Back aboard, we headed for the South China Sea. Our commanding officer lined us up one day.

Map of Vietnam

"I want you to take a look at that man on your right and take a look at that man on your left. Two of you are most likely going to die or be seriously wounded. You might not be coming back."

The words sank in, but as young, strong Marines, we felt invincible.

That is, until we sailed into a typhoon. The ship's steam engine stalled three times during the storm, leaving the big tub at the mercy of the sea, shifting first one way, then another, and bobbing up and down, like riding a buckin' bronco. I was in the bowels of the ship with all these Marines puking their guts out, chucking vomit everywhere.

Since leaving high school, I had walked away from my Christian faith. I walked away from church, giving up God along with my childhood toys. I was a hard-drinking, smoking, raunchy-mouthed devil dog jarhead, not an angel or a hoity-toity Christian. However, He never left me. God never left me nor did He forsake me. He was committed to me, in spite of myself.

That night, sitting on my bunk, the third one up, I prayed, something I hadn't done for a long time. The rocking ship didn't worry me, but the number of Marines losing their lives in Southeast Asia did.

"Lord, if you'll help me and protect me and see me safely through this war in Vietnam, when I come back I'll be what you want me to be and serve you for the rest of my life. I'll preach the Word. Amen."

I repeated the words Isaiah had said, "Here am I, Lord, send me." Thank God, He is patient.

When we reached Vietnam, we slid over the ship's railing and climbed down rope ladders into landing crafts, which carried us to a secure beach at Da Nang in the northern part of the country. We arrived during the relatively cool, mostly dry season, which lasted from November to April, when warmer temperatures brought monsoons. It was pouring down rain and the mud was nearly a foot deep in places.

***

I didn't know much about Vietnam. I finally grasped the idea that we were trying to save the South Vietnamese people from communism, since they wanted to live in a democracy. Those who disagreed with the North Vietnamese Army (NVA) were tortured or killed.

I was assigned to Lima Rifle Company in the Third Battalion, Third Marines in Quang Tri Province, where the unit had been fighting since October with heavy casualties. The battalion commander was Lieutenant Colonel Earl R. DeLong. Lima Company was commanded by Captain John Walter Ripley, a Virginian, and an amazing and fearless man who later became a full-bird colonel. We all respected him. I only regret that I was such an immature knot-head Marine at that time.

Captain Ripley loved all his Marines, and the 200 or so of us in Lima Company in 1967 became known as Ripley's Raiders. He complimented us whenever we did a good job. We might have done stupid stuff occasionally, but he stated that none of his Marines ever failed him. He later earned a Navy Cross for bravery after exposing himself for three hours in April 1972 to repeated enemy fire while setting 500 pounds of explosives underneath the bridge in Dong Ha.

He was about nine years older than me, and far more mature. He enlisted in the Marines at seventeen and graduated from the U.S. Naval Academy in 1962 with a bachelor's in electrical engineering. Commissioned as a second lieutenant, he joined the Third Battalion in October 1966, serving as Lima Company's commander. According to his biography, *An American Knight*, he patterned his aggressive leadership after his hero, Stonewall Jackson, a Confederate general.

When my fellow replacement Marines and I arrived in Vietnam December 19, 1966, twelve long days since leaving San Diego, we found that the region had suffered heavy rainfall during the first half of the month with temperatures between seventy-six and eighty-nine degrees. Right away we were ordered to replace Lima Company's squad on Razorback ridge, a huge rock towering above the jungle. Wearing helmets and boots, carrying eighty pounds of gear on our backs and rifles in our hands, we climbed almost straight up at times, using toe holes, vines, and bushes.

The military used the ridge as an observation point. We ran patrols off the top, climbing to the 300 foot level for observation, running night ambushes into the jungle. Ponchos kept the heavy rain off our bodies, but the gray cloud cover created an eerie atmosphere.

The third day on the Razorback marked the first time I actually realized that somebody was trying to kill me. Lead started flying as heavy small arms fire targeted us from the valley. Bullets pierced the rocks around me. Ping! Zang! I slithered to a hollowed out section. Other guys crawled behind sandbags. Bullets whizzed past my ear, piercing my poncho. We couldn't dig into the rocks for protection. We felt exposed day and night. Unable to pinpoint the enemy's location, 200-300 yards down in the valley, we still returned fire. Then our squad radioman called in artillery. One bullet hit a Marine in the foot, either by a ricochet or direct hit. We had to haul him off the ridge to safety.

We spent two weeks up there in late December. As the New Year dawned, our company remained on the Razorback. We conducted a lot of patrols and ambushes into the jungle, where we found and destroyed a cave that the Viet Cong had used recently. I carried an M-14, then an M-16, and finally an M-79 grenade launcher, so I was known as a bloop gunner. We carried .45-caliber guns, long machetes, and military K-Bar knives. We fought the enemy as well as snakes, rock apes, tigers, and other predators. We also contended with bugs: leeches, mosquitos, and many others.

They finally climbed down off the ridge, one squad of a dozen to sixteen Marines at a time.

Phillip LaFerriere and Ron Brandon, on patrol in Vietnam

***

Lima Company did a lot of patrols, ambushes, or recon missions. We also participated in twenty-two major operations, battalion-sized or bigger. Captain Ripley was a risk-taker. His Marines saw more action than most. Captain Eddie McCourt described Ripley as "fearless" and a magnet for the Viet Cong and North Vietnamese.[1]

"My Marines and I used to request to be assigned to one of Lima Company's flanks because we were sure to see a lot of action," McCourt said.

"People find it hard to believe that I never slept in Vietnam,' Ripley said.[2] 'Never was I fully unconscious. Anytime the handset on the radio clicked, I was fully awake immediately."

His men learned to rest lightly too, since they were never safe in the jungle, whether on patrol or at the base camp. The captain made it a point to become acquainted with his Marines, caring for them like a father, acknowledging their fears while encouraging them to fight back and keep it from controlling them. He led from the front, never backing down from a fight.

During the first four months of 1967 the Third Battalion faced continuous combat on the north-south grid line between Cam Lo and Con Thein which wiped out nearly two companies.

---

[1] According to *An American Knight: The Life of Colonel John W. Ripley,* by Norman J. Fulkerson

[2] According to *An American Knight: The Life of Colonel John W. Ripley,* by Norman J. Fulkerson

***

The Lima Company command post sat between the Rockpile and the Razorback outside of Dong Ha, near the demilitarized zone. We kept a Marine squad on top of each peak to observe enemy activity. Captain Ripley rotated the squads on the peaks every two or three weeks.

From the base camp during January, we ran company and squad-sized patrols and ambushes. We trudged through mud up to our knees, dodging shrapnel that flew at us constantly. Snipers fired at our positions often. Throughout January we continued to run a lot of recon patrols and ambushes. If we stumbled upon the enemy we'd call for air strikes. Most of the enemy just shot at us and ran, disappearing as fast as they could. We found big enemy base camps, well-built bunkers dug in and fortified, and plenty of Viet Cong gear and equipment—Chicom grenades, Chinese-made 82 mm mortar tubes still in their packing crates, Russian-made AK-47 rifles, and lots of ammo. We would confiscate the arms or destroy them.

During January 1967, when I had been in the country only three or four weeks, we started back up the Razorback after a night ambush patrol. The enemy threw small-arms fire at us. It was like being picked off by snipers. We'd return a few rounds and keep climbing. Three Marines were wounded.

One time we were at the 200 foot level, but the enemy was positioned 100 feet above us, firing down at us. We ran a patrol up the mountainside and cleared the area after calling in air support. Fighter planes dropped bombs and strafed the area, doing serious damage. They lowered the elevation of the Razorback by several feet!

***

We provided cover for engineers ordered to blow a cave and build an ammo bunker at the command post. We crossed the Cam Lo River and local streams in recon patrols, reporting on water depth and currents and the firmness of banks. We kept one rifle company on the Rockpile and Razorback at all times. Those squads at times took heavy automatic-weapons fire.

Ron in Vietnam with Rockpile on left and Razorback on right

When we saw enemy troops, usually in gray, green, or khaki uniforms, we always reported their activities. We usually called in mortars and other artillery on their locations, firing on them at the same time. Then we searched the area and counted the dead and wounded.

We often found Soviet and Chinese-made weapons, which we destroyed. Sometimes we discovered bags of rice and vegetables, maps and paperwork, radio equipment and other supplies. We forwarded anything relevant to intelligence officers. We also faced small-arms fire from Viet Cong and fired back.

New Marines rotated in for guys who were leaving—either after their tours ended or in Medical Evacuation (Medevac) helicopters or body bags. We had a lot of guys leaving on Medevac choppers, usually wounded in action. Most of the guys only slightly wounded chose to stay in the field and keep fighting.

***

I remember my first up-close encounter with the enemy.

During my second month in the country, we were on a reconnaissance patrol and ran into a large unit of the North Vietnamese Army (NVA), so we pulled back a hundred or so yards and dug in for a daytime ambush. Concealed in the jungle, we saw two NVA soldiers walking toward us on a trail. They were maybe nineteen or twenty years old, dressed in nice new uniforms. We let them walk to within forty feet of our position and opened fire. They were dead before they hit the ground. They took a lot of bullets.

I had to search one of them afterward to make sure he was dead. I found his billfold with Vietnamese money and a picture of a woman and child. I figured it was either his wife and child, or maybe his sister and her kid. I felt bad that we hadn't tried to take them prisoner, but in jungle warfare, in the rice paddies and mountains, things just happened fast sometimes. War is hell; not much time for thought.

We were in a lot of firefights, close combat with an enemy eager to fire on us. But usually, after shooting, they ran for their lives. They knew our standard operating procedure: make contact, call in artillery, and blow the crap out of everything in front of us. Then we'd attack. A lot of times they would *di di mau*, a Vietnamese expression that means "get out fast."

Captain Ripley often ordered his men to dig foxholes, and then dig another one a bit farther away after dark. Although we complained, when the enemy bombed the first foxholes, we realized the captain was trying to save our lives. One Marine was digging a foxhole when a grenade exploded, wounding him.

Toward the end of February, the Third Battalion, Third Marine Division concluded what was known as Operation Prairie II. By then I'd seen plenty of bloodshed, Marines killed, others wounded, and enemy bodies scattered throughout camps.

***

February arrived with drizzle and overcast skies. We saw the sun only nine days that month. Low fog hampered our ground patrols and Medevac choppers.[3] We operated north of Thon Son Lam on the Razorback.

Patrols found more enemy bunkers, many hidden by thick branches and dirt. We always destroyed machine guns, mortars, ammo, bunkers, and fighting holes. We called in air strikes on possible ambush sites. One time we even found a hammock and a bottle of rice wine.

We always detonated enemy explosives found along the trails or road. Our patrol found three Chicom grenades, each shaped like an old-fashioned potato

---

[3] According to *Ripley's Raiders Vietnam Chronicles* compiled by Russell J Jewett.

masher, tied to trees with vines, triggered by stepping on a tree limb eighteen inches off the ground. We destroyed them before anybody was hurt.

During February, we coordinated relief lines between Lima and Mike companies, starting when it was dark, relieving security units on the Rockpile and defensive positions near Razorback Ridge. We moved most of Mike Company to Lima Company's positions. Platoons relieved from the observation posts served as guides in coordinating movement of vehicles and equipment.

We regularly conducted search-and-destroy operations of VC and NVA complexes, starting in the early morning hours under cover of darkness. Sometimes we were restricted to one meal a day with no resupply anticipated. In mid-February, we found and destroyed a complex of thirty enemy sleeping bunkers, NVA uniforms, boots, rice, batteries, hammocks, and paper with blood on it. The complex was hidden from the air by the jungle canopy. We forwarded maps enclosed in plastic and writing notebooks to intelligence at G-2. Other times we forwarded fuses or other weapons. We destroyed additional enemy base camps, bunkers, fighting holes, caves, and tunnels.

One day our company captured an unarmed Vietnamese national in black clothing carrying a rucksack filled with food. We also apprehended an old man, a woman, and a child. As we continued along the trail, our point man received fire from an NVA soldier. We killed him with small-arms fire. During the firefight, the woman and child escaped.

We lost three Marines on February 19—William M. Branock, Peter J. Liberati, and Johnnie Mason—while eleven suffered wounds when friendly artillery rounds—one volley of six rounds and another of ten—landed amid Lima Company. I dropped to the ground immediately when I heard the incoming rounds of artillery. Shrapnel ripped through the air, trees, and branches. Then I heard the terrible screams of wounded and dying Marines. The smoke cleared and I slowly moved forward toward the sounds of agony. I saw a Marine with his rifle in his arms, leaning against a tree trunk. Only about an inch of his neck was still attached to his head, which was slumped forward. He was dead from a piece of shrapnel that had cut through his neck. How had he managed to kneel down against that tree and then die with that kind of wound? I could not make sense of it.

As ordered, I began picking up body parts: hands, arms, legs, torsos, heads and placing them into body bags to be loaded onto medivac choppers. Screams could still be heard from those who had lost legs or arms and yet had survived the artillery fire; it was a grizzly sight and as I did my grim duty, my hair stood up on the back of my neck; I sensed the spirits of dead Marines moving around me. Something seemed to die inside of me that day. It was so horrible, so traumatic that I was never the same again. I didn't care if I lived or died after that ordeal.

Poor weather at the landing zone delayed evacuation of the injured. We also had to use some explosives to knock down trees to make a clearing for the choppers. We finally evacuated the injured and one VC suspect to be interrogated by the South Vietnamese Army known as Army of Republic of Vietnam (ARVN)[4]. We heard that the ARVN sometimes interrogated enemy soldiers in helicopters and, after questioning, tossed them to their deaths.

At the end of the month, we returned by truck to Cam Lo.

---

[4] Ripley's Raiders *Vietnam Chronicles*

***

In March, search-and-destroy operations continued as enemy forces approached Third Battalion Third Marines.[5] They hit our company with small-arms automatic weapons fire and grenades.

On March 2, 1967, fighting began about 7 a.m. when a sniper targeted Lima Company. After a Marine captured an NVA sentry who carried a complete radio set with Chinese markings, message book, list of radio frequencies, communications logbook, codes, and other documents, Ripley realized we had found a large battalion-level base camp. We hit the jackpot that day.

The NVA fled, but not far, opening fire on Lima Company. Ripley ordered us to fix bayonets. Because of fierce hostile fire, he waved off a chopper crew trying to drop medical supplies. Instead, the crew kicked the supplies out the door, but a mortar hit a box and it exploded, blasting Marines with shrapnel. It even hit Ripley and broke some of his ribs. The fighting continued. We followed bloody bandages along a trail and engaged about a hundred NVA soldiers. We called in mortars and artillery fire and afterward found fifteen NVA bodies.

As we advanced, the enemy lobbed forty rounds of mortar fire at us. We hit the ground, looking for cover, but we were out in the open. I heard the mortars firing, making a very distinct "bloop" sound as they exited the tubes. I was in the first squad and mortars fell like hail all around us. I dropped to my knees, deaf to everything except for the ringing in my ears. Chaos and terror surrounded me; my body shook as if in a seizure.

"Get up, Marine!" a sergeant from the rear said as he shook me hard. "Snap out of it!"

When the smoke cleared and shrapnel quit flying, I looked around and saw dead and dying Marines everywhere—in front, in back, beside me. In our squad of sixteen, ten Marines died and five others were wounded. I was the only man still standing.

I knew almost all of these guys in my squad who died—John W. Barker, Richard B. Blinder, Forrest Goodwin, Richard S. Graham, John W. Hanscom, Jackie L. Harris, Terry G. Heekin, Robert E. Martin, John P. O'Donnell, and Richard W. Strahl. It was like our whole first squad got wiped out. I was a rifleman at that time.

The nearby command post received ten 82 mm incoming mortar rounds. Altogether in Lima Company, a dozen Marines died and twenty-eight were wounded. Most everyone suffered an injury. Even Captain Ripley was hit. I escaped any injuries, by the amazing grace of God.

We targeted the enemy with mortars and small arms, but couldn't ascertain the damage. We couldn't see an enemy to shoot without possibly hitting one of our own guys. We retreated to safety, pulled out our dead and wounded, and called in Medevac choppers. We loaded our wounded onto choppers and put the dead into body bags. No time for tears. No goodbyes.

The NVA regiment, suffering heavy casualties, retreated across the DMZ. We moved out to pursue them before they crossed, targeting them with a vengeance, grief fueling our rage. *You killed our guys; prepare to die!* We chased them down and killed them. If they ran fast and hard enough to conceal themselves until

---

[5] Ripley's Raiders *Vietnam Chronicles*

dark, sometimes they escaped. We boxed them in when we could. We seldom took prisoners—only once, that I recall. We just killed everything that moved. My heart hardened.

We found and destroyed more enemy weapons—anti-tank mines, mortars, submachine guns, grenades, ammunition, fuses, firing devices—as well as gas masks, pots, pans, communications equipment including a radio set, shovels, a trench periscope, and food. We forwarded a code book to intelligence.

That day is when the company earned its moniker Ripley's Raiders, a name worn with pride. We entered the fight that day with more than 200 men, but only 15 remained standing at day's end.[6] I was one of them.

The next day, March 3, we had another Marine killed and four wounded. Our company received twenty-five incoming 82 mm mortar rounds and fired back. I was still a "bloop" gunner, carrying the M-79 grenade launcher as well as a .45-caliber pistol.

Air reconnaissance showed about 250 enemy troops in green and khaki uniforms carrying away their dead and wounded, so we attacked to the north and called in artillery.[7] We stumbled across graves as we chased the enemy, killing them as they fled. We confiscated more weaponry and food, destroying it. We lost another guy; two more were wounded. We ran into the enemy again, fired back and killed eight, but three of our guys were hurt.

Later, our company's tanks approached the village of Thon Bai An from the south. The troops climbed down and, when a tank continued, it hit a mine, exploding into flames, killing one crew member and injuring three others. Our company moved into the village, receiving small-arms fire and ten 60 mm mortar rounds. Seven of our guys were hurt. We saw an NVA soldier near our tank and fired. He was carrying five 60 mm mortar rounds with fuses, 200 rounds of belted .30-caliber ammo, five Chicom grenades and a pack of gear.

By March 5, we had eighty-seven confirmed NVA kills and twenty-nine probable deaths. The battalion also took two NVA prisoners. But we paid a huge price in Marine bloodshed. We lost huge numbers of guys, killed and wounded. The Marines suffered the heaviest casualties of any branch in Vietnam.

Notice the tank behind Ron in Vietnam

***

We left Cam Lo by trucks, returning to the command post, and some guys rotated out after completing their tours.

Old six-ton trucks with benches on both sides hauled us to Cam Lo. Sitting with our gear and guns beside us, we rumbled over dirty bumpy roads, bouncing into knee-deep chuckholes filled with muddy water.

---

[6] According to *An American Knight: The Life of Colonel John W. Ripley,* by Norman J. Fulkerson

[7] Ripley's Raiders *Vietnam Chronicles*

Sometimes NVA soldiers, Viet Cong or even civilians walked up to the trucks and tossed in grenades. One time a kid, probably nine or ten, swung his arm onto the bed of the truck. A Marine snatched out his machete and chopped off his hand. Blood gushed from his arm. It was self-defense. Kill or be killed. He could have held a grenade or satchel charge in his other hand or beneath his shirt. We never knew for sure, but we knew that children had killed truckloads of our men in similar ways. Although the NVA wore uniforms, the Viet Cong dressed in black pajamas, just like the villagers, but participated in guerrilla warfare. Psychologically, it was devastating to be forced into killing potentially innocent people.

***

On March 13, a message from the regimental commander, Colonel Lanigan, arrived addressed to "the gallant officers and men" of the Third Battalion Third Marines:

"Your rapid response to a changing situation, your rapid move into position and subsequent attack to relieve pressure on other units and your rapid and aggressive movement against a determined enemy was the key to forcing the enemy to leave prepared positions and attempt to flee to the safety of the DMZ. Through all of this you gained the admiration of all who observed you. Your action throughout was highly commendable. May God bless all of you and your comrades who died to gain this victory. (It is a comforting feeling for a Regimental Commander to have a battalion of the caliber of the Third Battalion Third Marines always ready.)"

Our battalion continued search-and-destroy missions, investigating all the draws and trails leading from the valley and up the slopes of Dong Ha Mountain and Mutters Ridge. Ammo and food were rationed to prevent running out and we each carried at least four pairs of socks.

We were at about the 200 foot level one night when we heard a bunch of noise below us. It was pitch dark, so we thought they were sneaking up on us. We opened up with automatic weapons, rifles, and grenades. Then…silence.

The next morning, we looked down to where we'd heard the noise—red hairy rock apes littered the ground, dead. The apes, which stand about five feet tall and walk on two legs, probably smelled our empty C ration cans, which we tossed down the hill, and drew near to forage for food. We thought they were the enemy and opened up, killing them. The apes are officially known as Batutut or Ujit, similar to our mythical Bigfoot or Sasquatch.

***

We saw the French influence everywhere—in the bridges, Catholic churches, and beautiful building architecture in the middle of nowhere on old dirt roads.

One time, fortifying our bunkers and doing patrols from our command post, we saw a French priest riding a bicycle along what was called Route 9, which more closely resembled a dirt logging road. He was traveling from Khe Sanh to Dong Ha. He simply pedaled the bicycle past us Marines, keeping his black smock away from the chain, acting as though he didn't have a fear in the world. We thought he was extremely brave, especially with enemy troops, booby traps and mines everywhere.

During another patrol, moving through an old French rubber plantation, we knew the village we planned to destroy sympathized with the Viet Cong. Before we invaded, our planes dropped pamphlets warning villagers to leave. Most did.

As we approached, we took enemy fire from the village. We dropped to the ground, crawling on our stomachs through jungle and rubber trees, firing weapons. When I was close enough, I lobbed a grenade into a hooch. After it exploded, I slithered forward to peer inside. I found a woman and young child, dead, thanks to my grenade. I was so angry. They were trying to kill us. Kill or be killed. But I never forgot that scene, even as we continued our "snoop and poop" operation through the jungle.

When we found the dead bodies of NVA or VC, we had to approach cautiously, since the enemy often booby-trapped their dead, hoping to kill careless Marines.

When we found tunnels, we sent in a few Marines known as tunnel rats, smaller guys who could scramble into the tunnels with flashlights, set charges, and back out before they blew. I never had to go, since I was such a big guy. I'd just toss in a grenade and try to collapse it.

Once in a while, we engaged in hand-to-hand combat with the enemy. But that didn't happen too often. We primarily fired weapons in the general direction from which small-arms fire had come, hoping to hit and kill a target. We couldn't usually even see each other.

***

On March 15, our company found a cylindrical explosive device about an inch and a half long concealed in a partially burned red wax-like Vietnamese candle. It had been purchased earlier in the month along with five other candles at the Vietnamese national store in Dong Ha next to the barbershop.[8] The booby-trapped candles were forwarded to G-2.

By March 18, when Operation Prairie II officially ended, the NVA had lost 694 men with 20 captured. The Marines lost ninety-three men, with 483 wounded, most killed or injured by mortar fire.[9]

In anticipation of sweeping north to Con Thien, the Third Marines Third Battalion and the First Battalion Ninth Marines both moved from Dong Ha to Cam Lo.

Lima Company sent a patrol to high ground. We saw North Vietnamese Army personnel on a hill shooting down at us, which was hairy. So we called in artillery fire on them before we rushed up the hill. Another unit heard drums and chanting east of their perimeter for about twenty minutes. Maybe it was Buddhist monks, calling down curses on us Marines. We'd heard that they'd hexed us.

We continued searching and destroying enemy bunkers, weapons, and food. Before destroying the bunkers, often made of logs and dirt, we tried to determine how recently they had been used, which we reported to headquarters. We established night camps and outposts with observation positions.

At first light March 22, Lima Company spied about thirteen NVA soldiers in khaki and green uniforms, but when we planned an ambush, the enemy's point man spotted us[10]. We fired at him and he fell, wounded, while his comrades fled southeast along the trail. We ordered artillery fire on the enemy position. We later

---

[8] Ripley's Raiders *Vietnam Chronicles*
[9] Ripley's Raiders *Vietnam Chronicles*
[10] Ripley's Raiders *Vietnam Chronicles*

found an old base camp with thirteen bunkers, mortars, mines, carbines, ammunition, gas masks, grenades, and seventeen half-pound blocks of TNT. We also found uniforms, clothing, and documents. We destroyed the mines and ammo, and sent the rest of the material to intelligence.

We often discovered mines in the road along Route 9 and dug them up. As part of my job, looking for suspected mines, I dropped to my knees and used my bayonet to probe the earth for something metallic, hoping it didn't explode when I hit it. We always disarmed them before digging them up.

***

We eagerly anticipated resupply of food, gear and men. New recruits kept arriving to replace those who had survived their year in hell, every one of them changed forever. In the midst of this search-and-destroy operation, I was pleased to reconnect with an old buddy from Bremerton, Ted Shindelus, who arrived in Lima Company March 22. Like me, he was a big guy, six-foot-five and 240 pounds.

We found more enemy weapons, uniforms, hammocks and moldy food, which we destroyed. We also found more graves of NVA soldiers, eight one day, ten the next. When we encountered the enemy, we fired. Every day we lived on edge, looking behind trees and bushes for the enemy, wondering if a gun was pointed at our heads.

We ran into a well-entrenched NVA company southeast of Con Thien with machine guns, bunkers, and nests with light mortars dug below ground, making them hard to find. We called for artillery before assaulting the company along with men in Kilo and Alpha companies. Three Marines died and seventeen were wounded.

Lima Company directed small-arms and 60 mm mortar fire to the east, found a dead NVA soldier, and established night defensive positions. We secured the road north of our position and called in air strikes on Ghost Mountain. Boeing F4Bs dropped general purpose bombs and napalm on the target, but another F4B, after dropping his bombs, turned around for a strafing run. Although the forward air controller gave a wave off, he had fired a short burst of 20 mm into Kilo Company's left flank, killing two Marines and wounding another.

We called in our fighter jets—Phantoms and Crusaders. One Crusader flew in strafing the enemy, but overshot the enemy lines and fired his wing cannons at us. They didn't realize we were as close to the enemy as we were. The pilot flew so low, guns blasting; I could see the moustache on his face through the cockpit.

Shells whizzed past me. Turning, I saw a huge cannon shell blow through the chest of my buddy, Clarence Bursaw, leaving a hole clean through. He had traveled over the Pacific Ocean with me on the old troop transport ship. He was from Minnesota, a few years older than me, known as "Junior" at his Minneapolis area high school. We had partied together on Okinawa during our eight-hour
shore leave. He was just behind me to the right. He was dead before he hit the ground. I saw him beside me, the hole in his chest, but we couldn't stop. We were assaulting the enemy position. But as I fought, my mind swirled with questions: *Oh, man! Oh, man. Our own guys are killing us! What are we doing here?*

We kept shooting, ignoring the pain, the grief, the sorrow, burying it deep inside. Confusion morphed into anger, aimed at the enemy, but deep inside, anger at the pilot, the country, the world, and the senselessness of a mistake that ended the life of a friend.

Our company received about forty rounds of incoming 82 mm mortar fire from the enemy so we shot back with our 60 mm mortars. Four of our Lima Company guys were hurt. A Marine from Command Group Alpha security patrol detonated an explosive device while moving through a hedgerow. Harassing mortar and sniper fire continued for days, until the enemy finally withdrew during the evening of March 26 into the demilitarized zone, leaving behind twenty-eight bodies, two of them women wearing NVA uniforms.

When the firefight ended, we had to put on gloves and walk around picking up arms, legs, hands, feet and torsos, trying to keep the bloodied limbs of each guy together to put inside one body bag.

We used explosives to knock down trees on the forested mountainside to create a landing zone so a chopper could retrieve the remains. No time to weep. No wailing aloud. No time to grieve. Stuff emotions inside and go on, knowing that tomorrow it could be me in a body bag. Shut down the feelings; avoid friendships. A whole lot of good Marines died in Vietnam.

I became like a killing machine without emotions. I never cried one tear the entire time I was in Vietnam. Not once.

The next day, Lima Company did a platoon sweep and found an enemy body dressed in a brown uniform, dead about seventy-two hours. We found a demolished AK-47 and four Chicom grenades with trip wires set as mines in a hedgerow. We blew them up.

Then our company saw an enemy soldier wearing a tan uniform, carrying a pack and running down the trail behind civilians. We didn't fire to avoid hitting innocent people. At first light we searched the village of ten huts, three sheds, and a large bunker with a fifteen-inch-thick reinforced roof. We found one NVA uniform with hat and sneakers, three ponchos, tools and an unusual amount of food for a village where only two men, eight women, and twenty children lived.[11] We destroyed the village and sent the civilians to Con Thien for resettlement.

Between March 18 and 28, during Operation Prairie III, our searches resulted in sixty-five NVA killed and twenty-eight others likely dead. But we lost good Marines too—more than a half dozen from the Third Marines Third Battalion, including Kilo Company's Clarence Bursaw and a Private named Gary Ken Newman, both killed by friendly fire, their cause of death officially listed as "misadventure." Others who died were Lance Corporal Raymond Louis Macklin and PFC Frederick Wilson Bergess, Company K; Gunnery Sergeant Chester Raymond Pavey, Company I; Corporal Warren Demarest Vought Jr., Company M; and Second Lieutenant David H. Cooper II, Company H.

We pulled out of that area March 28 and returned to the command post at Thon Son Lam. We continued patrols and ambushes, destroying bunkers, fighting holes, weapons and equipment when we found it.

***

In late March, back at our base camp, we received about forty rounds of incoming fire.

Several of us off-duty Marines sat inside our bunker, trying to take a break. We didn't have electricity so we used candles beneath ponchos to prevent any light from leaking, giving away our position to the enemy. We used battery-operated

---

[11] Ripley's Raiders *Vietnam Chronicles*

radios and record players. As we drank beer, jamming and dancing to the Supremes, a mortar round landed right on the bunker, blowing off half the roof, caving in the rest on top of us. We dug ourselves out. Nobody was hurt that time. But you never knew when something could happen.

One night, a Marine sat on the crapper, a ten-man toilet built in the compound away from the bunkers, and lit a cigarette with a lighter, trying to cup it with his palms. Bam! One rocket smashed into the crapper, blowing it to heck and back. I considered it a miracle shot, hitting that thing with one round after catching just a split-second glimpse of light. A couple of Marines died. We learned a hard lesson that day. It could have been any one of us; we all smoked.

***

During April, Lima Company engaged in Operation Prairie IV, which included bloody fights with heavy losses near Khe Sanh referred to as the Hill Fights.[12]

The enemy launched more ambushes on trucks, tanks, and equipment, using mines, hand explosives, mortars, and small-arms and automatic weapons. We operated near the command post early in the month, conducting patrols and ambushes, discovering more dead enemy soldiers and machine guns. Then we left by truck for Thon Son Lam.

On April 9 we moved to Ca Lu to relieve K Company and resumed search-and-destroy missions. Starting near Hill 492, we swept all the trails in the vicinity. We found enemy camps with well-built camouflaged bunkers, reinforced with logs, dirt, and waterproofing, grass and wood huts, and dozens of fighting holes, which we destroyed. We sent the gear to G-2. Second Platoon fired on two NVA soldiers, but they killed one of our guys, Robert K. Hice.

We had linked up with Kilo Company on patrol, pushing through heavy brush in the jungle, a combination of rice paddies, trees, and brush. Someone hit a trip wire on a Chicom grenade set five feet off the ground as a booby trap. It exploded. Shrapnel blew forward into Ted Shindelus's back, shoulder, and right arm. It hit four other guys too. The wounds were minor enough that the guys continued with our unit. Although I was closer than anybody, none of the shrapnel hit me. It shot one direction—forward.

After returning to the base camp at the Rockpile, Lima was assigned to relieve Kilo Company at the Ca Lu outpost not far from Laos, just south of the demilitarized zone and expected to be a less demanding assignment than our three weeks near Con Thein.

***

Shortly after he arrived on April 15, Corporal David Schwirian was ordered to lead his squad on a nighttime patrol toward Khe Shan to set up an ambush in the bush along Route 9 west of Ca Lu, nearly three miles from the outpost. High cliffs stretched above one side of the road and the Quang Tri River flowed on the other.

They arrived at the ambush site and dug in, rain dribbling from the dark sky. They checked in every hour with a simple radio handset double-click to indicate all was secure. Schwirian dug into a foxhole at the center of his squad, his radio operator Steve Fickel and a corpsman nearby. In the stillness of the night, he reached over toward his radio operator to see if he had checked in.

---

[12] Ripley's Raiders *Vietnam Chronicles*

Schwirian let loose a blood-curdling scream! Mixed with his yowl were low guttural growls.

As Schwirian had stretched out his arm, a Bengal tiger latched onto it from behind and shook him like a rag doll, ripping out his muscle, severing a nerve. When he punched the growling big cat in the muzzle with a right cross, it let go of his arm and lurched backward. As Schwirian dropped to the ground, the other Marines opened fire and the animal bounced down the hill.

Their corpsman, "Doc" Daniel Fuss, rushed to Schwirian's side, trying to wrap up his bloody arm and radio for help at the same time. He also wrapped his head, turning it away from the wounded arm and shoulder, and gave Schwirian morphine. One of the men radioed the command post, saying they needed to return.

Wrapping his arm around Schwirian's waist, Fuss lifted him to a standing position. Another Marine pulled his good arm over his shoulder, and the two of them helped him hobble back toward base camp.

Two-thirds of the way to the base camp, Schwirian collapsed from loss of blood. His squad used ponchos as a makeshift stretcher to carry him to the camp, crossing a bridge single file in the dark, rushing to the relative safety inside the perimeter. It took them nearly three hours to reach the camp. Upon examination in the light, Fuss saw claw marks, torn flesh, and a clean bite that ripped out muscle from the bicep.

A chopper couldn't be sent until morning, so Marines carried Schwirian to the Rockpile, where he was evacuated by a dump truck accompanied by a Jeep to Delta Med at Dong Ha. After treatment there by Lt. G. Gustave "Gus" Hodge, he was transferred by chopper to the USS *Sanctuary*, where he spent April and May before being sent home to Pennsylvania, where he was discharged after nearly losing his arm. His story appeared in national publications such as *Readers Digest* and *Time*.

We always referred to him afterward as Tiger Dave.

In the morning, our squad returned to the attack site and found tiger tracks measuring four-and-a-half inches in diameter. We followed them, hoping to find the tiger and kill it. We figured it had to have been seven feet long and weighed a couple of hundred pounds.

A few days after the attack, we heard about villagers in the upper Ba Long area sleeping in the fields at night to prevent wild animals from destroying their crops before harvest. They were warned to return to their villages by dark because we couldn't guarantee their safety if they stayed overnight in the fields.

***

We were ordered to call in artillery during search-and-destroy patrols when making contact with or sighting the enemy and also to request air strikes on suspected targets whenever weather permitted.

Lima Company dispatched a fire team from Second Platoon April 25 to reinforce a road maintenance team under fire. The enemy ambushed an engineer unit north of Route 9. A dump truck with a trailer hit a mine that blew off its front tire so it veered out of control. Two 72 mm rockets hit it. Rescuers faced heavy automatic small-arms fire, mortars, and grenades. The NVA tossed a gallon-sized can filled with explosives into a truck. A three-quarter-ton personnel carrier with a trailer also hit a mine.

Lima Company provided security for the two damaged vehicles at the ambush site. Five died—two Army and three engineer personnel—and twenty-four were wounded in action. No U.S. traffic was allowed beyond the Ca Lu command post without prior approval and then only with sufficient security.

The next day, the Eleventh Engineers salvaged the demolished vehicles with a security force of six vehicles, twenty engineers, and a fire team from Lima Company. A bridge was blown during the night. Lima Company apprehended an ARVN deserter, who was forwarded to the Fifteenth CIT in Cam Lo.[13]

The Eleventh Engineers repaired the blown bridge but received a sniper round that grazed an engineer in the forehead. Marines retaliated with small-arms fire and 81 mm mortars.

***

Enemy activity decreased slightly in May, but increased on Mutters Ridge and in the Ba Long Valley. Lima Company sent squad-sized patrols and ambushes into the Quang Tri River area along Route 9, which extends west through the province from Dong Ha to the Laos border, linking Dong Ha and Khe Sahn bases. It covered sixty-three kilometers with thirty-six bridges.

On May 6, Lima Company reported an M42 command truck had turned over on Route 9, injuring several men. A recovery vehicle had to lift the M42 off four men pinned beneath it—one Marine and three Army personnel. Two Marines died that day—Jay T. Hensley and George A. Lewis.

Daily patrols and ambushes continued. Lima Company provided security May 11 for the Eleventh Engineers Rough Rider convoy of sixteen vehicles passing through Ca Lu toward Khe Sanh. Three days later, we received an order that all patrols and ambushes have at least twelve men, including a corpsman.

On May 16, the village chief of La Cat notified a Lima scout that the VC had buried an object in a nearby field. A patrol dug up an armed six-inch round antitank mine with plastic wrapped around it, buried at the end of a bridge near the road. A vehicle would have triggered it while crossing the bridge.

The following day, a recon Marine was brought into the command post with eyes swollen shut from insect bites. Poisonous spiders never bit me, but I remember plenty of leeches sucking the blood from my body, clinging so tightly they left scars when pried loose with a knife. We dodged a poisonous snake nicknamed two-steppers because, once bitten, you could walk two steps before you died.

Enemy rockets struck the rear of Third Battalion Third Marines at Dong Ha May 18, damaging a radio Jeep and generator and demolishing a command post tent. A Marine, Jacque J. Ayd, was killed.

Several times during the month, Lima Company provided security details for Rough Riders to Khe Sanh for Eleventh Engineers bridge and road repair platoons. One platoon was working on the most critical bridge along Route 9, which spanned a gorge east of Khe Sanh.

Two civilians were apprehended for questioning after they claimed they were following a trail to their fields to prevent animals from eating their crops. A farmer from Ba Tan was also interrogated. He said seven VC armed with Chicom rifles moved southeast along the road through Ba Tan and ordered children to tell

---

[13] Ripley's Raiders *Vietnam Chronicles*

them the time, size, and direction of the Third Battalion Third Marines patrols.[14] He was released after questioning.

[14] Ripley's Raiders *Vietnam Chronicles*

5
Casualties and Ambushes

In late May with temperatures over a hundred, I collapsed onto my bunker, still wearing my ragged and dirty clothes after returning from patrol near Cam Loon. I blacked out; that's the last I remember.

A week later, I woke aboard the USS *Sanctuary* hospital ship, floating off the coast of Vietnam.

I looked down to see my body packed in ice, under my armpits, between my legs. I passed out again. I had been medevacked from Ca Lu.

When I woke up again, I was no longer in ice, my temperature having dropped from 105 to normal. As I recovered on the hospital ship, I ran into Tiger Dave, whose arm was wrapped tightly, as if in a cast. Before I was ready to return to duty, I witnessed a horrible event. Since the ship was only three to four miles off the coast, we could see that a 'fire-fight' was in full flare. Explosians, bright flashes, then total darkness. Suddenly we heard the distinct sound of rotor blades. Womp! Whumph! Wump! We were able to make out a double-prop Seaknight chopper, low, just above the water, about a mile or so away, coming toward us. It dropped like a rock, hit the sea, and vanished. It all happened so fast it was hard to believe.

Ron on USS Sanctuary
May 1967

We found out that morning that two pilots, two crewmen and ten wounded marines were on board that chopper. One wounded marine survived. We fished him out of the water on the double. The rest perished by drowning. At least ten boats searched for days and only recovered dead bodies. It was another of many traumatic experiences in Vietnam

Doctors never figured out what caused me to collapse or my fever to skyrocket, but after two weeks, when it dropped back to normal, I rejoined the fight.
***

During the summer, we were dug in at the company command post right off of Highway 9, doing guard duty watching the perimeter in shifts of four off and four on during the night. Triple concertina barbwire, claymore mines, and tripflares protected us from surprise attacks.

We spent a lot of time in Vietnam digging foxholes and building bunkers in the bush. Life there was hard work—loading and unloading helicopters, emptying ammunition boxes, hauling C-rations to keep us nice and thin and healthy.

When I left for Vietnam in December 1966, I weighed 230 pounds, but fourteen months later, I returned home weighing only 185 and looking like a rag doll. That's what happens when you eat only C-rations. Once in a while we received our beer ration—two cans of beer a week—and if we were in a rear area where we could find it, we'd buy a bottle of whiskey off friendly villagers. We primarily drank water treated with chlorine-based Halazone tablets to remove contaminants. It left a nasty taste but we needed to drink, especially in the hot season when temperatures could top one hundred degrees.

Sometimes we filled our canteens from creeks or rain-filled bomb craters, dropped in a few Halazone tablets, shook it up good, and then guzzled. Other times we drank from the river.

On at least one occasion, it was real hot and we were all so thirsty, with a real shortage of water, that we had to literally fly in what they called a "water buffalo"—a big tank of water—by helicopter so we could fill up our canteens with actual fresh water that we didn't need to treat or pull out of a swamp or a creek or a river.

Another time, as I was drinking from the river, I looked up to see two bodies floating downstream. You never knew what you would see next over there.

***

Malaria swept through the American camps during June and July, carried by the ever-present mosquitoes, and created a need for more medevacs by choppers. Another Marine showing signs of appendicitis had to be airlifted.[15]

We continued with patrols and ambushes, and provided security for the Eleventh Engineers who were called to repair damaged roads and bridges. We always had to watch for booby traps hidden alongside the trail under leaves and grass.

A Marine in Lima Company, while passing a civilian convoy in early June, saw a man he thought was a Viet Cong spy so he detained him and sent him to Cam Lo for interrogation.

Three Montagnards—Vietnamese who lived in the mountains rather than the flatlands and hated the Viet Cong, NVA, and Communists—showed up at our base June 15 seeking food and protection. They had been laborers at an outpost for five years but ran out of food and traveled up the Ba Long Valley.

On June 23, I was leading a patrol when I heard a racket ahead in thick elephant grass about twenty feet off the trail. I couldn't see what it was, so I opened fire, killing my first water buffalo. The official report says the animal charged the K-9 scout dog accompanying our patrol, so we killed it to protect our war dog and handler. However, after the Battalion Civil Affairs officer investigated, we had to pay the farmer for killing his animal.

A patrol saw a Vietnamese man in black pajamas fleeing from a hut and running down a trail into brush as they approached. The patrol found papers that appeared to be propaganda.

An overnight mortar attack injured six members of a Rough Rider convoy battalion and caused minor damage to three vehicles June 26.

---

[15] Ripley's Raiders *Vietnam Chronicles*

On June 27 the enemy fired fifty rounds of mortars on the Khe Sanh base camp, killing four Marines and an RVN liaison officer and wounding seventy-six. One of the dead was George T. Mangrum of Lima Company; eight others in our company were hurt. While medevacking the injured, a helicopter crashed because of mechanical failure. Lima Company provided security while the wounded were evacuated to Da Nang and Phu Bai.

That same day, Lima Company received a visit from Floyd Patterson, former heavyweight champion of the world, accompanied by Hugh O'Brien, who portrayed Wyatt Earp in the television series.

During June, medevac choppers carried away five Marines with possible malaria, one with possible heat stroke, another guy coughing up blood, and another with possible appendicitis.

***

Lima Company continued providing security for Rough Rider convoys and Eleventh Engineers during July.[16] We continued with patrols and ambushes.

Everyone remained on alert status on Independence Day, anticipating possible attacks. One Lima Company patrol literally ran into a hornet's nest, with four guys stung on the head, face, arms and back. They were treated with Benadryl injections and resumed their patrol.

Thirteen refugees who said they escaped from the Viet Cong west of Ca Lu and evaded them for ten days arrived at Lima Company's position, where they were given food and medical attention before being sent to the Cam Lo Refugee Center.

We often called in artillery support from Camp Carroll, where Lima Company was assigned for three or four weeks one time to guard the perimeter. In addition, when we were there in July 1967, I received a telegram from the States. I was a new papa! I had a daughter! Ronda was born in San Rafael July 9, 1967.

I visited the local village to buy a box of cigars and then entered the CO's hooch, where the platoon sergeant, gunny, and company radioman were seated, along with a few other Marines. I passed out cigars to celebrate my daughter's birth.

Bloop! Ka-boom! The enemy fired four 102 mm rockets at us. We dove into trenches to avoid the rockets. We hunkered down as shells exploded around us.

"Well, we sure celebrated my daughter's birth,' I said to a fellow Marine. 'So did the Vietnamese! They sent us some fireworks."

They blew up the hooch where we had been standing, but nobody was hurt badly.

We left Camp Carroll two days later.

Search-and-destroy missions continued through the valley west, northwest, and north of the Dong Ha Mountain complex. We found more bunkers and campsites with fighting holes, which we destroyed.

We swept Route 9 in advance of Rough Rider convoys and provided security for engineers. The enemy planned an attack on a convoy traveling Route 9, but a mortar triggered prematurely, warning the Americans of danger. The convoy received small-arms fire but returned to Ca Lu. The next day, our company found Chicom mines rigged with trip wires alongside the road, set to ambush troops seeking cover on the south side of the road.

---

[16] Ripley's Raiders *Vietnam Chronicles*

We also found a minefield with thirty Z-10 Chicom mines spaced about 150 feet apart on the south side of Route 9, with five-foot-long trip wires about a foot above ground. We destroyed all the mines.

As Lima Company swept Route 9 en route to Ca Lu July 24, we found and destroyed claymore mines, bunkers and more than five hundred fighting holes. But an explosive device detonated and killed one Marine—Francis J. Ludwig—and wounded another. Three days later, patrols found more fighting holes and bloody bandages.

Marines with the large snake that crawled over Ron at 3 AM

***

Several times our company called in Puff the Magic Dragon, an AC-130 aircraft with deadly Gatling guns mounted in the side of the fuselage.

One night we were stationed on the Razorback, next to the Fishbowl with Mutters Ridge to the north, when we heard a racket. We called in artillery to drop bright parachute flares that turned night into day so we could see what was happening and target enemy locations. We thought we saw movement of a large NVA unit, so we called in Puff, which flew at the slowest possible speed so their guns hit their target. Spewing bullets, with every fifth round a tracer containing red powder, the plane left a trail that made it look like the sky was bleeding amid a cloud of smoke and terrifying racket. Deadly, these guns killed hundreds of VC at a time, shooting everything it passed as if mowing grass. Then we'd go in and mop up, though we found very few still breathing.

Other times the fighters dropped napalm and we heard horrible screams as enemy soldiers burned, but they died pretty quickly. The B-52 bombers also were effective. We often followed the bombers, finding entire squads of NVA troops lying side by side in perfect marching order, not a scratch on them, dead from concussion of the bombs. Other times we encountered gruesome gory scenes with flies, maggots and other bugs crawling inside their mouths, noses, and eyes. It was a grisly sight.

***

We also encountered snakes. We'd go into the bush for a week or two at a time, often crossing rivers with water up to our necks, so we lifted our weapons above our heads as we slogged through the water. Some of the shorter Marines had to grab onto taller guys so they wouldn't drown. Climbing ashore, we'd find leeches latched onto our arms and legs, sucking our blood. We'd take a cigarette butt and try to make them let go. If we scraped them off with a bayonet blade, part of the critters remained under our skin, festering and creating infection. They left small round marks on our bodies that disappeared only years later.

We saw mosquitos that sometimes seemed as large as flies, and spiders as big as your hand. We were always dealing with centipedes, scorpions, and weird bugs. We also saw all kinds of snakes—two steppers, pit vipers, and big boa constrictors. We used to say Vietnam had a hundred types of snakes—ninety-nine of them a venomous variety that could poison, swallow or crush you to death.

One night, while lying on my back zonked out on some ammo boxes at the base camp, I felt cold clammy paws prancing across my forehead. I woke up in the pitch black, listening to the rustling of rats chirping and cheeping. Then I felt something heavy slithering across my thighs. Although I had a bayonet and pistol beside me, I froze, hoping the big snake would keep slithering through the front of the bunker without stopping for a bite of me. It did. The critter had slid through a back ventilation hole into the bunker.

"Snake!" I hollered out front to another Marine, a guy from Louisiana who knew all about snakes. He tore out of there so fast, poncho flying behind him. He just vanished! It was pretty funny, although that snake crawling over my legs scared the crap out of me too!

We set off flares to see where the snake was and to ensure nobody was crawling through the trip wires. I couldn't fall back to sleep that night. The next day, a bunch of Marines captured the boa constrictor and put it into a box. I think they finally let it go.

***

We saw a lot of action in Vietnam. I was on twenty-two major operations with names like Operation Kentucky, Operation Lancaster, Operation Prairie II, III, and IV.

In late July, a firefight between the Vietcong and Mike Company closed Route 9 for a time. That month saw one Lima Company Marine evacuated with first and second-degree burns on his body, seven with possible malaria, two men with temperatures of more than 104 degrees, one man with possible appendicitis, another with an eye infection, and another with an arm injury.[17]

The major effort in August was keeping Route 9 open, with sweeps, patrols, and ambushes conducted regularly.

We continued to sweep the road whenever Rough Rider convoys passed through, traveling between Khe Sanh and Dong Ha, but they were delayed when air cover was unavailable.

Marines continued to need evacuation for medical reasons—high temperature, high fever, neck swelling, and other ailments. On August 13, Lima Company requested medevac for seven Marines with non-battle injuries—heat stroke, a bee sting, a fractured wrist, a fractured hip and leg, and three possible malaria cases. The Medevac helicopter approaching the landing zone caught fire because of a malfunction of the rear rotor gearbox and plunged rapidly to the ground. After Marines on the ground doused the fire, they loaded the ill and injured men onto another chopper for evacuation. One platoon stayed in place to guard the downed helicopter until it was retrieved.

---

[17] Ripley's Raiders *Vietnam Chronicles*

The next day, two Marines needed medevac—one for malaria and one for dysentery, and the following day, a Marine was evacuated with shigellosis, a bacterial infection which caused stomach cramps, diarrhea and fever.

***

On August 21, twenty-six "grunts" from a Third Marines Platoon left Camp Elliot to connect up with the colonel and his command post group. They had jumped on an M42 Duster (a self-propelled anti-aircraft gun tank which held six people) to go one-and-a-quarter miles ahead on Route 9. Our undermanned platoon had one Marine killed in action—PFC Benjamin "Benny" Romero-de-Jesus. One of the Marines, our squad leader Charles "Duf" Hudson, recalled lying spread-eagle across the road, trying to stop Benny DeJesus's bleeding as he died. Seventeen of our guys were wounded (actually eighteen, but Phil Laferriere didn't report his wounds). Other units reinforcing us also had men killed.

That same day, a convoy passed our base camp between the Rockpile and Razorback heading to Khe Sanh. Three trucks in a resupply convoy were ambushed by an entire battalion of dug-in NVA firing small arms, grenades, mortars and rockets. Some of the guys jumped off their rigs and radioed the command post for help, reporting they were under fire.

The entire Lima Company immediately saddled up double-time and took off, sweeping the area as we moved through with two twin 40 mm Dusters to reach the stranded Marines. Several other Marine units were involved—the Third, the Twenty-Seventh, the Ninth Marines, the Fourth Marines, and I can't remember who else. We surrounded this NVA battalion and swept forward.

An aerial observer spotted forty to fifty fighting holes and bunkers, from which automatic weapons erupted. The observer called in air strikes, and after that we engaged the enemy, taking small-arms and rocket fire, with both twin 40s hit. The enemy soldiers had dug into foxholes with spider traps, little covers that they'd pop up to shoot at us and then drop into for cover. Two tanks and two twin 40 mm left the command post, moving south, to fight the enemy.

"Fix bayonets!" Captain Ripley ordered. "Charge!"

All 180 or so Marines in Lima Company grabbed steel and slammed it onto our rifles, then let out a blood-curdling yell like a Confederate rebel cry and smashed and thrashed through the jungle, killing everything in sight.

I carried an M-79 grenade launcher, or bloop gun, which resembled a short-barreled shotgun, and fired rounds as quickly as I could. One round landed on a three-crew machine gun nest, killing all of them. I stitched them, firing three rifle rounds into each body to make sure they were dead. We didn't want anybody shooting us in the back as we moved forward in echelon formation, a large wave firing to clear our path.

Captain Ripley was right beside me as we moved through this enemy territory. We practically annihilated that NVA battalion, although a few escaped.

Unfortunately, we found one of the Marines from that convoy—a sergeant, brutally tortured. The Vietnamese could be every bit as vicious as the Japanese in WWII. They had stripped him down naked and strung him up spread-eagle on a big tree trunk. Then, while he was still alive, they disemboweled him, cut off his private parts and stuffed them into his mouth. He died from blood loss and shock. It was a horrible, vicious act.

Ripley's eyes watered. We went berserk. We took no prisoners, killing everyone we found. We truly were devil dogs then, ferocious, vicious, angry and completely nuts. We never stopped until we were commanded to regroup.

That was only one of the few times I had fixed bayonets to charge.

Kilo Company brought two tanks from the command post to reinforce Lima. Mike Company's convoy casualties were evacuated to Ca Lu. Air strikes destroyed three bunkers, damaged another one, demolished eight fighting holes and two automatic weapon positions, and killed at least six enemy soldiers.

A truck and driver thought to be ambushed hadn't left the command post yet. Two other drivers arrived at Ca Lu. But the driver from Ninth Motor Transport was not at Ca Lu; he was missing in action. (Lance Corporal Leonard R. Budd was a POW in North Vietnam for six years.)

A Mike Company Platoon captured three NVA soldiers. The enemy withdrew and Mike Company returned to Ca Lu with the destroyed convoy trucks. Six men were killed—three Marines and three others—and thirty-five were wounded. We had 129 confirmed enemy kills and 305 who probably died, with one prisoner of war sent to be interrogated.[18] Lima Company apprehended five Vietnamese men and two boys in a civilian truck claiming to be woodcutters. Marines found spent brass in the truck's bed and forwarded the detainees to the Fifteenth Counter Intelligence Battalion.

Our search-and-destroy patrols continued, with the battalion being mortared five times and receiving sporadic small-arms fire almost every day. We returned to Camp J.J. Carroll August 28 and then moved on to the Ca Lu outpost again.

***

One time we were patrolling what we called Ghost Mountain and, after hiking fifteen or twenty miles in one day, we took a break. The next day, we started climbing, pursuing a large group of NVA. Halfway up the mountain, a soldier jumped out from behind a huge tree, where he had been hiding, with a Thompson submachine gun. He emptied the entire banana clip into our squad, probably twenty or thirty rounds, wounding one Marine in the back of the neck. A Navy corpsman 'Doc', the first to react, snatched his .45 pistol and pumped six rounds into that guy, killing him before he could reload to shoot again. We really appreciated Doc after that. He took good care of our wounded Marine.

Another time we engaged an NVA battalion from a ridgeline, shooting across a valley at unseen men who were firing back at us. We called in air support strikes. Fighter jets dropped napalm, setting off huge fires, and then we'd move in. We found burnt trees and dead bodies everywhere. We had 109 confirmed kills in one particular area, with another 305 suspected killed.

One time near the fire support bases near Khe Sanh, the enemy attacked our outer perimeter at Con Tien by the hundreds. We were ordered to fix bayonets because we thought they might break through the wire and perimeter. But after the firefight, the wires were littered with the dead bodies of NVA who tried to storm the base. It was really grisly.

On August 29, Lima Company was assigned temporarily to First Battalion, Ninth Marines to relieve India Company, providing defense at Camp Carroll and the Khe Gia Bridge.

---

[18] Ripley's Raiders *Vietnam Chronicles*

Ripley at times provided hot coffee to men returning from patrol to keep up their morale.[19] The cook provided hot water for shaving, which Ripley required his men to do. He wanted his Marines to look and act respectably. Ripley also wrote to the families of his men back home, letters of condolence and others of praise.

It was easy for the men to feel sorry for themselves, far from home and constantly facing death, but what they did without didn't compare to the ultimate sacrifice some families paid when their loved ones never returned home alive.

Ripley was injured four times during his first Vietnam tour, returning home with a Silver Star, a Bronze Star with V for valor and a Purple Heart.

During the fall, we started building and defending the McNamara Line, fortifications along the DMZ in an area known as Leatherneck Square—Cam Lo, Con Thien, Gio Linh and Dong Ha.

The Viet Cong attacked the positions and the Third Marines, Third Battalion had to rescue the Second Battalion Fourth Marines before they were overrun. Third Battalion occupied several of those fortifications through May 1968.

The reinforced Third Battalion Third Marine Division earned the Presidential Unit Citation for gallantry, determination and esprit de corps under difficult and hazardous conditions, heroism similar to that for which the Air Force or Navy Cross is awarded. The citation recognized eighty-seven major operations from March 29, 1966, to September 15, 1967, for seeking and destroying the enemy in canopied jungles, rugged mountains and swampy lowlands. We defended key airfields and communication routes, conducted a pacification and revolutionary development program, freed Vietnamese villages, and captured tons of rice.

***

On September 7, 1967 a large enemy force ambushed a resupply convoy of two tanks, a fuel tanker, a Mite, two Quad-50s and two six-by-sixes on Route 9 heading to Ca Lu. Convoy personnel were pinned down by enemy fire. A squad with 81 mm mortars left for South Bridge. Small-arms fire attacked an India Company Platoon and later Mike Company from both sides of Route 9. Mike and India companies also received incoming mortar fire. The Mike Company tank commander was wounded.

Lima Company left Camp Carroll by truck convoy and linked up with India. Four Marines needed medevac, but the helicopter received small-arms fire. A Mike Company Platoon moved with all convoy vehicles back toward the Ca Lu outpost, which fired on the enemy. Mike received recoilless rifle fire and called in medevac choppers. All units returned to their command posts.

But the Lima Company command post received incoming mortar rounds three times. Twice the mortars fell outside the perimeter. During the third attack, the only attack at the post in nine months, twenty rounds of 102 mm rockets hit inside the perimeter, and enemy soldiers were seen near the defensive wire of the post. Two Marines were killed during the mortar attack—Lee B. Jarvis and Albert C. Lawson—and fifteen others were wounded.

Thirteen Montagnards, who get their name as mountain people by the French colonialists, arrived at our camp; they were detained under guard and interrogators discovered they walked from a village up the road to the Third Battalion

---

[19] *An American Knight: The Life of Colonel John W. Ripley, USMC.*

Third Marines command post about the time the convoy was ambushed. They were forwarded to intelligence at Cam Lo.

With arrival of the monsoon rains, the malaria rate increased. Building materials were in short supply. The battalion evacuated forty-two confirmed cases of malaria, draining its manpower. Another Marine was evacuated with a high fever and gastroenteritis September 11th, and one with a high fever left September 15th.

A patrol searched Viet Cong villages and burned both of them. An Arc Light request for B-52 heavy bombers was made on twelve separate NVA sites suspected of launching ambushes on convoys along Route 9 between the Rockpile and Ca Lu between August 21st and September 7th.

***

A Lima Company Marine accidentally discharged a .45-caliber pistol October 1, wounding one Marine in the right forearm. He was medevacked.

A convoy of the Third Marines, including Lima Company, left Thon Son Lam to Dong Ha October 10, joining with the Ninth Marines to relieve the Third Battalion Fourth Marines at C2 and C2 bridge areas. Commanders were cautioned to maintain flank security. Each Marine carried a gas mask, entrenching tool, three meals, and they were ordered to wear helmets and flak jackets.

On October 14, a Lima Company battalion moved out to defend the C2 Bridge, fortifying positions, laying wire and clearing fields. They provided security for convoy resupply of Con Thien. Two companies swept north, one each to the east and west, then determined a likely ambush site. The mission resumed the next day, with two meals instead of three. Aircraft flew overhead before a detonation killed three and wounded nine Marines near the C2 Bridge, which received nine incoming 122 mm rocket rounds. Artillery targeted enemy positions.

Lima Company spotted a column of troops to the southwest of their position. Marines directed an artillery mission. Lima Company heard movement southwest of their position and directed M79 and small-arms fire.

***

During our thirteen-month tour of duty, we were allowed to leave the country twice for rest and relaxation, better known as R&R. When I visited Hong Kong in the spring, my mom sent me $500.00, which was a huge amount of money in 1967, equivalent to $3,600 today. I knew it was a big sacrifice for the folks. Like other Marines, I spent the time drinking in bars and nightclubs and checking out girls. I bought nice clothes too and smoke jackets for the folks.

In October 1967 I stayed in-country at China Beach, where I saw lots of good-looking French-Vietnamese girls. In fact, I enjoyed it so well, I decided to stay an extra few days.

Even though we were on R&R, we still remained in uniform. I was walking past a pier with boats manned by Navy squids.

"I want a ride over there," I said, nodding across the water.

"Okay, sir. Hop onboard, sir."

Whoa! They think I'm an officer. Well, why not?

"What's over there?" I asked, pretending to be a first lieutenant. I felt like Lee Marvin or one of those other guys who acted in World War II movies. They treated me like royalty, so I stayed in my hotel in Da Nang a little longer, escorted back and forth daily to the Officer's Club, *The White Elephant*.

I figured a lot of guys were delayed returning, unable to catch a plane because it was full, so I'd just play that game.

But I paid for my pleasure. When I returned, I got busted again from Lance Corporal to PFC and fined a month's combat pay of seventy-five dollars.

I worked hard, earning another promotion to Lance Corporal later on.

***

One of my friends I knew well from sharing a bunker was Kevin L. Ferguson, an African-American guy we called Fergie who had served on embassy duty in France before he arrived at Lima Company. I remember us sitting at the base camp, drinking beer and smoking a cigar, showing each other photos and talking about our lives at home—my wife, his sister, and how much we both looked forward to returning home.

"I'm not going to die in this country,' he told me. 'I'm going home."

And I said, "I hope so, Fergie."

On October 16, about a month after he arrived, Fergie and I were with a squad-sized patrol at Con Thien. Three companies were conducting search-and-destroy missions; two reinforced the Second Battalion Fourth Marines, which made heavy direct contact with the enemy.

The command post received sixteen rounds of mortar fire and directed artillery and 81 mm mortars at enemy locations. Marines near C2 Bridge reported the accidental discharge of an M16 rifle, wounding one Marine who was medevacked. Marines near the bridge received two rounds of 82 mm mortar fire outside the perimeter.

As point man in our squad, I was in front when a mortar round dropped behind me point blank on our squad, the blast slamming me onto the ground. Dizzy, I staggered to my feet, falling down twice, my ears ringing.

I turned to look behind me and saw several Marines pummeled with shrapnel, gushing blood everywhere. One was Fergie. He died right there, right next to me. Still, we didn't have time to grieve. We just had to put it behind us, stuff it down, pretend it didn't matter, knowing full well it did. Like I said, I never shed a tear in Vietnam. His death was another brutal shock and very painful for me.

On October 30, a Lima Company patrol saw four NVA and within three minutes directed eighteen rounds of 105 recoilless at the enemy position.

***

In November the Third Marines Third Battalion continued defending the C2 Bridge with security patrols, ambushes, and sweep-and-clear operations. A liaison communicated between the command and Cam Lo district headquarters.

The battalion suffered an unprecedented number of casualties due to friendly artillery and mortars. We constantly needed replacements because Marines were killed and injured all the time. A lot of Marines fell in battle. Our whole company was considered wiped out on two or three different occasions.

I should have died either from enemy fire or our own, but I never was wounded—not once. It felt like I was somehow protected whenever enemy bullets, mortars, Chicom grenades or small-arms fire and even errant friendly fire hit our platoon. It seemed like I had a steel umbrella over my head, with just one escape from death after another. But I had become so calloused and hardened I didn't allow myself to think at all. I focused only on survival and killing, just like a zombie, a killing machine. I figured I was lucky; I never thought of thanking God for His protection.

On November 1, two men—Morrell J. Crary and Michael M. Horner—were killed and eight were wounded in action. When an India Company patrol spotted fifteen NVA, the Marines set up an ambush of an NVA platoon. Lima Company prepared to leave the C2 Bridge to assist and ran into the enemy, well dug in. We tried to surround them so India Company could withdraw, but it didn't work. Lima called in 81 mm mortars, artillery, and gunships.

The companies returned to the C2 Bridge, directing more 81 mm mortars and air support. But seven India Company Marines were killed, one was reported missing, and eighteen were wounded, fourteen of which required medevac. Lima Company had one Marine killed and one wounded. Eleven NVA were confirmed dead with another twenty-two probably dead. I remember that firefight. It was a big one. That was a bad situation right there.

The next day, India Company found and destroyed a mine rigged to a tree while searching for its missing man. They found his body and returned to the post.

On November 11, the battalion engaged an NVA company, driving them from their bunkers, using artillery and air support. Lima Company spotted five NVA in the open and requested artillery, but stopped it after seeing aircraft in the target area. Another patrol found and destroyed four NVA living bunkers and forwarded gear to intelligence. Four Marines were wounded slightly when a short round hit the battalion.

Marines ran into mines throughout the attack. We established a defensive perimeter, which the NVA harassed with mortars, rifle, and small-arms fire.

The next morning, the battalion returned to the bridge and a mortar round rattled inside our perimeter. Mortars flew between the enemy and the Marines, who moved back to the C2 Bridge, where they spotted two NVA. Marines pulled back their listening post and fired fifteen 81 mm mortar rounds at the enemy. The next day, Lima Company determined the most suitable ground for the battalion's perimeter.

On November 17, the battalion was assigned to the Cam Lo artillery base and bridge. Three days later, the Marines called for artillery fire on enemy locations not far from C2 Bridge, wounding one Marine slightly. The artillery mission error was due to transmission of erroneous firing data to the guns, causing a deflection error of two hundred meters.

The Marines assumed defensive positions at C3 Bridge, moving from C2 Bridge. Flank security was established from the C2 area and then redeployed south to the C3 Bridge.

On November 23, a Marine on a road sweep security team fell and suffered injuries. The Marines found a mine with twenty pounds of TNT and three blasting caps November 25. They blew it in place. Another group found a second anti-tank mine ten meters from the first. It was disarmed and brought back. A truck detonated a box-type mine and destroyed its front wheel but nobody was injured.

On November 27, the Third Battalion Marines detained thirty-one indigenous people suspected of Viet Cong connections at a dump area and turned them over to Cam Lo district headquarters.

***

In early December, we searched villages and destroyed fortifications, providing assistance and security to civilian personnel under the Chieu Hoi (open arms) program and taking custody of Viet Cong suspects. Each Marine carried normal arms and equipment, helmet, flak jacket, gas mask, poncho, notebooks and pencils.

One time at the command post near Cam Lo, we dug in near the river with antiaircraft weapons and tanks, running patrols and ambushes when a fight erupted between two Marines—a white guy and a black guy—when the cultural revolution and racial tensions in the United States spilled over onto the Vietnam battlefield. I helped break up the brawl.

That was just a year after the Black Panther Party began in California. They were extremists promoting violence and guerrilla warfare to overthrow the U.S. government only months before the assassination of civil rights activist Rev. Martin Luther King Jr.

The Marines didn't tolerate extremists on either end—Black Panthers or the Aryan Brotherhood—and booted members of both groups out of the corps. I'm really grateful the Marines didn't tolerate that kind of stuff.

I landed in plenty of fights before and after Vietnam. Only once, Ted Shindelus and I wound up punching each other while digging out a trench line. I don't remember what happened, but I charged uphill after him and he charged downhill toward me. He knocked me onto the ground and pounded me pretty good.

"Knock it off!" the platoon sergeant yelled. "Save your energy for fighting the enemy, not each other."

***

We seldom drank at the command post; we received two cans of beer once a week. During the fourteen months I was overseas, I probably ate only ten or twelve hot meals, usually on a holiday or when we served in rear areas such as Dong Ha. We only showered every two or three months, if that.

Our unit didn't do drugs, except perhaps while we were on R&R in China Beach. After R&R one time, I brought some really good weed back to the unit. We smoked it within a day or two. Very rarely did anyone do drugs in our unit at that time.

We seldom saw girls either since we were a recon unit, practically living in foxholes, wading through rice paddies, climbing mountains, and slashing through jungle. We weren't even close to cities like Da Nang, Dong Ha, or Saigon. The only women we came in contact with were usually trying to kill us. They chewed beetle nuts, which made their teeth stained black, and they were ugly.

We were always taking one numbered hill or another, month after month, patrolling Route 9 or the river that ran through Dong Ha, a village near the demilitarized zone. That's where Captain Ripley stopped about fifty NVA tanks singlehandedly by blowing up the bridge. But that wasn't until March of 1972, when he hung for hours beneath the bridge setting explosives.[20]

I was pretty immature and stupid at times. I wish I had been more mature when I worked under Captain John Ripley. Instead, I got in trouble.

---

[20] A feat recounted in *The Bridge at Dong Ha* by John Grider Miller.

On December 2, 1967, we were in a village so we bought some whiskey. Somebody else had booze sent from home, so we all guzzled down the alcohol. Then the guy who was supposed to go on duty as a sentinel had passed out drunk, so I volunteered to pull his duty. But I had been drinking too and I dozed off—an absolute no-no in a war zone. You just don't do that. I should never have volunteered.

They caught me while making night rounds shortly after midnight. I tried to explain that I was filling in for someone else, but they didn't care. I never should have fallen asleep.

I was busted from Lance Corporal to Private First Class and locked in the brig for thirty days, without my sixty-five-dollar monthly pay. That hurt my record. I felt terrible, guilty and ashamed. I was embarrassed to return home from Vietnam after losing my rank again and spending time in the brig. I should have been a Corporal or sergeant. By now I considered staying another year to regain my rank so I could return home with honor, but I was talked out of it.

So after a month in the brig at Da Nang, I returned to Lima Company to make up that one-month bad time. Then I returned home to the USA with a screw-everybody-I-hate-you attitude.

***

While I was in the brig on December 3, Captain Roger Zensen had replaced Captain Ripley as Lima Company commander. On December 10, I heard that an M109 driving recklessly struck an elderly Vietnamese man, the father of the village chief of Am Thi. The villagers were hostile, the responsible individual held.

The battalion conducted a sweep-and-clear operation in the area of Van Quat Xa and Van Ba Thung, alert for antipersonnel mines and booby traps. A civilian was killed and four others injured by an artillery round December 20. Three days later, Lima Company left the Cam Lo Bridge and joined an ARVN sweep before returning to the bridge without making contact with the enemy.

On Christmas Day, an outpost saw ten figures moving northeast in a rice paddy, and the next day, a Lima Company patrol learned from villagers at Thin Vinh An that Viet Cong squads had passed through.

The battalion also launched a civic action program hiring Vietnamese people to fill sandbags for bulgur and oil and providing medical care. It held a Christmas Day party for children of the Cam Thi village. I heard that an India Company patrol met twenty Vietnamese children trying to sell marijuana to them.

***

In late December 1967, right around Christmas, our prison work crew was allowed to join the troops in Da Nang when Bob Hope and the USO performed before 12,000 troops. The actor and comedian strutted onto the stage, swinging his golf club and cracking jokes about Vietnam, Da Nang, the military and us Marines.

He called Da Nang "Dodge City," saying he had to stop there because if he traveled any farther, he'd be in Cong country.

"These Marines are really tough. I asked one guy if he'd seen John Wayne. And he said, 'John Wayne? Who's she?' And their motto is *Semper Fidelis*. That means 'Oh, don't worry about it, Doc. Just nail it back on.'"

We laughed so hard at his jokes, recognizing a tad of truth in the humor, an underlying truth in his digs about combat in Vietnam and turbulence in the United States.

"Don't worry about those riots you hear about in the States,' Hope said. 'You'll be sent to survival school before they send you back there."

When the laughter died down, he continued.

"Everything's going up at home: prices, taxes, and mini-skirts. Mini-skirts are bigger than ever—even some of the fellas are wearing 'em. Don't laugh. If you would have thought of it, you wouldn't be *here*."

Among the celebrities we saw were actress Raquel Welch, singer Barbara McNair, singer and dancer Elaine Dunn, Les Brown and his Band of Renown, baseball player Earl Wilson, Phil Crosby (Bing Crosby 's son), and Miss World 1967 Madeline Hartog-Bel. They sang, danced and entertained with skits and comedy routines, making us laugh and providing a sense of normalcy in a world of chaos.

I remember seeing heavyweight fighter Floyd Patterson, who was with the Bob Hope show. I shook his hand, the same hand that won him the world heavyweight title and a gold medal in the 1952 Olympics as a middleweight. Paterson's fists were nearly twice the size of mine!

I also saw Rod Taylor, a well-known Australian actor. It was pretty cool. It certainly boosted the morale of the guys. On December 26, Bob Hope performed at Pleiku.

***

In the first week of January, the battalion fortified living and radar bunkers and developed a fire support plan and defensive schemes. On January 12, the Third Marines Third Battalion defended Hill 28 and Lima and India Companies defended the A-3 position.[21]

Lima Company then moved forward to defend the eastern sector of Hill 28 and continued security and sweep operations. One company routinely served as security for the Eleventh Engineers constructing the Main Service Route 566 between Route 1 and A-3. They swept all probable ambush sites and north-south avenues of approach. At least four squad-sized night ambushes and three fire-team listening posts were employed. Aerial forward observers covered the battalions AO (Area of Operations).

Our Battalion (which is a unit of men consisting of about three companies, a company being about 200 men, give or take, so about 600 or so men total in a battalion) received over fifty rounds of friendly fire, over twelve times, in or near the perimeter of A-3 and Hill 28, during the early part of the month. Enemy mortar fire and artillery was received on eight occasions, over 140 rounds, but most didn't strike the perimeter. However, the Marines sustained four casualties. Ground contact was limited.

***

One day I was point man leading a large patrol through rice paddies and canopied jungle when I climbed a hill and peered into a valley, where I saw a squad of fifteen or sixteen men. One of the men stood a head taller than the others—a black guy—and they all wore Marine Corps uniforms. I hesitated, trying to figure out if they were our guys or the enemy pretending to be our guys. Are these guys Viet Cong? North Vietnamese, American? Only a few seconds passed…

---

[21] Ripley's Raiders *Vietnam Chronicles*

I didn't shoot. I just kept staring at them, trying to decide one way or the other. One of the men turned and looked at me—and I knew. Viet Cong! I yelled to the rest of the guys behind me: "Gooks!" and opened fire.

It was a matter of total confusion. I never wanted to fire on my own Marines.

It turned out the North Vietnamese brought in some Cubans and Africans to fight beside them, which accounted for the taller black guy in that squad. Where they got the Marine uniforms I hate to guess—probably off of some of our guys they killed, or they had stolen them. That incident caused me a lot of grief, both then and after I returned home.

I just carried on, the best I could.

That same day, another patrol reported that a sniper team saw three NVA in the area and engaged the enemy with small arms. One of them fell. Lima Company small-arms fire kept the NVA pinned down until artillery could target the position. A direct hit was seen, killing three NVA soldiers.

***

In mid-January, the battalion received a lot of incoming artillery fire, both from the enemy and friendly fire.

Lima Company conducted short-range security patrols and established observation posts, searching for booby-traps along the way and using scouts extensively. On January 24, a sniper fired and wounded a Marine but he died before Medevac could be completed.

Near the end of my tour in Vietnam, on 24 January 1968, another Marine and I were at Con Thien, carrying boxes of ammunition or C-rations, when a sniper shot rang out. The Marine beside me fell, hit in the lower leg near his ankle. But the bullet ricocheted off the bone, tore up his leg and ripped through his lower abdomen into his chest. I knelt beside him, trying to staunch the blood flow, holding him in my arms as the light faded from his eyes, his life flickering out despite efforts by the field surgeon who raced from his bunker to help.

Another twenty-year-old Marine in his prime was dead.

I looked around, figuring that round was fired uphill from probably 200 yards away. We called in an air strike, firing mortar rounds, hoping to kill the gook who had fired the shot that killed a Marine.

Shortly afterward, I received orders to *di di mau*—get lost—as in leave Vietnam and return home.

On January 28, 1968 while other Marines headed into the jungle to do security sweeps and ambush patrols, I boarded a plane for Okinawa.

The Third Marines Third Battalion's first major battle during the Tet Offensive occurred January 30, 1968, about a week after the Tet Offensive began.

I left for Okinawa January 28, burned out and bent out of shape, angry and ready to explode.

6
Return to The World

I received verbal news that I'd be going home, followed by official paperwork.

I felt ambivalent about returning home. At first I didn't want to go back home, not until I could redeem myself for the blunders I had made, like dozing on duty or staying those extra days on leave without authorization. They busted me back to Private, and I wanted to prove myself, so a part of me wanted to stay. I knew I could do it in the combat zone, where I fought fearlessly.

But I wanted to see my wife, my baby girl, and my parents. We had been married only five months before I left for Vietnam. She wanted me home. So did her father.

My brother, Forrest, had joined the Marines right after graduating from high school. All of them told me "Don't stay over there. Come home."

So I did.

After fourteen months in Vietnam, I caught a C-130 at Dong Ha back to Da Nang. From there I boarded a government contracted United Airlines Jet filled with Marines, heading to Okinawa.

I stayed for a week or ten days in Okinawa, where I decided to spend a little money getting loaded at a nightclub. After leaving the club, I passed out and wound up missing my plane back to El Toro, California. I couldn't believe it: I had missed my plane back to the world!

That's what we called the United States, *the world*, since we were living in a combat zone in Asia, where it was hotter than hell. We all talked about going back to the world. But, I figured, *well okay, no big deal. So I'll just catch the next one.*

I boarded the next plane out and then, while flying 35,000 feet over the Pacific Ocean, all of a sudden, we heard a bang and the plane plummeted. I looked through the window at the wings, which flapped up and down like a seagull trying to take off. *Oh my God, the wings are going to get ripped off this plane!* The wings finally stopped flapping and the plane soared smoothly again. We had hit an air pocket which felt like we dropped 10,000 feet, like an elevator in a freefall. We saw the pilot leave the cockpit for the bathroom afterward, and the stewardesses had jumped into the laps of Marines. Nobody was standing in that commercial airliner when it dropped.

We finally landed at El Toro. When I stepped off that plane, I dropped to my knees and kissed the ground. I was so thankful to have survived fourteen months in Vietnam.

Nobody met me at the airport. How could they? I never let them know when I'd be back. I received thirty days leave after returning from Vietnam, so I flew from El Toro to San Francisco, where Bonnie was living with her parents at Mill Valley in the Bay area, not far from my folks.

Bonnie met me at the airport and, for the first time, I held my baby girl, who was already seven months old. We packed our belongings into a car and trailer and drove to El Toro, where we found housing on the base for married Marines. It angered me to see how protesters treated the veterans returning home from Vietnam, guys like me who had simply served our country.

I didn't know for sure what I wanted to do. I had a choice of several duty stations, but I picked El Toro, which was a bad mistake. I never should've gone there. I didn't know anybody. I should have gone to Mare Island Naval Station or a Marine base near my hometown, close to family members and friends.

As it was, I picked El Toro for my last duty station—the Third Marine Air Wing adjutant's office. I still had a year left in the military so I worked in an office as a clerk-typist—a Remington Raider! I had a top secret security clearance working nights in crypto-intelligence typing up pilot's orders signed by a colonel. At lunch I played basketball with my bosses, a captain and a major, and we tried to kill each other on the court, playing intermural sports for an hour. Then we showered quickly, threw on our uniforms, and returned to the office. It's amazing when I stop to think about it, how the master sergeant hand-picked me out of a line-up of some 100 men all returning from 'Nam. My military record was not that good. After nearly three years, I was still a Private First Class, when I should have been at least a Corporal by then. I knew how to type, though, from classes in high school. It was more of the 'Father's Grace,' that I got that job. Wow! What an amazing God; He was so good to me!

When I was sober on the job, I was an excellent Marine earning high marks for efficiency, proficiency, and what all. But I just couldn't stay out of trouble when I got to drinking. I should have been promoted to Lance Corporal; instead, I was busted to Private after I was caught gambling with some other guys in the barracks where I was visiting. Gambling was illegal. I was fined and given office hours. Three months later, I was Private First Class again, a salty PFC, which is what they called a Private First Class with three years in the Marine Corps.

Another time, returning from town after a drinking binge at a nightclub, I knew I'd be arrested for drunken driving or public intoxication if I stopped at the main gate, so I just floored the accelerator and ran the gate. A bunch of MPs started chasing me, so I switched off my lights and took left and right turns, finally pulling over without using my brake lights. I lost them!

But, in typical cocky fashion, I decided, *Well, I got away with it that time. I'll leave and run the base going out. No big deal.*

A few hours later, after downing a few more drinks, I tried to exit the base. But when I roared up to the gate, they were waiting for me with a shotgun and .45 pistols drawn. They would have fired if I tried to run that gate, so I slammed on my brakes. They threw handcuffs on me and tossed me into the brig.

The next day, the captain I worked for in my office job visited the brig and managed to have all charges dropped. I faced no consequences. Why had he gone to so much trouble to get me out of trouble? If not for the 'Skipper', I'd have been court-martialed and given a 'bad conduct discharge' otherwise known as a B.C.D. He did me a huge favor; I wish to God I'd had sense enough to realize what he'd done for me. But by that time, I was so gone in my drinking, my selfish and self-centered attitude, I couldn't appreciate anything. I wish to this day I had thanked him.

Life at home wasn't much better. I returned home from Vietnam[22] a much different man than I was when I left—meaner, harder, madder. I felt torn between my wife and my child. I wanted Bonnie's attention, but so did my daughter, Ronda.

---

[22] See Appendix I for "Interesting Thoughts and Facts about Vietnam Vets."

As a baby, she needed her mother. As an emotionally and spiritually wounded veteran, I needed my wife. I nceded help. A lot of it! I didn't like Bonnie's divided attention.

Although I loved my daughter, I couldn't stand to be around her, especially if she cried, screamed, or fussed as babies do. Ronda was like any other baby who wailed when hungry, tired, or out of sorts. It drove me berserk. I'd go ballistic, shouting and yelling, hollering for Bonnie to hush that kid. It reminded me of kids in Vietnam, shrieking in terror, crying and dying. I heard their terrified screams, but shut out the shock, clamping down any emotional response. Yet now when my own baby screamed, my emotions erupted. I blew up. I was a sick soul.

When Ronda cried out, it set me off. I developed an angry attitude and stayed away from home. I crashed at my parents' home to escape the noise. I drank with friends, bombed out on drugs, and cozied up to lady friends often. I felt like a zombie, doped up, zoned out, and entirely unfeeling. I wanted to stay that way.

One time I slapped Bonnie. She was yelling at me and I backhanded her. She went flying across the bed. That was the first and last time I ever struck her. I caused her plenty of pain then and later.

I was shell-shocked and angry, and attempted to escape by drinking too much. One time I was driving down the freeway in a Volkswagen Bug when Bonnie decided to shut the sun roof. I screamed and nearly hit her, I was so angry. She told me she just wanted to shut out the noise and the wind. She had no idea why I was so angry.

Sometimes I returned home at night, drunk, and sat on the side of the bed. Tears streamed down my cheeks as I rambled about how the enemy soldiers used kids as shields.

Bonnie didn't know what to do. She didn't want to hear my horrifying war stories. I never talked about 'Nam except during drunken episodes.

When Bonnie walked into our bedroom one night, she found me crumpled on the floor next to the bed, weeping and moaning.

"What's wrong, Ronnie?" She knelt beside me, rubbing my back as my shoulders shook, sobs racking my body. Between jagged breaths, I told her.

"I shot a kid. I killed him. He was my prisoner and he tried to escape, but he was just a kid."

I shoved away from Bonnie's arms. I didn't deserve her sympathy. I didn't deserve anything good.

Sitting up, I palmed my tears, swiping them away, hardening my heart.

"I need a drink." I stood and stormed out the door, focusing only on the need to drink and numb the pain.

One night she picked me up at the Marine base and left Ronda at home, sleeping. I was drunk and wanted to drive, so she let me. I drove past the gate guard, who ran to the front of the car, a gun pointed at us. He ordered us out of the car and searched both me and Bonnie. She was so embarrassed and told him our daughter was home sleeping. They sent someone to the house to check on her.

"I can't tell Ron what to do,' Bonnie told the guard. 'I can't fight him!"

They finally let us leave.

The worst thing happened one night when I had a terrible accident.

I drove a Volkswagen bug into town with a Marine buddy, a guy who, like me, had served in Vietnam and survived. We worked together in the Third Marine

Air Wing at El Toro. After partying in town, where we had both been drinking, I was driving us back to the base on the Santa Ana Freeway because we both had duty in the morning. We had become good friends.

I struck the highway's center divider. The car flipped over, end over end, again and again.

"Jesus!" I yelled. "We're about to die! Save me!"

After passing out, totally drunk on whisky, why or how had I cried out the words "Jesus, save me?"

I was deeply backslidden—I'd walked away from God and the Church. I drank, gambled, cursed, smoked, and sinned sexually on a regular basis. But those words still cried out of my spirit, as I was about to die. Amazingly, God heard and answered. He delivered me from death!

What kind of God was this? Why did He even listen to a guy like me? Could He possibly love me that much? Was this thing called "Grace" that real? Grace is defined as undeserved favor. Was I that valuable, that important to God? To Father God? What was inside me that would make me cry out to God at all? I didn't give it much thought at the time. But years later, I would give God's grace a great deal of thought.

The car landed upside down. I crawled out the driver's door with only a few scratches and looked for my buddy. The right-hand door hung open; he had been thrown onto the road. I saw him moving, so he was still alive—that is, until a big Buick sedan built like a tank driving sixty miles an hour ran over him, dragging him down the highway.

I witnessed the entire thing, watching him die right in front of me. Cops rushed to the scene, lights flashing. They asked me what happened and spoke to the other driver too. It turned out the Buick's driver, who had been drinking, ended up serving time in prison for vehicular manslaughter.

I was locked up in the Tustin Jail for three days, facing charges of vehicular manslaughter. I called Bonnie.

"I do remember one night getting a call from Ron asking me to pray for his friend,' Bonnie recalled. 'They had been in a terrible accident. His friend had been thrown out of the car on the Santa Ana Freeway. He remembers someone telling him his friend was hit by another car.' Bonnie continued, 'I believe he was in jail and drunk. I was so upset, but I told him he should pray that his friend did not die, knowing that Ron would be responsible."

Bonnie called my mother, who flew down from Santa Rosa to Tustin and hired the very best attorney she could find. I think it cost Mom and Dad about $5,000. Since my buddy was still alive when thrown from my car, officials dropped the charges against me. NCIS from the military also investigated the accident and arrived at the same conclusion, exonerating me of all charges.

But, I felt responsible. He never should have died. I was drinking and wrecked the car, which threw him onto the highway where he died. He might have survived the wreck, but I'll never know for sure. I felt so guilty, surviving when yet another of my Marine buddies died—this time because of my driving. I didn't cry. Just like Vietnam. I stuffed it like I stuffed everything else. I felt dead inside.

I returned to my Marine Corps duties. I pulled myself together long enough to finish my stint in the Marines. After receiving an honorable discharge from the Corps, I went completely berserk. I was an emotional, mental wreck.

Later, my Marine buddy's parents tried to sue me in civil court for wrongful death. I wrote them a letter and basically told them I was very sorry for their son's death. They dropped the law suit against me, but I believe they sued the Marine Corps and the guy who ran over their son.

Bonnie finally told me she would leave if I didn't find help. My mom set up an appointment at the Veterans Administration Hospital in San Fernando Valley, which was later heavily damaged in the February 9, 1971, earthquake.

Bonnie practically dragged me to the appointment. I didn't want to go.

The visit didn't last long. After the doctor talked with me, he basically said, "You're in a state of shell shock and we can't do anything for you."[23]

He diagnosed me as "clinically insane" and suggested committing me at the Atascadero State Hospital on the central coast of California. I didn't want anything to do with staying in a nuthouse.

"I left there feeling very sad, but before I left I told the doctor I did not believe his report,' Bonnie recalled. 'I was glad there was a God and I believed *His* report. My faith would not accept such a bad story."

At that time, doctors didn't diagnose Post-Traumatic Stress Disorder, or PTSD, the way they do today. They simply acknowledged that I had done my duty in 'Nam, but now I needed to deal with whatever feelings I had stuffed—spending every day of my life for a year in combat, wondering if I would die that day. I've learned since that PTSD used to be known as combat fatigue, and veterans do not openly share their suffering with others, partly because civilians cannot comprehend the mental and physiological trauma a combat veteran has experienced.

Vets with PTSD desire closeness but find it very difficult.

Symptoms of PTSD[24] include depression, hopelessness, mistrust, hypervigilance, irritability, flashbacks, startle reflex, nightmares, anxiety, survivor guilt, and intrusive memories. I couldn't let anyone close, after losing friends, bantering with them one day, holding them as they died the next. I was so angry, burying the hurt, pain, and terror beneath an unquenchable rage. The naïve young kid I had been died in Vietnam. I returned a monster. I trusted no one. I hated everyone. Stress set me off.

People told me to shake it off, forget about the past. Live for the future. But I didn't know how to do that. How could I quit looking over my shoulder every day? Hyper alert? Jumping when a car backfired? How could I keep images of bloody body parts at bay when they invaded my sleep? Wondering if what I just

---

[23] Porcupine photo used by permission from Tom and Pat Leeson of www.leesonphoto.com

[24] See Appendix II for more details on PTSD symptoms.

saw actually occurred today or was a flashback to the past? How could I stay calm when I had lived for a year on adrenaline? How could I silence the echoes of screaming Marines in pain and agony? Keep my fists from clenching and stomach from knotting when I walked outside? Why was I still living when so many good guys died?

I wanted to vent. I wanted to fight. I wanted relief. So I drank, numbing my feelings. I knew lots of veterans; I grew close to none of them. I made no friends.

When I was in 'Nam, I had heard that Buddhist monks cursed the U.S. military, saying they would be angry, violent men, suicidal, wanderers unable to settle down, filled with anxiety and fear, haunted by nightmares, unable to find peace in life. I've heard Buddhist monks wouldn't curse people, but I believe in the city of Hue in 1962, monks were quoted as cursing those who killed innocent people; other monks burned themselves to death in Saigon protesting the government and U.S. troops. Curses are real and mentioned many times in the Bible, though ineffective against Spirit-filled Christians who have taken up the whole armor of God as described in Ephesians 6.[25]

Chuck Dean, a Vietnam veteran involved in Point Man International Ministries, wrote a booklet called *America Ambushed*, in which he described how an ex-Buddhist monk in late 1989 told an American pastor that an entire sect spent years casting demonic curses on American troops in Vietnam. Those curses are eerily similar to symptoms experienced by Vietnam veterans with PTSD.

Veterans returning from Vietnam committed suicide in high numbers—150,000 of the 2.7 million who served there—according to a 1990 book by Dean called *Nam Vet*. A 1987 study by the Centers for Disease Control indicated suicides among Vietnam veterans within the first five years were nearly double that of nonveterans—1.7 to 1—although fewer killed themselves after the first five years than nonveterans. But a May 3, 2012, ABC News article quoted John Draper, project director of the National Suicide Prevention Lifeline, as saying suicide rates among Vietnam veterans are the highest of any particular group. And the National Vietnam Veterans Readjustment Study reported that 31 percent of all men who served in Vietnam developed PTSD even though only half of those had been in combat units. Rumors circulated that Vietnam veterans accounted for a quarter of the nation's prison population, but those statistics weren't verified.

Some veterans dispute these statistics, but I believe the curses were in fact real and effective, causing many problems for myself and fellow veterans. A large number of veterans became angry, resentful, wandering alcoholics. They divorced in high numbers and suffered physical, mental and emotional maladies. Years later I had the curse broken off of me through prayer.

The point is, those who served in Vietnam had a tough struggle returning to normal back at home, especially with so many people protesting and treating troops with utter contempt and disdain. When I first joined the Marines, I could go into a bar and get a free drink before I sat down. After Vietnam, I had to bring my .45 pistol with me to buy a drink. Okay, that may be a slight exaggeration.

One time, while visiting my folks on leave, I was wearing my full dress uniform when Dad and I decided to drive somewhere in his truck. Bang! A truck

---

[25] See Appendix III for a graphic of the 'Whole Armor of God.'

backfired, but within two seconds, I had jumped from the truck and dove beneath it. Dad climbed out, looking underneath the truck, his brows creased.

I stood up, brushing dirt and debris from my uniform. I grinned at him, though rather wobbly, I imagine. I tried to explain.

"Hey, that sound I just heard was like a mortar attack, the kind that kills everybody," I said. "That's why I went underneath the truck. It was just an instant reaction. Sorry."

Dad just nodded his head and started the engine. As a World War II combat veteran, I knew he understood.

After the year ended, I was honorably discharged from the Marines. I had reached the rank of Lance Corporal twice and was promoted to Private First Class four times. I had no trouble earning promotions; I just couldn't manage to keep the ranks once I achieved them.

We moved off base into Santa Ana for a while, then into the Simi Valley home of Bonnie's sister and her husband, where we rented a bedroom. I didn't like staying there; I didn't like the husband, even though his boss gave me a construction job building pool decks, working with steel and pouring concrete. It was backbreaking work, but we ended the day with drinks. Then I left that day job for my night work as a bouncer at a nightclub, Jack's Office. I slept maybe five or six hours a night and started the same cycle the next morning.

Bonnie became pregnant with Ronnie Jr., who was born in Ventura, California July 29, 1969. Bonnie and I didn't really fight, mostly because I was gone most of the time. I worked days, then nights, and spent time drinking in bars when I wasn't working. If I returned home at all, it was late. We didn't have much of a marriage. Bonnie insisted I couldn't handle life outside the service. As a kid, my mom set all the rules. In the military, the Marines established right and wrong. On my own, without rules, I ran wild. I was totally out of control.

I felt really bad for my wife. I couldn't love. I couldn't care. I couldn't trust anyone. I neglected her. I neglected the kids. I cared only for my own sorry self. She should've divorced me then, but she didn't.

I thought about working for Dan Terzich, my former Boy Scout master and a Mill Valley detective who later was promoted to police chief. I took a written test as part of my application for the California Highway Patrol. They invited me to attend the academy in Sacramento, but I never finished the process.

I can identify with the statement by a character in George V. Higgins's 1970 novel, *The Friends of Eddie Coyle*: "This life's hard, but it's harder if you're stupid."

And I was stupid.

Instead of becoming a police officer, I was on the receiving end of a police call after screaming at my wife and kids loudly during a drinking binge, threatening to hurt them. My wife called the cops, who arrested me. I swore I'd never hurt my kids, ever. However, in my drunken anger I had slapped my young daughter's face. It was the first and last time I did that. A drunk for a dad is bound to leave emotional damage. It hurts my heart that I hurt theirs. I used a belt very rarely on my boys. I never belted my daughter. I always told them why I was spanking them, and added that I loved them too, which of course I did.

About that time, my brother visited us in Santa Ana for a week. He was still in the Marine Corps, preparing to leave for Vietnam. Forrest didn't say anything about my drinking; he knew I wouldn't listen.

I grew hard, and self-medicated with drugs and alcohol to dull the pain. I even introduced him to our good-looking neighbor, Beverley, who drove a sports car. She was older than us, but she and Forrest hung out together a lot for lunch and dinner, tooling around Santa Ana.

I took Forrest with me drinking or gambling in card games. I had a Dodge Polara with a 383 engine, black, fast enough to outrun the California Highway Patrol, which I did one time. You cannot outrun those police radios though!

"He scared the daylights out of me the way he drove,' Forrest recalled. 'He drove like an insane person. I'm serious. Sober or drunk, everywhere he went it was 80, 90, 100 miles an hour."

Sometimes I picked up my girlfriend. "He was married at that time,' Forrest said. 'It really shocked me. I had no idea he was doing that. And we would go to that bar and sometimes within minutes he was in a fight."

Sometimes I dropped Forrest back at Bonnie's and returned to the bar or my girlfriend's. Bonnie talked to Forrest about my behavior, but he also knew about it from my girlfriend. Bonnie suspected I had a girlfriend, but I never actually told her.

"I don't know how Bonnie tolerated Ron's behavior as long as she did,' said Forrest, who also served in Vietnam and later returned home an angry, restless, and drunken playboy, even though he hired on as a cop with the San Rafael Police Department, won awards for his shooting, and learned martial arts, teaching fellow officers for the department.'

'My girlfriend was a few years older than me,' added Forrest. 'Sometimes I showed up on her doorstep at three or four in the morning after a four-day bender. When she answered the knock, I'd stumble inside and collapse, passing out for a day.'

'She was a real down-to-earth, level-headed woman who cared about Ron,' Forrest said. 'She was afraid that he was really going to get into some serious trouble if something didn't happen in his life to stop him."

She was right.

7
Arrested

In November of 1969, working as a bouncer at Jake's Office, I spied a familiar face sauntering into the bar—one of my old Marine buddies, a good friend I served with in Vietnam. Even though he's dead now, I won't use his name, out of respect for his family. Instead I'll call him John.

After we closed down the place, John and I pounded down some whisky, rehashed old times in the hell that was Vietnam, and shared what we knew of the guys who survived, and those who didn't. He returned to his home in Los Angeles after his discharge.

Under the influence of toking a little weed, I complained about working two jobs, just to pay the bills. That's when John gave me the brilliant idea to do something stupid: he said we could get easy money and an adrenaline rush by pulling some armed robberies.

He wanted to do something exciting, risky and dangerous, just like everyday life in Vietnam.

Excitement, adrenaline, and easy money sounded great to my intoxicated brain. Besides, this was one of the guys who razzed me about hesitating on that hill when I was point man, that maybe I had been scared. If I refused to join him now, he'd consider me a coward for sure.

"Let's see how brave you really are," John said. I agreed, not so much for the money as to prove my bravery. I wasn't scared of anything or anybody and no one was going to call me a coward again. Robbery? I had never given crime a thought before now.

So why not? We risked our lives for a country that could care less about us when we returned home. I hated authority. I hated cops. I hated judges. I hated the world. I was one ugly whack job. I even hated myself.

John drove to a large service station in Los Angeles with about a dozen pumps. I carried a big Bowie knife while he sat unarmed in the car as the getaway driver, parked maybe fifty yards away from the station so they couldn't identify him or the car. I headed to the gas station, opened the door, and stealthily approached the clerk running the place. I grabbed him by the front of his shirt, jerked him up to me and stuck the knife in his face.

"This is a robbery." I growled, reeking of alcohol and marijuana.

The guy in his early twenties, about my age, acted pretty terrified. He didn't squawk or fight, just opened the safe and gave me all the money. It was a little over 300 bucks.

"Now go sit down in the bathroom and don't come out for ten minutes!" I ordered him, gesturing with my knife toward the restroom door. "Then you can do anything you want."

As the guy beat it to the bathroom, I added, "I've got a buddy of mine sitting in a car with a rifle trained on you so don't try anything stupid."

I ran out of the station, hopped in the car and John sped away. We laughed. That was so easy, after what we experienced in Vietnam. After all, nobody was shooting back at us. We kept at it, hitting one station after another, leaving Los

Angeles County for Ventura County, robbing four stations in a row. In the early morning hours, we split the money and parted ways.

I don't think John ever pulled another robbery. I never squealed on him. He never spent a day behind bars, as far as I know. But he stopped committing crimes after one night. I didn't.

It was easy, exciting, empowering. I used whatever weapon I found—a Bowie knife, a butcher knife from the kitchen, a gun. My modus operandi was to grab the person, scare them half to death with the knife so I commanded 100 percent of their attention, and then demand the money.

"Don't try anything stupid! I have a partner with a gun on you."

I didn't, but they never knew. It was a horrible thing to do, but I didn't care at the time. I didn't even bother to disguise myself. I was a dummy, an ignorant amateur. I was bound to get caught.

In addition to armed robberies, I pulled a few burglaries. One night I heard from a friend about a big party at a giant house so I joined in the fun, drinking and partying. I finally passed out, but when I awoke, people had passed out and drifted into bedrooms. Looking around, I saw about a dozen women's purses scattered around the large living-dining room where everyone had been dancing. With nobody around to see, I picked through those purses and pocketed the cash and any jewelry or other valuables that I found inside the purses and the house. Then I left, no one the wiser. I got away clean with about one thousand dollars cash and hundreds of dollars' worth of jewelry.

When I finally drove home to our place in Santa Ana, Bonnie asked me, "Where'd you get all this money?"

"I won it in a poker game," I told her. She seemed to believe me.

I wasn't working then; I had quit my jobs, too wrapped up in drugs and alcohol to hold a steady job. Although I didn't consider myself to be a burglar, I never missed an opportunity to take what I wanted. I just didn't give a darn about anyone or anything. The world owed me. I didn't care if I self-destructed.

I always drove fast hot-rod cars, ignoring speed limits, stop lights and stop signs whenever I felt like it. I owned a '69 GTO Pontiac "The Judge" with a souped-up 400 engine. I eluded the California Highway Patrol and local cops on more than one occasion. I could make anyone eat my dust—and I did—especially when I was drinking.

One time I drove my car into a park to lose the sheriff's deputies and jumped out and ran. I then reported the car stolen and it worked. I didn't get busted—not then, anyway.

Then my luck ran out.

In November 1969, I pulled a robbery with a knife at another service station, but this time the guy had tripped a silent alarm. I ordered him to give me his money and hide in the bathroom for ten minutes. But he ran out immediately as I was racing to my car, loaded on booze and drugs. I saw cops surrounding my car, lights flashing, and I tripped, fell, and scrambled toward some bushes. It was dark, so I tried to make myself scarce. I tossed the knife away so they wouldn't find it, which helped me later in court. I hid behind some bushes, trying to conceal myself, but this attendant I had robbed ran toward the bushes carrying a steel-tipped hunting arrow.

"He's over here!" He hollered to the cops, gesturing toward the bushes. "He's over here!"

I started to stand and he stabbed me in the rib cage with the arrow, drawing blood. It left a scar for a while. The cops yanked me from the bushes, slapped on handcuffs, and hauled me off to jail. As I sat in the back of that squad car, I thought about finding that scrawny attendant and taking revenge. The cop car stopped at the Parker Center Police Station, which was known as the Glass House and held a reputation as an evil place to incarcerate men.

Everybody knew about my arrest, or at least it seemed like it, since it had appeared in *Van Nuys News*. A headline in the November 1969 newspaper blared "Man Arrested in Robbery of Gas Station."

"A 23-year-old man who allegedly held up a Studio City gas station and escaped with an undisclosed amount of money early Friday was apprehended moments later, according to North Hollywood police.

Arrested on suspicion of armed robbery was Ronnie F. Brandon of 1850 Duncan St., Sim, who allegedly held up a Union 76 station at 12080 Ventura Blvd.

The attendant said he saw a man walk into the station restroom. Then a short time later the man approached him, police said, and after a short conversation, the man pulled out a knife and stuck it against Armstrong's stomach.

He demanded money and forced the attendant to give him the cash in the register," reports stated.

"He then made Armstrong go into the restroom and left, walking east on Ventura Blvd. Armstrong, however, chased the bandit and caught up with him near a motel complex at 12020 Ventura Blvd.," police reported.

"Police arrested Brandon and transported him to North Hollywood station where he was booked. 'Money and a knife were booked as evidence,' police said."

Bonnie received a call from the cops.

"The police called me and said he was in jail; would I come get his personal belongings?" Bonnie recalled. "He had robbed a gas station attendant with a knife."

Bonnie was angry, disappointed, shocked. She couldn't believe what she read in the newspapers. Shame enveloped her, especially since her family heard what I had done.

Once I sobered up, back into my right mind, I thought about the dishonor that I had brought on my family, the Marine Corps, myself. I hated myself and I wanted to die because I had stooped so low engaging in a life of crime. I felt so miserable and alone.

I had no one to bail me out of jail, even though the cost was relatively low. By then my folks finally had enough, after helping me on R&R in Hong Kong and then with the high-priced attorney when I was involved in that fatal accident. I never repaid them, and now here I was robbing people. That was it. Bonnie didn't have the money. Nobody would help, and I swore I'd kill my wife, my parents, and everyone else for not bailing me out. I was angry, full of hate and murder and viciousness because it was all about me. I was totally selfish, self-centered. I didn't think about anybody else or care about anyone else. I never wanted to see my family again and signed a paper to that effect, refusing visits.

I was miserable in the Los Angeles jail, up five or six stories, and it was a real pit, a dungeon with three of us packed into a one-man cell. I slept on the floor. Disgusting meals arrived through the bars, food unfit to eat. My dog would have bitten me if I had tried to feed him those meals. We washed our laundry in the toilet, which we scrubbed clean every day before scrubbing our drawers, T-shirts and socks with soap. We hung it on the bars to air dry.

My anger and hatred festered. I hated the guards, judges, and attorneys. I hated everybody. I hated the world. I talked trash; every other word spewing from my mouth started with some nasty curse word. I felt deep-seated guilt and shame from Vietnam, especially looking at how far I'd sunk. But I also felt sorry for myself. I didn't even have a dime for a commissary treat. Nobody gave me a cent. Nobody visited me. I was alone.

Initially I faced five or six charges of armed robbery, but they dropped most of them when, after three months in jail, I pleaded guilty to a reduced charge of one count of armed robbery without a weapon. I couldn't really deny the charge, since I was caught right away by the police. I figured I'd probably have to serve ten to fifteen years because I had committed a horrible crime. I terrified people.

Bonnie attended the sentencing, where the judge lectured me about my heinous crime and irresponsible and violent lifestyle, drinking and drugging when I had a family depending on me.

"I don't understand why a person of your caliber would stoop so low as to do these things," the judge said. "You're an honorably discharged Marine. You have no criminal record."

"I remember a long walk from the parking lot to the gates, thinking how much I loved Ron and believing God would see us through this time,' Bonnie said. 'I remember during his time there he was served papers, being sued for the death of his friend back in the Santa Ana accident. Because he was incarcerated, they could not do much about that."

I was shipped from Los Angeles County Jail on a bus with a bunch of other convicts to what was known as Chino Max, a prison where we stayed two months while a team of hippies, who hated the Vietnam War and the military, evaluated us to determine what type of incarceration we needed. Because of the violent nature of my crimes, this team of so-called experts, who probably burned their draft cards, deemed me an extremely dangerous threat to society. They recommended incarceration in San Quentin, a maximum-security prison for hardened criminals. Was I a hardened criminal?

Thinking back so often to those days spent in the 'glass house' or L.A. County jail, I've often wondered what would have taken place if I would have had a good attorney, a high-priced attorney to represent me. After all, the VA doctors, the psych's, had clearly stated that I "was suffering from shell shock, temporary insanity, and needed to be hospitalized for mental health care in an institution." If this information had been brought forth in the court room before the judge, would it have made any difference?

I was assigned a public defender also known as a 'public pretender' by the cons, who had barely spent 10 minutes with me prior to the supposed trial. Out of three months spent in that horrible jail I got to talk to my attorney for maybe 10 minutes on two occasions. He did literally nothing for me. If the judge would have known about my emotional war wounds, my service in Vietnam, would things have gone differently? Would I have gotten the help I so desperately needed? Was incarceration in the harshest prison in the United States justified? Was justice served? I suppose many will think it certainly was. Some will, however, think differently I believe. At any rate God was still with me. He would not fail me either.

8
San Quentin-The Big House

In mid-1970, guards hauled me to San Quentin in a bus they called the Grey Goose, a long ride to the prison north of San Francisco referred to as the Bastille on the San Francisco Bay. I looked at the thick, eighteen-foot-high concrete walls surrounded by concertina wire, long narrow windows and guys in jumpsuits, each looking like they'd kill you as soon as look at you.

San Quentin, right next to Alcatraz, was the roughest, evilest imposing fortress-like prison in the state. I was a bit nervous. Some guys chained together on that bus at the ankles, waists and wrists were first-timers like me; others were returning for a second or third time.

We walked in pairs as guards with fingers on the triggers of their shotguns and rifles followed us from the guard towers, preventing any attempted escapes. I thought about trying to make a break for it; I'm sure other guys did too. But we never had the chance.

Ron Brandon, inmate, San Quentin 1970-72

We passed through a series of huge iron doors. One by one they closed behind us with a loud bang, the echo punctuating the cold hard fact that I was now inmate Ron Brandon, #28750. Ugly-looking convicts with tattoos all over their bodies helped the guards herd us like sheep into the processing center, where we were fingerprinted, photographed, and then issued ID cards.

As the last inner door clanged behind us, my thoughts of escape dematerialized. I realized I'd never leave this place until they let me go. It was totally self-contained, a city within a city. After shaving all facial hair, we put on prison-issued blue jeans, blue shirts, caps to cover our heads and black boots for our feet. We each received a heavy wool jacket for cold, windy breaks in the concrete yards. San Quentin is surrounded on three sides by San Francisco Bay.

I was assigned to a cell on the fifth tier in South Block, where close to a thousand men were jailed, 200 on each floor, half on the front side, and half on the back. Hard Cases were locked down in the adjustment center, and those in trouble landed in the hole. Eventually overcrowded, guys were stacked in bunks in the gymnasium and outside in tents in the lower yard. In 1970-73, 7,000 men were jammed into a prison built for 2,500.

Each cell housed two guys in bunk beds, but it was small, built for a Chinese midget. I could touch the sides of the walls by stretching out my arms. They were 12 feet deep. Each cell had a small steel desk and chair bolted to the wall, a toilet with a sink and metal mirror, and two cabinets where guys kept their stuff. Iron bars faced the center of the block, looking onto the cat-walk across the way. The cells had double locks that guards could open all at once using a manually operated lever. They also held keys to each cell door, which a trustee convict opened when it was time for guys to eat or go to work assignments.

Here I was, back in Marin County, but it wasn't exactly the homecoming I envisioned. I had read about San Quentin, which sat on San Francisco Bay, and knew it opened as a prison in July 1852 with sixty-eight inmates. In the 1950s, the prisoner population topped 5,000. Today it houses more than 4,200 prisoners, with 734 on death row, and a staff of 1,700 working there.

In the dining hall hung six twenty-foot murals painted by Alfredo Santos, a heroin dealer incarcerated in the prison during the mid-1950s, just before Merle Haggard, the country singer, served his three years in San Quentin for grand theft auto and armed robbery. Johnny Cash had recorded his *Live at San Quentin* album in February 1969, just a year before I arrived at the prison.

San Quentin is the only place where men are executed in California—initially by hanging, then by gas chamber, and now by lethal injection—so I expected to see a bunch of mean and nasty guys. But I was one mean, lean fighting machine, a former Marine. Vietnam prepared me for that place. I was ready for it.

It was a vicious, deadly, wretched place, especially during the upheaval of the 1960s and 70's when racial segregation ended in schools, public buildings, and even prisons. But as they desegregated, racial tension erupted into violence and inmates formed gangs with others of similar skin color. You had the Mexican Mafia, Black Guerilla Family, and Aryan Brotherhood, which formed at San Quentin in 1964. Sometimes the Aryan Brotherhood allied with the Mexican Mafia against the Black Guerilla Family. The Hells Angels stuck to themselves or joined the brotherhood. These gangs hated one another, stabbing, beating, and killing over any perceived slight.

We all learned to do the crabwalk, keeping your back to the wall as you walked. Some guys tucked thick newspapers and magazines into their waistbands and shirts to thwart potential stabbings, but I never did that. You could be stabbed for being white, for being black, for being tall or short, fat or thin, or just for being in the wrong place at the wrong time.

I tried to steer clear of trouble, but one time I couldn't avoid it. One of the tough guys wanted to prove his mettle by taking on a big guy. He wasn't too bright. I pummeled this inmate so hard I ripped a tendon out of my finger joint in the tussle. Doctors operated on my finger in the San Quentin Hospital because it balled up. It took a month to heal. The other guy survived with cuts and bruises. I think he learned a lesson. He lost five front teeth in the fight.

Another time in a holding cell, jailers brought in sack lunches of peanut butter and jam and bologna without mayonnaise on white bread, maybe an apple and a cookie. One black guy who stood three inches taller than me tried to grab my lunch, thinking I'd just hand it over. I threw a right cross and hit him so hard in the jaw I'm sure he saw stars. He staggered and fell to the floor. He didn't mess with me anymore. Nobody else did either.

During riots, guards tossed tear gas grenades everywhere. We could scarcely breathe or see through watering eyes as we vomited snot, saliva flying. Guards opened up with submachine guns once so everyone had to dive underneath the tables when a fight broke out and someone jumped a guard. One time in the grassy lower yard we used as a ball field, a guard on the tower fired when he saw an inmate moving in to stab a guy. Zzzing! The bullet whizzed right past my head and ka-plunked into the grass a few feet from me. I don't think he even cared whether he hit an inmate, but he just ripped up grass.

Fights were common, usually over silly stuff, probably to break the daily routine. One time two guys started boxing like pros and a guard rushed in to break up the fight. Some inmates liked to intimidate others into giving up money, cigarettes or their bodies for homosexual acts. Convicts sold their "girls" to others for sex.

Ugly stuff took place in prison. I tried to avoid it. I didn't join gangs, but affiliated loosely with the Aryan Brotherhood for protection. I didn't want to engage in any stupid rituals like beating up my mother or stabbing a guy simply to join any gangs. I had friends in the brotherhood, but never joined. They were very anti-black, which I'd never been. I grew up with blacks, Mexicans, Indians, and whites. I never had problems with anyone in high school or the Marine Corps.

In prison I saw human beings of all races at their worst, vicious men committing atrocities and unspeakable acts. So I developed a lot of hatred for blacks and homosexuals. I grew even more calloused and hardened.

I feel sorry for police officers like my brother, who deal with society's worst all the time. They see ugliness—murder, robbery, domestic violence—every day. It's easy to develop a twisted view of humanity. God help our law enforcement community.

I was shocked to recognize a guy from high school at San Quentin. He had been a senior when I was a freshman. He was a white guy in the Aryan Brotherhood, and a Black Panther stabbed him in prison. He lived through it. He even tried to go after the black guy and stab him back but the guards jumped him.

Never a dull moment in prison; I had one goal, the same as in Vietnam: survive each day.

I went through lots of roommates. Guys who caused trouble wound up in the hole. Others transferred out. Still others were sick and taken to the hospital.

One roommate I had for a while was a guy incarcerated for a violent crime. After he discovered I had attended the Assembly of God Church, we talked a bit about religion and the Bible. I knew a bit about God and the Good Book, even though I didn't have a personal relationship with the Lord the way I should have. I had a lot of head knowledge but hatred had hardened my heart. Sometimes we debated the Word. Finally, he issued a challenge.

"Tell you what, I'll read your New Testament if you read my Book."

So I said, "Okay, you're on. You start reading that and I'll read your Book."

I laughed so hard I almost fell on the ground reading his Book. I thought it was a comic book. I am not kidding.

"What's wrong with you?" he asked.

"Man, I can't believe this stuff!" I responded. "You actually believe this crap?"

I insulted him and made derogatory remarks about his beliefs. We never physically fought; we were about the same size. He razzed me about being a Holy Roller and a hypocrite, since I didn't practice what I was preaching. We laughed and got along well after that.

San Quentin seemed like a continuation of Vietnam, a struggle to survive in a dangerous situation. As a former combat Marine, I earned respect from some of the guys who never served. Inmates always read the file of new guys to the prison to find out the crime, and then passed it around the joint. Gossip spread. People knew I was an ex-Marine convicted of armed robberies with a knife.

In prison, knives rule, and those who can handle them are feared. So are murderers, the most violent criminals, followed closely by armed robbers. The less violent the criminal, the less respect the criminal received. Rapists and child molesters lingered at the bottom and seldom lived long, often winding up stabbed to death or forced into isolation for their own protection.

I saw guys stabbed several times. One time, walking out of South Block on the way to the yard, all of us were stopped and forced to the wall so guards could pass carrying a black guy on a stretcher. I saw eight or nine homemade knives, called shanks or shivs, sticking out of his body. Guys from the Aryan Brotherhood plunged the knives into him. I imagine he died, but I don't know for sure. They were hauling him to the hospital. San Francisco was home to top knife-wound surgeons who gained plenty of experience treating San Quentin prisoners.

They also treated plenty of gunshot wounds of inmates shot by guards during riots or other upheaval.

People died every day, killed with a knife in the back, a throat sliced by a sharpened spoon, a beating that splattered brain matter against the walls. I nearly died several times in San Quentin. God was constantly looking after me.

I've always been a hard-working guy, so naturally in the prison nothing changed. I tried to find a good job so I banged on the bakery door. When it opened, I saw Manuel Saenz, one of the Sunday school teachers from our old Mill Valley church. He had baked our wedding cake five years earlier. I had forgotten that he was employed as San Quentin's head bakery supervisor and vocational instructor! I never expected to see him again, certainly not in San Quentin.

"Ron, what are you doing here?"

I asked Manuel (Manny for short) the same thing, shook hands, and then gave him an abbreviated version of what I'd done in Vietnam and since returning to the States. We talked a bit and then he offered me a job working in the bakery as a clerk-typist—a Remington Raider again. I didn't know at the time that all the guys working in the bakery then were Mexicans, or what we called Chicanos at the time, and they didn't want a white guy working there.

Rather than politely asking me to leave, they concocted a plan to kill me.

At the end of his shift, I was typing away in the office and Manny was ready to leave the bakery through the giant metal door—the only way in and out. He told me later the Lord stopped him while he was opening the door.

"*Manny, if you leave, your crew is going to kill your clerk.*" He heard God speak to him clearly.

"What do you want me to do, Lord?"

Backing up, he closed and relocked the door. He called together his crew of a half dozen guys and spoke to them in Spanish.

"You guys all know who I am. You know I'm a Christian. You know I'm a pastor of a church."

They nodded and he continued.

"Well, the Lord just spoke to me and he told me what you guys were getting ready to do—that you plan to kill my clerk."

He said they looked at each other, shaking their heads, babbling denials.

Manny continued. "Now I'm going to give you a choice. You can hand over those shanks right now and I'll drop this whole thing or you can go ahead and pursue this and you will all stay in prison for the rest of your life. I will guarantee it."

Slowly the men pulled out the big old shanks (knives), and handed them over to Manny, who stuffed them in a sack and got rid of them. For the next few days, I kept receiving strange looks from the guys in the bakery, but I didn't know any of this had occurred. I quit shortly after this and transferred to a different job in the kitchen. It wasn't until years later that Manny told me what happened. I was in awe when I realized God protected me in prison as well as in Vietnam. Even after I had turned my back on Him. He loved me despite my evil lifestyle. He intervened to save me, even though I had turned my back on Him. He loved me!

I worked out in the gym, fondly called 'the iron pile,' trying to stay in shape as much for protection as anything. I was benching 400 pounds and was proud of it. I played football, basketball and baseball. Football was my main sport. I made first string on the San Quentin Pirates football team, which was pretty good since most of them were lifers. I started in our first game. We were in a semi-pro league, but of course all our games were played at San Quentin. We were always the home team. We didn't get paid either.

One day playing against a California college team, I played defensive end and dodged around blockers to sack the quarterback. I drove him into the ground and the whole prison went berserk, jumping up and down, shouting and screaming, tossing items into the air. It was an awesome sight. Their encouragement convinced me even more to keep trying to tackle the quarterback.

We also played a team of law enforcement officers—prison guards, sheriff's deputies, highway patrol and city cops. These games grew rather rowdy as inmates took revenge on the guys who threw them into prison in the first place. Three cops hit hard during that game landed in the hospital. The inmates applauded like mad.

We also had inmates who dressed as female cheerleaders, waving pompoms and urging our fellow inmates to root for the home team. Inmates also served as referees and umpires. It was *The Longest Yard* for real, just like the movie in which Burt Reynolds played quarterback.

One guy on our team, a big black guy named Joe Raddee, was imprisoned for armed robbery. He played fullback. When I tackled him one time, it felt like hitting a truck or a wall. It jolted me. The Baltimore Colts later drafted him but he never played for them. I heard later that he knocked over a jewelry store in another armed robbery and wound up back in San Quentin.

I enrolled in college courses to earn credit, but I couldn't come close to graduating. I completed a lot of courses, however, with good grades. Dr. Harlan Hogue from U.C. Berkley taught one of my classes on Old Testament Prophets and I actually earned an 'A-' in his class.

After my kitchen job, I was assigned to work in the photo identification section, processing new inmates who had transferred into the prison. I took their photos and fingerprints and issued ID cards. One day in April 1971, I was working away when the guards brought in Charles Manson, a dippy-looking skinny little rat-like guy.

"Who are you?" I asked, contrasting him with my bulky six-foot-four physique.

"I'm Charlie Manson." I was not impressed or even slightly fearful.

"Get over here. We're going to take your photograph and take your fingerprints," I barked at him.

Of course I had heard about the loony leader of a commune of nutcases who butchered seven people, including actress Sharon Tate and four others at her home, as well as Leno and Rosemary LaBianca in August 1969. They also killed other people. Manson, an evil man whether drunk or sober, was convicted of the murders in 1971 and sentenced to death.

He had his sentence commuted to life in prison when the California Supreme Court ruled the death penalty unconstitutional in 1972. Palestinian-turned-Jordanian citizen Sirhan Sirhan, a San Quentin death row inmate, the guy who killed Robert F. Kennedy in May 1969, also exchanged a death sentence for life in prison. Even though California voters reinstated the death penalty by passing a constitutional amendment, no additional executions took place in California until 1992.

Manson was sent to death row at San Quentin, but after his sentence was commuted to life in prison, they transferred him to Folsom State Prison.

Because high tensions kept resulting in stabbings and deaths, we were locked down in our cells for several months, forced to eat sack lunches. We left our cells only once a week to shower. Through a tiny window in the cell, I could peer into the upper yard, a covered concrete yard where inmates gathered at times to buy canteen items.

On August 21, 1971, I looked into that yard and saw a bunch of convicts carrying stretchers. I counted seven of them, and it looked like every one of these seven guys lying on stretchers was dead. It turned out a riot had erupted in the adjustment center during a failed escape attempt by cons.

George Jackson, founder of a Marxist prison gang called the Black Guerilla Family and a member of the Black Panthers, had met with his lawyer that afternoon to discuss his civil suit against the Corrections Department. His lawyer slipped him a .32-caliber pistol that he had hidden inside a tape recorder and Jackson tucked it into his afro hairstyle beneath his cap. After his lawyer left, Jackson pulled the gun and ordered guards to open all the doors in the solitary confinement wing. During the ensuing riot by more than two dozen prisoners, Jackson attempted to escape but was shot to death. What became known as the San Quentin Six beat, shot, tortured, and slit the throats of guards and inmates they considered informers. In addition to Jackson, three guards and three inmates died. One of Jackson's cohorts was convicted of murder, and two others of assault. I knew some of those guys.

After the bloody battle and fatal riot, we were locked down for six months. Six months was a long boring time, only to be let out to shower once a week. We had bag lunches with no TV, radio or anything except books.

Seagulls liked to fly over the inmates when they stepped outside for recreation, plopping poop on prisoners. One day I was talking to a guy and—splat! A big old bomb splattered on the side of my head, white dribbling past my ear onto my chest.

All the inmates burst out laughing.

"Hey, Ron, that's a sign of good luck," one guy said.

"Okay, come on. Give me some more luck." I said.

Bonnie visited me maybe half a dozen times at San Quentin, traveling at first from Simi Valley, squeezing a visit or two in between caring for our two kids and working at a department store. It was harder when the bank repossessed our car. That's when Bonnie moved to her parents' home in Mill Valley. My brother Forrest helped her load the U-Haul and drove it north. By then Ronnie, my oldest son, was a year old, Ronda three.

She visited me with her father too, even though she described San Quentin as "a scary place for me."

"We were able to visit by talking on a phone through glass dividers," Bonnie remembered. "There was tight security. When Ron was first there, a lawyer had brought a gun in his briefcase to one of the prisoners."

Bonnie worked at a factory in Corte Madera at night while her mother watched the kids. She remembered the shame she felt when her sister Callie married the year she moved back home. "I was so upset to be in the wedding and seeing all my cousins come through the line to greet us, I had to go have a good cry," she said. "It was very emotional to be back home, having a husband in prison in my home town, and I was embarrassed."

I was amazed that Bonnie didn't file for divorce, but she stuck with me.

My mother visited me once. My dad was up to his eyeballs in work. Besides, he couldn't visit, since he drove a truck for Nielsen Freight Lines and made regular deliveries to the prison. After he suffered a nasty injury, he was bedridden for several months.

My brother Forrest visited me in San Quentin after he was discharged from the Marines in 1970. He filled me in on his experiences in Vietnam and our parents. Mom had kept him informed of my illegal activities.

"I just couldn't believe it,' Forrest said. 'That was not the Ron I knew. I couldn't see him committing serious felony crimes and going to prison. I knew he was a fighter, but I couldn't see him committing these serious felony crimes. It just blew me away."

Forrest described San Quentin as "a scary place."

"They had so many heavy-duty prisoners in there at that time: Black Panthers, Symbionese Liberation Army people, the Weathermen, Hells Angels. They had a lot of gangs. It was a heavy hard black hole."

He scarcely recognized me and I didn't say much. I had become a cold-blooded character. I cared for nobody and nothing.

"I could see from his posture and demeanor that he was always on edge every minute I was sitting talking to him,' Forrest said. 'He wouldn't relax. He was constantly looking around seeing who was getting near him, who was standing up, who was sitting down. It was crazy."

I warned Forrest to keep his voice low during our conversation. I told him I was proud he was working as a cop for the San Rafael Police Department and knew he'd do a good job. But I didn't want him to tell anyone because if inmates knew my brother was a cop, I'd be dead in a minute.

"He had really changed,' Forrest recognized during their earlier visit in Santa Ana. 'I couldn't relate to him. It was like his mind was somewhere else all the time. He would look at you, but he wasn't there."

After more than two years of living day by day, trying to work hard and keep my record clean, I heard I'd be appearing before the parole board. I prayed, asking God if He could intervene and help me with this parole board.

"Lord, have mercy on me. I need to get out of this prison. I don't want to be here anymore." I didn't pray much, but I was dead-serious this time.

He heard my pleas, in spite of who I was. The Lord spoke to me in that East Block prison cell on the fourth tier, right below death row. Sometimes God speaks to me now through the Scriptures, words jumping off the page into my heart. But that time I heard His voice in the Spirit, right in that little cell. He reassured me that all would be well; He would let me leave the prison. It was profound. *Who am I, a criminal, that God would visit me in a cell in San Quentin, and show His favor toward me and hear my prayers?*

I felt a sense of peace then, so certain that I told all the guys that the parole board would let me go home. I know they thought this ornery former Marine had a screw loose. One of the guards who had been an Army captain during World War II even wrote a nasty letter to the parole board, trying to keep me behind bars longer. He didn't think it was safe to release me. He said I posed a danger to society. But my mother also wrote a letter to California's governor, Ronald Reagan, explaining that her son had served in Vietnam and returned home a different man—lost, confused, and angry. She said she didn't know me anymore, especially when the boy who loved God and gave his heart to the Lord attacked and robbed people for money. Reagan wrote back to my mother, and to the parole board, a letter that carried weight.

God kept His promise. Although I was sentenced to five years to life, I was released on parole after two and a half years in San Quentin, the last six months spent on work release, leaving each day to work and returning to the prison's minimum-security barracks each night. I was able to see my wife and family every week.

Ninety-five percent of the time, inmates convicted of multiple acts of violent crime, such as armed robbery, serve eight to fifteen years. Very few serve less. My record of conduct while in prison had been good overall. But, to go to a parole board with only two years' time served on an armed robbery, and have a guard write a letter totally negative, meant only one thing to me! *Parole denied. Come back in two years.* And yet, I walked. Was it my mom's appeal? The Governor's? Or did God act on my behalf? After all, He had spoken to me months prior to the parole board hearing and said "*I'm setting you free!*"

Ronnie Jr. was only five months old when I was sent to jail. He was three when I left San Quentin in 1972.

9
A Revolving Door

Released from San Quentin in 1972, I returned to Bonnie, who was living with her folks in their large house. My parents were done with my antics, deeply hurt and ashamed by my behavior. They were people of honor and integrity, with a criminal for a son. They never gave up hope for me.

Bonnie's parents weren't entirely happy with me either, but as a minister, my father-in-law believed in second chances and redemption. He had worked at Mare Island Naval Shipyard as a civilian contractor for more than thirty years. I think he was relieved when Bonnie and I eventually moved into our own apartment.

I found a job as an assistant auto mechanic at a huge Chevron gas station. We had sixteen gas pumps and four or five lube room bays with hoists. A retired Navy chief named A.J. Merritt ran the huge operation. He knew I'd been in prison, but he hired me anyway. We worked well together.

Bonnie was working in a factory at Corte Madera. Apartment life proved stressful, especially with two little kids running around—soon to be three. Right after I returned home, Bonnie became pregnant again, this time with our second son Daniel, who was born in September 1972.

We split up, but didn't divorce, just separated. I moved into my parents' home in Rohnert Park and started attending a private Christian college full time while working part time. Later, I moved into a home with some other students and studied theology at the Genesis Bible College in Santa Rosa run by Jim Argue. I paid my way through school, trying to decide if I wanted to become a missionary, pastor, or teacher. We had phenomenal teachers, like David du Plessis, the father of the modern Pentecostal movement, and David Wilkerson, author of *The Cross and the Switchblade* and founder of Teen Challenge in New York. We learned from other well-known religious leaders, such as Australian-born Winkie Pratney and Tony Salerno, founder of Agape Force, Joy Dawson, Bob Cornwall, and Judson Cornwall.

Kelly and Ferral, Ron's youngest siblings

When I was going to Genesis Bible College, I stopped by to see my brother Forrest in San Rafael. Like me, Forrest liked to drink just as our father had, whose name he carried.

Some of the problems with Forrest happened at home after I joined the Marines. With me gone, he was stuck with all the babysitting, yardwork, and other chores. Mom and Dad relied on him to watch the younger kids—Kelly and Ferral—while they worked. His days were regimented by Mom: walk home from school, watch the kids, do the chores, day in and day out. His senior year Mom hired a babysitter and let him go out for football in the fall and track in the spring.

He served as president of Christ's Ambassadors Youth Group and even led services at church for thirty young people. He prayed every day that Mom would start attending church and that our dad would quit drinking.

Mom butted into his relationships with girls, probably worried he might marry and she'd lose her babysitter. One time, Mom, wearing an old bathrobe and giant curlers in her hair, showed up at the high school where Forrest was talking with his girlfriend.

"You should've been home twenty minutes ago!" Forrest climbed into the car, fuming over her deliberately humiliating him. He hated her from that moment, turning his back on his parents and later on God.

He joined the Marines the day he graduated, eager to leave home. After graduating from boot camp in San Diego, he attended missile and radar training school in Fort Sill, Oklahoma. In 1967, he was stationed at Adak, Alaska, Marine Barracks, Military Police, as a turn-key and chaser; and later served in the 2nd Marine Division, Camp Lejeune, North Carolina, in field artillery and as a radar operator. He drank heavily by then, after hours, playing pool and drinking beer.

Like me, he landed in trouble for drinking once—the night he and his friend left a bar drunk and climbed aboard a forty-foot fire truck with the engine running and drove off, lights flashing and sirens screaming. MPs pursued them until the drunken Marine driver of the fire truck rammed it into a snowbank right below their barracks. Since Forrest had worked in the brig, the major showed him leniency by giving him office hours in lieu of a court-martial and ordered him to refrain from drinking alcohol for the next six months.

Forrest visited me in El Toro before leaving for Dong Ha in Vietnam, where he served with the First Battalion Headquarters office of the Third Marine Division. As a missile radar screen operator, he monitored enemy activity like tank and truck movement on radar. He also disassembled radar sets and worked in counter mortar radar. After four-and-a-half months in Vietnam, Forrest was transferred to Okinawa in early November 1969 and was promoted to sergeant. Forrest was a good Marine and was offered promotion to E6 if he signed up for four more years. He turned all offers down. In July 1970 he was honorably discharged.

While in Vietnam, Forrest sent a letter home to Mom, telling her how much she had hurt and embarrassed him, how angry he felt toward her, and how much he hated her.

After he returned from Okinawa in 1970 until late 1973, Forrest drank heavily.

The day I visited him in the summer of 1973, I started talking to him about how important it was to get right with God. We had both grown up in the church, loving Jesus Christ and embracing Judeo-Christian values.

"I was a stone cold alcoholic at that point,' Forrest admitted, even though he worked as a cop. 'I was drinking and getting drunk every day of my life."

He didn't appreciate his older brother's intervention.

"I got really angry with him for confronting me with that,' Forrest said in retrospect. 'I didn't want to stop drinking or go back to church."

At that time, I laughed, letting it go.

"I wanted to lay it out for you, Forrest. You can take it or leave it. But life's so much better if you take God's grace and go with it."

As I prepared to leave, Forrest grabbed my arm.

"Ron, you're always welcome to come here, but don't you ever bring that up again," he said. "If you have to bring it up, then don't come here."

I had a tremendous experience at Genesis Bible College and learned a great deal about the Bible. I studied hard, reading the Bible from cover to cover, passing tests on each chapter. I was earning decent grades. They packed a four-year program into two years, which I had almost completed.

But I still wasn't done doing stupid things.

Perhaps because my mind whirled, telling myself I was a deviant, not like these other Bible College guys, I started doubting my calling to Genesis. *I never would change my worthless ways. Who did I think I was, trying to finish college and follow God? Why would He want a lowlife like me?* I was having intrusive thoughts, hearing the enemy telling me lies in my head. Realizing what I had done, I sought help with a college counselor.

"Hey, I'm really having some difficulty here,' I said. 'I'm struggling."

But like the doctors at the Veterans Administration hospital, the counselor didn't know how to help, other than encouraging me to stand firm and reassuring me that I could handle anything. I don't know what I needed, but he didn't offer it. Maybe he considered me a ticking bomb, ready to explode. He said a short prayer for me and that was it.

I reverted to my old lifestyle and, the day after Christmas in 1972, burglarized the house where I was living, taking items that didn't belong to me. I needed money, so I took cash that somebody left lying around the house. I also stole a movie camera, radio, and other items of value.

It was almost like a demonic attack—a test—and I flunked. I caved into the temptation, followed Satan instead of God, pocketed the money and stole the stuff. I moved back to my folks' house in Rohnert Park and resigned from school.

I returned to Bonnie and the kids for a while, trying to sober up. I tried again to go straight. I enrolled in classes at the College of Marin in Kentfield. I rode a bicycle to school and even played football on the college team. After completing a handful of courses, my demons surfaced again, especially when I heard that the cops were looking to arrest me.

That's when I called my brother Forrest. After his discharge in July, 1970, Forrest was working for a landscape maintenance company in Corte Madera when Mom called him one night to say she had seen a newspaper ad for San Rafael police officers.

"You know, you might take a look at this,' she told him. 'You might find it interesting work. It certainly pays a lot better than what you're doing."

He was one of about 300 to apply for the seven open jobs. He was hired. Within three months of leaving the military, starting October 1, 1970, he was an officer with the San Rafael Police Department. They asked him about having a convict for a brother, but he said I was responsible for my own actions and needed to pay the penalty.

Would he be able to arrest his brother? Of course, Forrest answered. "He's my brother and I love him, and I'll always love him, but I would deal with him just like I would anyone else."

Nine months after the burglary, I was arrested at the San Rafael Police Station after turning myself in to my brother. He booked me into the Marin County Jail and I was released on my own recognizance.

In September 1973, I pleaded innocent, but changed to a guilty plea the following month after the charge was dropped from a felony to a misdemeanor. In December a judge added on two years of probation and ordered me to pay $550 in restitution which I did.

Part of me had wanted to turn my life around, which is what Bonnie thought I was doing. But between the combined effect of Vietnam and San Quentin, I felt wild inside. I drank, did drugs, and bought a Harley Davidson, and started running around acting crazy. I hung out with some Hells Angels, other Vietnam veterans like me with attitude. We rode our bikes right through the front door of this huge Sausalito bar and parked. We loved that place, pounding down one brew after another. The bartender never said a word. Of course, we tipped him well. We also frequented a place called Smitty's Bar and a waterfront nightclub called Zack's, both of which are still there. But the bar we rode into has closed; maybe that's why.

One night I was arrested for having a weapon with me at Zack's, which I had considered robbing. I changed my mind when I saw an old high school classmate, George Duke, playing piano. We were drinking, dancing, and enjoying ourselves when one of the bartenders evidently saw the gun inside my jacket and called the cops. Police officers entered the bar with guns drawn and pointed them toward my head, then hauled me off to jail, where I spent a couple of weeks behind bars.

We drove our bikes as fast as they'd go, racing down the highway, sometimes stopped by cops and ticketed for speeding, reckless driving, or drunk driving. We just had to pay a fine and maybe spend a night in jail.

As an ex-con, I had trouble finding jobs. I faced one rejection after another, but sometimes I lucked out. For a while, I drove a truck for a guy named Luigi Baker, a successful waiter in a restaurant called Tarantino's Restaurant on Fisherman's Wharf in San Francisco who saved all his money and bought a moving business. We loaded and unloaded trucks while moving people in California, Nevada, and elsewhere. I could lift pianos, heavy hutches, refrigerators, couches and just about anything and haul it up several flights of stairs.

Luigi and I became good friends. He owned a beautiful home in Tiburon, California, right across from where I grew up in Mill Valley. We both rode motorcycles, so one day, after a few beers at a bar on Throckmorton Avenue, we decided to ride up Mount Tamalpais. I led the way up the windy, curvy road with a drop-off on one side. We enjoyed the thrill!

Boogying around a long sweeping curve at a good clip, I hit a slick of oil, my bike skidding flat on the pavement, into oncoming traffic. I held tight to the bike, sliding along the pavement, with my head inches from the cars whipping down the hill. Someone had evidently leaked a lot of oil all over that road.

Then Luigi, who had seen me slide, hit the oil and ran over my legs. He remained upright since I kind of gave him traction. I stood, checked my arms and legs, then picked up the bike and inspected it. We laughed and I hopped back on the bike.

Another time, I was riding fast down a road in Guerneville, California, on my Harley—or maybe it was a Triumph—and I had been drinking, but I wasn't drunk. I was dressed like a biker, probably heading to another bar for more booze, when four rednecks in a pickup tried to run me off the road. They succeeded. My options were to either hit them head-on, veer off a cliff, or swerve into a bank on the side of the highway. I chose the last one, ramming into the bank at high speed and flipping through the air head over heels. I just happened to land perfectly, rolling onto my shoulder and then up to my feet. Even though I wasn't wearing a helmet, I walked away with only a couple of scratches, though the motorcycle was demolished. Those mean ornery dudes laughed like hyenas as they zoomed off.

One day, driving on an overpass atop Highway 101 at the Belvedere-Tiburon Exit near Mill Valley, I saw a carload of drunken Mexicans driving the wrong way in the fast lane at maybe twenty-five miles an hour. I saw California Highway Patrol cars pulled off on the side of the road, but they didn't stop the Mexicans. I just envisioned a head-on collision with unsuspecting drivers motoring north from San Francisco in the fast lane.

I zipped onto the highway, also driving the wrong way, so I could pull alongside that car. I knew just enough Spanish from high school classes and the San Quentin bakery to catch their attention.

"*Vamoose!* Let's go! Follow me."

I gestured frantically at the guys. "You're on the wrong side of the freeway! You've got to get over."

Finally, I exhaled a pent-up breath when the driver turned the wheel to follow me off the freeway. Just as they reached the side of the road, cars flew down the highway at seventy miles an hour in all three lanes. These guys thought they were driving in the slow lane.

I jumped back on the highway, this time heading the right direction, and took off. I didn't want to talk to any cops about anything. They'd probably give me a ticket for driving the wrong way.

Even when I worked, I never stayed at a job long. I couldn't afford my lifestyle, drinking, gambling, and partying, so I figured the fastest and easiest way to find money was to take it. I put a hard shell over all my feelings and emotions in 'Nam. I didn't think about anyone—my wife, my kids, my victims. So when I returned home, I never empathized with the terror I caused the people I robbed. I didn't give a rip about anybody except me. I would step on someone's face, take all their money, and never think twice about it. That's the way I was.

But when I sobered up, I always felt guilty. I never repented. Instead, I'd just shut down, buy booze, smoke pot, or once in a while drop acid or snort cocaine. I'd go to parties with white cocaine in bowls for the snorting, weed available for the taking, sometimes laced with other drugs. When I was high, I felt nothing, absolutely nothing.

One time when I smoked pot, my heart raced so fast I thought I'd die. I went to the VA hospital, where they examined me and told me to lie on a bunk. After three or four hours, my heart slowed and I left. I wanted to kill the guy who laced that weed. I wanted to break his legs. I looked, but I never found him.

In April of 1975, I took off again, just driving north. I reached the southern Oregon Coast and knocked over a big casino-lounge where people danced, ate, and gambled. Brazen, I pulled the car to the front door, left the engine running, and ran inside carrying a .45-caliber pistol.

"This is an armed robbery!' I barked to the cashier. 'Don't move. Give me all your money!"

Gathering the money, I turned around and ran back to the car. I should've been shot; I don't know why I wasn't. Most of the people drinking and dancing had no idea what had just happened. I think my take was about a thousand dollars.

I didn't plan the robberies. I just found myself broke, so I spontaneously decided to find money—whether at a gas station, a nightclub or a bar, it didn't matter. All I cared about was me, my next drink and running.

I hated authority figures. I hated the word "no." I could do anything I wanted to do and nobody could stop me!

Driving back to California, I stopped to drink along the way. I didn't have a job. The lounge heist gave me enough money for gas, food, and booze to last awhile.

But then it ran out.

I drove over to Bonnie's, where she was staying with her folks. We had been separated, but sometimes I stayed with her. Then I'd disappear for a few days, or weeks.

"Well, where have you been?" she asked. I didn't tell her anything.

"Aw, I've been on a trip up north."

I lied a lot to Bonnie, to her parents, to my kids, to everyone. But I couldn't keep lying to myself.

On the night of June 19, 1975, I walked into a nightclub in Eureka to shoot a little pool. I plopped two bits into the jukebox, punched in three Merle Haggard songs, and closed down the place. By the early morning hours, I sat alone at the bar with one other guy a little older than me, and the lady bartender refilled our drinks.

As she started to close down, I saw an opportunity and seized it. I pulled a loaded gun from my jacket and pointed it at her.

"This is a robbery,' I told her. 'Give me all the money."

I gestured toward the bleary-eyed guy at the bar. He raised his arms over his head. "Whatever you want me to do I'll do it."

"Go behind the bar and lay down on the floor!"

He scrambled off the bar stool and dropped to the floor.

The bartender, a lady who, it turned out, owned the place, pulled cash from her drawer—about 200 bucks. I left in a hurry without hurting anyone.

The next morning, I sobered up, replaying the evening in my mind, over and over. I never would have killed any of those people. I couldn't have done too much damage with a BB pistol, which is what I had. I might have cranked off a round or two in the air as a threat to gain cooperation.

I drove north into Oregon, feeling nervous all the time, knowing I had committed two robberies, just waiting for the cops to arrest me. I couldn't stand it. Finally, I picked up the telephone.

"Hey Forrest—I messed up, you know?"

"What'd you do now, Ron?"

"Well, I pulled some armed robberies, bro. What do you think I should do? All these cops are going to be looking for me. Two armed robberies and they're more likely to shoot me than talk to me."

"Ron, you know I'm a cop,' Forrest said. 'You can turn yourself in to me. Where are you?"

"I'm in Oregon, Forrest. I don't have any money."

"You need to hock your radio to pay for gas, but whatever you do, you need to get down here legally,' Forrest warned me. 'I'll pick you up and take you back to Eureka."

I used my knife to pull the radio out of my car. I even sold my spare tire. It was enough. I headed toward San Rafael and picked up a hitchhiker on the way down. The guy gave me a little money for gas.

I knew that, unlike me, Forrest had quit drinking and turned his life over to God. That had happened in December of 1973, only three or four months after our talk. He attended a birthday party at the home of a fellow police officer, where everyone drank and Forrest got loaded. He passed out at the party and a couple of his friends threw him in his car and took him home. The next day that he worked, Forrest was the butt of jokes. He couldn't remember anything about that night. He couldn't believe some of the things they said he had done, but they were honest guys, so he started pondering it.

"And I got to thinking, *'I'm carrying a gun. I mean I can't remember anything and I do something and kill somebody or something or shoot somebody and I can't remember, I'm going to be in a lot of trouble.*"

One night, alone in his basement apartment, Forrest wondered how he could stop the merry-go-round of binge drinking. He was smoking three or four packs of Cools a day and drinking every night. It was bound to catch up with him. He looked at his gun lying on the nightstand, seeing one way out of the endless cycle.

In the pitch black night, he suddenly recalled a wagon lamp he crafted for our mom at Vacation Bible School when he was little. It worked. When you plugged it in, the light shone. He felt so happy then. Where had that cheerful boy gone? He hadn't felt real joy for a decade—not since he had turned his back on God.

He dropped to his knees and prayed. He even asked God if He was real, brokering a deal of sorts.

"God, if you're real and you're really there and you still love me and I could get this thing squared away, you've got to show me somehow right now," Forrest recalled saying. "I need something desperately."

Sudden light pierced the darkness, so bright he couldn't open his eyes. He felt an overwhelming sense of God's presence.

"It just broke me and I started weeping and weeping and weeping and weeping,' Forrest recalled. 'I couldn't do anything but weep. And then that presence went away and I prayed a prayer of forgiveness asking God to forgive me, come into my life, take charge of my life, and turn me around."

He moved back in with our parents. He attended church regularly. He never drank another drop of alcohol. He has never smoked another cigarette to this day, forty years later.

"I knew it was my mission in life to pray for my brother, so I began very intently and intensely to pray for him and I never stopped,' Forrest said when interviewed. 'And I still do almost every day. The intercession that went up for him was hell on earth."

Forrest continued, "God would wake me up at two or three o 'clock in the morning and bring me into prayer in my office in my home. I would intercede for Ron and sometimes it felt like I was in combat. The spiritual warfare was so heavy and intense it would wear me out. I would be sweating by the end of the time of prayer. That went on for years."

Forrest suffered terrifying nightmares of guys chasing me with knives and guns.

"And I would wake up and I would know that I needed to go pray for him right now,' Forrest said. 'I felt sure that God was intervening and that Ron's life was being spared."

I didn't know about Forrest's nightmares. I just knew he could help me out of the mess I'd made.

So when I called him up, I told him what I had done, both at the casino in Oregon and at the bar in Eureka. The next day, he picked me up and drove me about 250 miles from San Rafael to Eureka, where I had robbed that bar. Forrest wore plain clothes instead of his uniform after he persuaded his chief to give permission for him to drive me north to Eureka.

We talked along the way—about the folks, the Corps, Bonnie and the kids—and stopped for a large lunch.

"I was a Christian serving the Lord at that time, so we had a good talk all the way up to Eureka that day,' Forrest said, acknowledging the terror my victims must have felt. 'I felt bad for them and Ron at the same time."

After Vietnam, I had erected a barrier to feelings, which Forrest recognized.

"I don't think anybody, in my opinion, short of God Himself, could've demolished that barrier. He would not talk about 'Nam and he wouldn't deal with any of his issues really."

I described what I had done at that bar and told him it was a BB pistol, not a real gun.

Forrest dropped me off inside the Eureka Police Department. I sat in the Humboldt County Jail for three or four months awaiting trial.

The Eureka Times-Standard wrote June 28, 1975, about my first court appearance for robbing that Eureka nightclub. Facing robbery charges, I was held in Humboldt County Jail on $15,000 bail, which was later increased to $25,000.

I wasn't entirely cooperative. In August when my lawyer and the prosecuting attorney wanted to postpone my preliminary hearing to a later date, I objected. The court dropped the charges of armed robbery for lack of prosecution, but my victory was short-lived. They refiled the charges the next day.

One time while locked in the Humboldt County Jail, a couple of us guys gathered the ingredients to cook up some home brew. We worked as trustees in the kitchen so we'd snitch sugar and empty containers, then stick in apples or other fruit and pinch some yeast to aid the fermentation. Then we waited, hiding it from the guards as it fermented enough to give us a buzz.

When we finally drank it, we got pretty loaded. We even hatched an escape plan since quite a few of us knew we'd be heading back to prison. We talked of tying together sheets and blankets to drop ten stories to the ground. We had it all worked out, but one of the guys told on us. We wound up locked down and never added attempted escape to our records.

Here I was, twenty-nine years old, sitting in jail again, waiting for a judge to decide what would happen with my life. This time I knew a judge wouldn't give me probation. The court sentenced me to five to life, weapon not proved. I was sent to the Northern California Reception Center at Vacaville, where they evaluated male inmates to determine where they should go. I was there about six months going through testing and evaluations. They determined I was totally sane.

Coincidentally, I was there at the same time Charlie Manson arrived there from Folsom Prison. He'd been sent to Vacaville, a medical prison for male inmates, in March 1974 for a few months because of his deteriorating mental condition and then sent back to Folsom in October. In May 1976, they brought him back to Vacaville, and this time he stayed there for nine years.

Not me. They sent me back to San Quentin.

This time, I figured they'd keep me locked up ten years at least. I felt hopeless—more so when they sent me to San Quentin again. When I was there, I saw Sonny Barger, the guy who was considered the godfather of the Hell's Angels. He had been sentenced to ten years to life for selling heroin in the summer of 1973, but he was released in 1977. The guys in these gangs were tough and dangerous; Forrest had dealt with both the Hells Angels and Black Panthers as a cop in San Rafael.

I was there when Muhammed Ali visited in early 1971. He was world heavyweight champion and I shook hands with him. That was really something.

About that time, my dad changed. He had been injured badly in work-related accidents when a forklift driver dumped that load of lumber on him. Suffering severe pain, he underwent several major surgeries and drew closer to God. He quit drinking and gambling. He attended church regularly and read his Bible.

Because I had turned myself in, they considered me less dangerous. I was sent from San Quentin to a medium-security work camp, the Sierra Conservation Center at Jamestown south of Fresno in the Sierra Foothills.

10
Released Again

My dad had taught me to box and I studied martial arts in the military. So at Jamestown, a medium-security prison at the foothills of the Sierras, I participated in the heavyweight boxing program. The prison had a legal full-sized boxing ring in the gymnasium. A lightweight boxer named Danny O'Malley served as my trainer. He and his four brothers were all crooks, cat burglars who pulled high-stakes, big-money jobs, scaling down the side of San Francisco high rises to steal jewelry and money. They were good at their work. They were pros.

Danny taught me a lot about boxing. I punched the speed bags, worked out hard all the time and even knocked out some heavyweight inmates. One time I had a fight with an African-American who had also been in the Corps. We were just about the same size. Both of us were tough. Both of us were determined to fight to win. It turned out to be a black and white thing although neither one of us could have cared less about color. The other inmates didn't see it that way though.

The bell rang and we went at it. Our fists flew and we pounded each other for three rounds. He came at me, hit me with all he had, took a break, covered up, and I came at him with punishing rights and lefts with all I had. Then it was my turn to cover up and back up. He tried everything he knew to knock me out but couldn't do it. I tried to knock him out but he refused to go down. Then finally I got in a lucky punch. I hit him with a right cross hard to the head, followed by a left upper cut to the jaw. He staggered. I hit him again in the head. He backed up and I had him on the ropes. He covered up and I pounded on him. Then I got tired. I backed up. All of a sudden he hit me with a lucky punch right in the heart. It dropped me like a rock. The fight was called. He won. I felt good though. I had thoroughly pounded him and he had thoroughly outdone me! We were both badly beaten up, bloodied, bruised, and exhausted. It had been a great fight! The inmates cheered of course at our good sportsmanship. We tapped gloves and both raised our arms together.

Later I talked to 'Joe,' the guy I had fought. He told me that he had served nearly four years in the Corps, did a tour in 'Nam and had come home with a habit. He was doing drugs. He had been given an 'undesirable discharge' when he left the Corps. He was doing 5 years for drug charges. I knew exactly what he was going through. Darn few former Marines ended up in prison. However, I met one other. He had been a fighter pilot during WWII. He was in prison due to drinking and driving, accidently hitting and killing someone on the road way. It was his first time in trouble with the law ever. I felt bad for him. We used to work out together.

I didn't like to just sit around there at Jamestown, so I usually found a job or something to do inside the joint. I worked out in the iron pile, building muscles, and participated in sports. I was captain of the football team one year and coached the team another year. I took college courses when I could. Forrest visited me once.

Jamestown offered vocational programs, teaching inmates firefighting, plumbing, carpentry, welding, and other trades. After four or five months, I chose to learn auto mechanics. My instructor and I got along really well. He provided hands-on, in-class training for a year. At the end of the course, we earned a grade and certification. He said I'd make a great mechanic someday.

After two years at Jamestown, I prepared to go before the parole board a second time. I figured they'd keep me locked up, knowing I was a big dummy who couldn't learn to live a decent life, even after receiving a break once.

This time I landed in front of the parole board after serving three years altogether. I prayed before I entered the room. "God, have mercy on me. Get me out of this place before I kill somebody in here." Just like my last stretch, all of a sudden I'm praying again for God's help. *Give me, give me, give me.* I was seeking God's hand, not His face!

Running the board of all people, was a former Marine captain who had served in Vietnam. We started talking about the Corps and the Bible. He drilled me, asking questions to see if I meant the words I said. He acknowledged that I was probably dealing with the stress from Vietnam.

"You're in here because you've gotten to drinking, self-medicating," he said. "If we give you parole, will you straighten up and stop doing this kind of stuff?"

Absolutely, sir,' I responded, saluting. 'Aye, aye, sir. I will not break any more laws. I will even, as a matter of fact, get out of your state."

I told him I planned to return to my family and work as an auto mechanic. By then "Bonnie and the three kids were living at the Springs of Living Water in Richardson Springs, California, where Bonnie worked and the kids attended school. But the director there didn't want me at their Christian campus in northern California. He wrote a strong, nasty letter saying in no uncertain terms that he didn't want me at their place.

The Marine captain on the parole board read the letter aloud to me. My immediate reaction was *I'm going to strangle that punk*. I was angry. The man had never met me, but wrote a letter shredding me as if he'd known me all his life. I knew he had talked to Bonnie and examined my record before writing the letter, and from his perspective, I'm sure he felt justified in writing that letter. It stung having to hear it read.

Despite the director's efforts, God granted my prayer, and I was paroled after serving three years, even though it was my second incarceration. I should have done ten years at least for the horrible, violent crime I committed. This had to be the grace of God!

"With the time remaining to serve, subject can gain a saleable skill and reinforce the gains that he has made to date in maturity and insight,' the hearing panel's report stated. 'If he could control his alcoholism, he probably would not have any further negative contacts with the law."

After completing the courses in the California State Automotive Trade School, I left Jamestown with a mechanic's certification and found a job through the Sacramento Valley Work Release program. I could always find a job with that training. Mechanics were in big demand, so even with a felony record, I could find work. I still had trouble obtaining other good-paying jobs, such as that of a truck driver, because of my record. But as a mechanic, nobody cared whether I had done time as long as I could do the job. The government assisted me in purchasing hundreds of dollars' worth of tools.

I worked for a Cadillac, a Ford, and a Chevy dealership. I never stayed long in one place, maybe six months to a year. I'd quit and move somewhere else, finding another job. Often my drinking and drugging interfered with my work and I'd lose the job. Another time our entire shop was laid off. On one job I missed too many days of work and was fired. I wanted a change. I later learned that this was symptomatic of PTSD.

I think Bonnie had mixed emotions about having me return. During work release, I visited her two or three times a month, using a car my dad gave me. He still accepted me as his son and he still loved me. I think Mom was embarrassed and ashamed to have a convict for a son. She was a very proud woman. We had a wall between us a mile high and five feet thick until the day she died.

I was granted parole on April 7, 1978, with one special condition: "Totally abstain from use of any alcoholic beverage or liquor."

After I was released from Jamestown, I tried to change. I never committed another violent crime.

I couldn't stay away from the booze though. My drinking buddies and I engaged in a few barroom brawls, pounding heads and releasing steam. We'd break chairs and mirrors, break bottles of booze over the heads of other guys. Somebody cut my head open with a whack from a booze bottle. It was crazy stuff.

One night in 1979, I had been drinking at a nightclub in Santa Rosa with another former Marine. When the bar closed at two in the morning, we rolled outside toward my car, which was parked along the street near a dark alley.

As we approached the alley, three guys jumped us—one armed with a machete, another with a tire iron or crowbar, and the third with a gun. They sprang from the shadows, intent on robbing us, but they didn't get far. I disarmed one of the guys and pounded on the other two. The guy with the machete sliced my arm in two places before I knocked him to the ground with a solid kick to the groin. My buddy Max took a blow to the head, which knocked him out cold. One of the other assailants ran off when his gun jammed.

Instead of scaring me, I went nuts. All that pent-up anger and hatred poured from my body into my fists as I pummeled those guys in that alley.

Cops raced to the scene, slamming on brakes, screeching to a stop. They pulled me off the guy I was pounding, and I remember lots of blood and teeth flying around, none of my own. They yanked my arms behind my back, and arrested me for attempted murder. They hauled me off to the Sonoma County Jail in Santa Rosa.

Fortunately for me, a witness the next day shared what he saw—two unarmed guys walking along when they were attacked by three others wielding weapons.

I was released, all charges dropped. I had sixteen stitches in the back of my head after that fight, due to a blow from a crow-bar. My arm was bandaged up for a few days. Prior to the arrival of the cops, I had jumped in my car and tried to run over one of my attackers but he jumped out of the way somehow.

This incident must surely have been one of those times when my brother Forrest was praying hard for me. I should have been badly wounded, maimed or killed. I could easily have killed one of these jerks too and ended up back in a California prison for a long, long time.

But California court officials considered revoking my parole in June 1979 after reviewing my activities from February 8 through April 6 while living with my folks in Rhonert Park. Their report noted that while I was working at a Sacramento service station, I transferred to Redding in May 1978 and then lost my job the last week of January 1979.

"He started drinking at that point and an activity report was submitted regarding his drinking on February 15, 1979,' the report stated. 'Subject returned to Sacramento February 3, 1979. He again took up residence at the Samaritan House. Subject made a few efforts at seeking employment but continued to find reasons as to why he would not hold certain jobs."

While at a Samaritan House one night after drinking, I punched one of the pastors in the gut. I don't know why I did it, just an impulse. About six residents of the house, mostly all ex-convicts sprang on me and taught me not to mess with any of their pastors again. I never did either! However, I was understandably kicked out of Samaritan House in March so they reported me to my parole officer. I had returned to Santa Rosa and asked for a transfer of my parole.

The parole officer's report read, "It appears Subject is jumping from place to place to avoid work." The report also noted I was in debt to the Sacramento office to the tune of fifty dollars.

I had wanted to live with Bonnie and the kids, who were at the Springs of Living Water. I had visited them frequently, and finally the assistant director relented and allowed me to move in after I completed work release. But they had no intention of making it easy for me.

I quit my mechanic job and moved to Springs of Living Water. Although they knew I was a trained mechanic, Cecil Cooper, the director, put me to work as a dishwasher.

In this place, dishwashers worked from five in the morning until ten at night, with a couple of breaks, cleaning and drying thousands of dishes, plates, glasses, and pieces of silverware. All of the dishes were hand-washed. The dishes were run through a machine for sterilization after they were washed. I scrubbed pots and pans. I wore rubber gloves to my elbows, washing, rinsing, and drying dishes, day after day, all day long.

I'm sure they thought I'd quit. But I didn't, even though I figured they were wasting my mechanic skills. But I kept at it—one month, two, three, and four. After the fifth month of washing dishes from sunup to sundown, refusing to quit, I developed an attitude. I knew they were trying to force me to quit, pressuring me to leave.

I felt angry, but I kept it inside. I just doubled-down and worked harder.

Our dish crew of four washed dishes for over 130 people on staff, three times daily, seven days a week. In addition, we had thousands of guests eating in our two dining rooms when we held big conferences with special speakers. With seven or eight large meetings a year, all lasting two or three days in a row, there were a lot of dishes to wash!

While I was working there, the parole officers saw progress on my part.

They wrote, "If he continues to follow his religious beliefs and stays away from alcohol, he should have little trouble in making a successful parole," they reported.

By the time I finally left, the director and I were on good terms, but when I started, I did not like Cooper. He wanted me to quit; I refused. I kept on washing those dishes, despite my anger, or perhaps because of it. Later, he actually said, "You're one of the best workers I've ever had in this place."

Bonnie and the kids all welcomed me home. By then Daniel, the youngest, was five. I hadn't seen him in three years. I was sober and working, which meant I was a good daddy too. I brought my wife and children presents. But while working at the Springs, I didn't have much money. My work paid for our room and board though.

Where we lived at the Springs, located near the Sierra foothills in Northern California, east of Chico, the weather could get really hot during the summer months; 110° or higher was common. Mountain lions, large rattlesnakes and raccoons were everywhere. One time I came home and found three rattlers in my front yard. I killed all of them, fearing for my family, but most of all young Daniel. He was just a small guy, a happy-go-lucky loved little boy, not only by Bonnie and myself, but by all the staff at the Springs! He was very popular. Proceeding into our cabin, I found at least eight raccoons all chowing down on my various cartons and bags of food, knocked down from the cabinets onto the floor and the dining room table. The raccoons were all over the table, counters, and floor! I grabbed a broom and chased them all off! They went slowly too, not in any hurry. (By the way, no one on staff ever was bitten by a rattlesnake during all the years the family was there); amazing huh?

Another time I was taking a short cut home through the woods, and caught a mountain lion dining on a freshly taken deer, a doe. The deer was dead, and half eaten. He growled and ran off when I approached. I was not afraid at all just irritated that the big cat had killed one of our friendly critters that inhabited the Springs.

Finally, after six months of washing dishes, they transferred me to a job in maintenance, helping on the road crew, filling chuckholes in the old cow trail that led to Springs of Living Water, a ministry founded by Cooper and his wife, Lillian. Today it serves as a training campus for YWAM (Youth with a Mission).

"The Lord did not open the door for Ron to come here,' Lillian Cooper once told Bonnie. 'Ron just knocked it down."

One day during my stay at the Springs, a mail bag came up missing. It had important mail and a great deal of money in it. So, after several people in our mail room looked for it, and could not find it, they began to suspect me of taking it or having something to do with its disappearance. I had nothing to do with it; however. I was practically accused of taking it, and hiding it somewhere. I was given the cold shoulder and treated like I was guilty without a trial, conviction, or any proof. Then after a couple of days, someone found the mail bag, with all of its contents, where it had been misplaced in a weird storage place. Not one person ever came to me and apologized. I felt like telling a few people where to go but held myself in check.

I don't think Bonnie put much faith in my permanent conversion either, having been through so much with me during our marriage. She was angry with me; I didn't blame her. She didn't trust me; I gave her no reason to. She loved me, but I don't think she liked me.

"It was horrible,' Forrest said. 'I couldn't believe she stayed with him at all—and that's from about two years into the marriage not twenty-two."

I couldn't believe it either. We were married about twenty-five years altogether.

Forrest visited us at Richardson Springs, along with his wife and little girl, Alicia. I think it was in 1979. We were living in a small cabin, and I had built a monster big deck over a creek that ran all year. Forrest and I had some heart-to-heart talks during that visit. I was really trying to straighten my life out.

Talk about a merciful, patient God.

Later I kept my promise to the Marine captain: I left California for the great state of Washington and never committed another crime in my home state.

11
Stevenson, Washington

After about eighteen months at the Springs of Living Water, we moved north in 1979 to Stevenson, where Bonnie's family had settled after Rev. Walton (Bonnie's father) retired in 1974. Bonnie and the kids had been at the Springs about four years by that time. We didn't even have a car, but a woman who was traveling north let us ride with her. She was a friend of Bonnie's family.

We looked forward to living near Rev. Walton and his wife. He was a great guy, even when I was a self-centered jerk causing heartache for his daughter and his family. Bonnie wanted to live closer to her parents. He seldom said anything to me about my behavior, or if he did, the words sailed over my head.

I was drinking occasionally again in the early 1980s. I found a job as a mechanic at Bingen, just twenty-five miles east of Stevenson, where we lived initially with Bonnie's folks. We later moved into our own house after I went back to work making some decent money. They were all really religious, so I began to stay away from home a lot.

I experienced flashbacks, recalling the guys who died all around me, the blood, the body parts, and the anger. And I felt guilty. Why was I alive when they died? Why did God keep me breathing when these guys, much better than I could ever be, died?

The memories hit me when I least expected them. For example, one foggy afternoon, chopping firewood on a hillside overlooking the Columbia River, I heard three or four National Guard helicopters conducting low-level missions up the Columbia River Gorge. I dropped my chainsaw, paralyzed. Instantly I was back in Vietnam, looking for the enemy, trying to find cover. I was back above the Cua Viet River, Hueys flying overhead. Boom! Artillery blasts. Mortar shells rupturing the ground. My hair stood on end, my breath burst in shallow spurts from my chest. I bent over, hands on my knees. "These are National Guard helicopters. That's the Columbia River. You're not back in Vietnam." I repeated the words, over and over, until I could breathe normally again.

When I recovered, I picked up the chainsaw, tossed it in the truck, and drove to the nearest bar as fast as I could. I needed to shake it off. I didn't want to fight the NVA again in my nightmares. If I drank enough, I passed out. Then I didn't dream.

I spoke to a couple of preachers about my attempts to straighten out, but they acted like they were afraid of me. They knew I was an ex-convict and Vietnam combat vet, so they never treated me like a normal guy. Nobody trusted me; they considered me scary. Of course, as a matter of fact, I was untrustworthy at that time and still doing evil things. I was a pathetic creature, still using and abusing people.

"I don't know how to deal with you, Ron,' one pastor said to me. 'I don't know how to talk to you. I'm not a combat veteran. I've never done time. I don't know how to relate to you. I don't understand what makes you tick."

Neither did I.

"I don't think I can help you,' he said. 'You might want to find a different church."

I tried in my own weird way to get help, but I always ended up self-medicating. No one seemed to be able to help me.

On February 11, 1983, I pleaded guilty to forgery in Stevenson, WA. I was given a deferred five-year sentence and placed on probation on the condition that I make full restitution and pay attorney's fees and court costs. I was ordered to spend one year in the Skamania County Jail to run concurrently with a sentence received in Clark County.

I violated the terms of probation because I wrote bad checks again in May 1983. I faced charges of second-degree theft and third-degree theft in Skamania County. The following month, the judge agreed to delay my sentencing by four months "while he enters an alcoholism program designed for veterans who have been in Vietnam." I was ordered to go to a Veterans' Hospital for drug and alcohol treatment, and a month later I completed the program in Vancouver, Washington. I was attending three classes each week as an outpatient and planned to live in a halfway house.

Although I had been ordered to take Antabuse tablets, Skamania County Sheriff's officials figured I was "tonguing" the tablets or simply spitting them out when I left, according to court documents. They were right.

"It appears we have at this time a probationer, dependent on alcohol. He has voluntarily discontinued his Antabuse treatment and returned to alcohol-related felony behavior by writing at least $735.00 in nonsufficient funds checks," the report concluded. I was ordered to return to the court to say why my deferred sentence should not be revoked.

While awaiting trial, Bonnie visited me at the Skamania County Jail. I told her to get out of my life. I was no good for her. So finally, after years of neglect, we were divorced.

After I committed the forgeries, I had driven to California, running from the law. I didn't want to go back to prison. I arrived with a wad of money, several thousand dollars, and checked into a hotel room, drinking. One evening I was in a nice nightclub in Yreka, California, when I met this well-off cattle lady named Cheryl Bea. She was going through a divorce and lived on a dairy farm in Yreka. We danced and traded phone numbers. I called her up and we dated every weekend. I fed her a pack of lies about my occupation. She had two small children.

Weeks later, I finally told her a bit about my criminal background.

"Listen, Cheryl Bea, we've got to talk. I've got some things I haven't told you."

I shared my background, my Marine Corps experiences, and my trouble with the law. "And right now, I'm on the run. I'm wanted. They're looking for me," I told her truthfully.

Her eyes widened.
"Well, what did you do?"
I said, "Forgery."
"Oh, okay,' she said. 'Well, that's not as bad as it could've been."
I shared the details of the crime.
"How long do you think you're going to do?"
I lied, "Probably two or three years." But to myself, I thought, *But I think it will really be five or more years.*
"'I'll wait,' she said. 'I'll wait for you."

"Are you sure, Cheryl?" I asked.

A few days passed, and she demanded, "Well, what are you going to do?"

I shrugged my shoulders.

"I think you need to turn yourself in."

And I said, "Well, let me think about that one."

So for about a week I got drunk every night. And finally I said, "Okay, I'll turn myself in."

It was 2 o'clock in the morning. I called the cops and I said, "I'm wanted. Come and get me."

I told them where they could find me. They arrested me and took me to jail. Then they transported me north to Washington. Some deputies came down from Clark County because the crime happened in Vancouver, WA. They came all the way down there and picked me up in California and hauled me back up. We stopped overnight at a jail and then they brought me to Clark County.

Cheryl Bea had fallen in love with me. I liked her a lot, but primarily I think I was using her. I wasn't in love with her. It was more Ron Brandon BS. I was just a con artist and a jerk. So I played her but I really didn't want to hurt her.

In September 1983, my attorney, Russell J. Grattan, wrote to the court, describing me as a Vietnam veteran and Marine who served on the front lines with no prior record before going to Vietnam.

Mr. Grattan said, "Mr. Brandon is seeking psychological help and also help with his drinking problem," the court records state.

I pleaded guilty to all the charges and the prosecutor recommended I be sent to prison for up to five years. Despite my attorney's arguments, the court agreed.

"The court cannot leave Mr. Brandon available to victimize the community,' the judge ruled. 'As the court sees it, the defendant is well on his way to serving a life sentence on the installment plan."

I was sentenced to five years in prison for forgery. I served two-and-a-half years from 1983 to 1985 at McNeil Island Corrections Center in an unincorporated area of Pierce County, Washington. From there, I was delivered to work release at *Progress House* in Tacoma, Washington.

McNeil Island was another scary place. It was really a dungeon. The U.S. government established a federal prison on the island in 1875. The state of Washington had just taken over the penitentiary in 1981 and turned it into a state prison. It reminded me of San Quentin: a big fortress, wall, catwalk, guard towers, and armed guards all over the place. It was a maximum-security prison, with both state and federal prisoners. But as a federal pen, it included a theater where inmates could watch movies on a big screen. The prison was spread out with a barber shop, commissary and gymnasium. It resembled a small city, kind of like San Quentin had been with the exception of the movie theater. We had a huge yard where we worked out. We also played sports, always as the home team. We played against basketball, football, and baseball teams from outside the prison. I played tackle football as an outside linebacker. I also worked out like a gladiator in the iron pile, jacking iron, and building muscles. We benched pressed, weightlifted, and performed squat thrusts, and curls. That's how I spent part of the next two years.

Just before I left, I jacked a bench press of 400 pounds. I was really into lifting, working out with eighty-pound dumbbells. I wanted to be strong and respected. I didn't want to waste my time in the joint and I found that lifting weights was a great way to burn off stress and anger.

Meanwhile, I attended classes each weekday offered through Pierce College in Tacoma. The instructors rode over on the ferry and actually taught in the prison. I admired and respected them a lot for doing this. I graduated, earning my associate of arts degree. I actually participated in the graduation ceremony in town with the rest of the students after I was released. I earned a 3.8 grade point average, taking classes in logic, history, astronomy, math, economics and English.

Ron on right, pumping iron at McNeil

I wanted to keep studying and earn a four-year degree. I never thought about obtaining a master's degree; that would have been daydreaming.

During my time at McNeil, I had three different jobs, the second two with actual pay, albeit fifteen cents an hour. That's twenty dollars a month! Big money for being a convict!

The first job was working in the gymnasium. The supervisor had been a former pro-basketball player for a few years. I liked the job, since I was always in the gym working out and the 'Boss' was cool. We got along well.

My second job was working in 'Receiving and Release' which was interesting; I checked out who was coming and going into and out of the joint. All packages came in through there too. My boss was a guard named Patnode. I liked this man. He had been a school teacher. Because he was a Christian, I sensed something really different about him. We got along great.

My third and last job there was 'Registrar' in the education department, helping convicts get signed up for classes through Pierce College.

I attended chapel a bit at the prison. I might have gone more, but I overheard the chaplain state that "I'm only here for the paycheck, not for any inmates."

My girlfriend, Cheryl Bea, was my main bank while I was locked up in the Skamania County Jail and later in McNeil Island. She sent me a lot of money, probably several hundred dollars every month, so I could visit the commissary to buy stamps, cigarettes and what we called wham-whams and zoo-zoos—small cakes, pies, candy bars, or other goodies to treat the sweet tooth.

I wrote real nice flowery letters to her and told her what I was doing, how I was going to school. We planned on getting married and she actually flew to Seattle, took the ferry, and visited me one time at McNeil Island. I really started to like Cheryl Bea and thought seriously of marrying her.

After two years in prison, I was given a prerelease job for a month near the Veterans' Administration Hospital at American Lake at the Western State Hospital. During prerelease, I worked to purchase clothes and received training before going on work release in Tacoma. I was released in 1985 to what was known then as the 6th Avenue work release, now called the Progress House Work Release. The owner, Roger Vogt, hired me as a full-time salesman for Vista Home Improvement Co. in Tacoma. I sold siding, roofing and windows for residential and commercial buildings. The company provided leads and I followed up, visiting homeowners and business owners who had shown an interest in new roofs, siding, or windows. Roger was bonded, licensed, and insured, but still he took a risk hiring an ex-con. I never let him down. I became a top salesman in the region, traveling throughout Lakewood, Tacoma, Puyallup and Seattle to peddle the products. I staffed booths at the fairs and malls, encouraging people to fill out cards.

I enjoyed dressing in a suit or a sport coat and tie, keeping my fingernails clean, making good money off commissions. But I was drinking too—hard liquor—which never boded well for my future. Whiskey, rum, and mixed drinks made me plowed whenever I didn't have to work.

While I was in prison, Cheryl Bea and I had planned our wedding. But when I got out, I realized marrying her would be a mistake as I would probably ruin her life. I knew I would hurt her; she didn't deserve it. So I called her to break it off.

"I'm sorry, but I've got to end our relationship. It's over. I'm going back to my ex-wife," I lied. I had no intentions of going back to Bonnie.

She was angry. I found out she burned all the photos I had sent her. She hated me afterward, I think. I'm sure she went on with her life and met somebody else. I hope so. Maybe she even got back together with her husband.

I felt bad about it, but I knew it was the right thing to do. I would have made her life hell. I wasn't ready to change my life. I'd done the right thing for a change.

In fact, while working as a salesman and living the single life in Tacoma, I had five full-time good-looking girlfriends. None knew about the others. They all drove nice cars, owned homes, and earned lots of money. I was earning decent money too, so I felt like a cool dude, a wild party animal who lived a crazy jetsetter life: drinking, partying, snorting cocaine. I was flying high, sleeping only a few hours each night, living a life of debauchery.

I wanted out of my job. I started to hate pressuring folks to buy my products. Since we were the 'Cadillac' of home improvement companies, we were charging customers too much. Restless and anxious, I realized something was missing in my life.

Shortly afterward, I quit my job in Tacoma and moved back down to Stevenson to be with Bonnie. Bonnie kind of forgave me. She took me back again.

Her family wasn't too excited about our reuniting after our divorce. They weren't real keen to see me back in town. I'd tarnished Bonnie's reputation along with my own. The cops knew me well. They never responded alone to a call involving me. They always arrived in pairs, or three or four or five. I had a bad reputation as a violent, crazy ex-con and Vietnam veteran.

"During that year Ron was in a halfway house in the same town,' Bonnie said, 'he bought me flowers and was sure I wanted to go back to him. He moved in with us and Ronnie Jr. told me later how I embarrassed him as all his church friends knew we were divorced."

By that time, Ronda had graduated from high school and she was engaged, so it was just Ronnie Jr. and Danny at home. I loved Bonnie and asked her to marry me again.

"I called my dad and asked him to come over after church one Wednesday night and marry us,' Bonnie said, and he did. 'It was a mistake and my children were not happy with the way their dad treated them."

Bonnie and I did okay for a while, but then I started drinking again, which always led to trouble.

Danny, Ron, and Ron, Jr.

"He spent so much time in the Stevenson jail, I was embarrassed," Bonnie recalled.

I would blow half my paycheck on booze, and then maybe pay the rent with the rest of it. Bonnie worked as a checker at Ann's Food Fair. Sometimes we hired babysitters until Ronda was old enough to babysit the two boys when the youngest was about ten. Other times Bonnie's folks or her sister watched the kids.

I was gone most of the time—an absent father. Once in a while I'd quit drinking, attend church, and try to straighten up. But it never lasted long. When I was home, I occasionally disciplined the kids when they were teens, spanking them with a belt, but never as hard or as long as my father did. I swore I'd never treat my kids like he treated us. A few times when Ronnie Jr. was in high school, I smacked him when he was cocky with me. I was a little rough with him, and I never should have been. My boys were good kids. I loved them with all my heart.

Bill collectors called. Bonnie was laid off when her checks were garnished to cover our debts.

"My boss was kind and let me draw unemployment,' Bonnie recalled. 'Then I was able to attend college for a year."

I was in and out of the Skamania County Jail, primarily on misdemeanors.

After I had finished another run of binge drinking, I stayed in hotels and wrote bad checks on our account. I knew we didn't have any money in the bank. I'd land in jail for unlawful issuance of bank checks, time and again.

The Skamania County Jail became a second home to me, since I was in and out so often. One time a fight broke out between two inmates, right in the open, but no guards showed up until it ended. When they hit the floor, one inmate straddled the other's body, wrapping his hands around his neck, strangling him. The other guy flailed his arms, trying to throw off his assailant, but to no avail. I watched the guy on the floor as his face turned blue. He was going to die!

I jumped on the inmate who was doing the strangling and punched him hard in the side of the head. He let go of the other guy's throat and I punched him again—hard. I probably broke two or three of his ribs. Then I threw him to the ground.

"That's enough! You're not going to kill the guy,' I said. 'You beat him up. You strangled him. He's just about to die. You're not going to kill him. Not in front of me."

He backed away, probably because I was six-foot-four with a reputation as a San Quentin con. Then the guard showed up, even though cameras were all over the place. That attacker was a little deranged; he later went to prison. I believe I saved that inmate's life. While waiting for a deputy to show up, the inmate would have surely died.

It didn't take long before I resumed my old habits, drinking and gambling what little money I had. Bonnie knew where this path led. Everyone did. So the family decided to intervene.

Bonnie told me they had scheduled a meeting with a psychiatrist who understood PTSD. So I walked in, thinking the meeting would involve just Bonnie and me and our kids. Instead, about fifty people walked in—Bonnie's family members, the Walton's and their friends, the church pastor, neighbors, and people from throughout the Stevenson community.

It was an intervention, with all these people sitting in a giant circle, sharing how much my actions had hurt them.

I was furious. They ambushed me. You don't ambush a Vietnam vet unless you're ready for fireworks. It backfired on them. I blew up. In front of everyone, I cursed out the psychiatrist. I wanted to punch him a couple of times.

"What do you think you're pulling on me?" I shouted. "You're telling me you're going to do this one thing and now you've done set me up with all these people here. Well, you can all kiss my ass and go to hell!"

I stormed out of the room. I was so angry I could hardly see straight. I left burned rubber on that driveway as I peeled out. I drove to the apartment where we were living, packed my clothes, and left.

I still talked to Bonnie occasionally, but I was in a black mood. Nobody ever apologized for ambushing me. That's what an intervention is—an ambush. It's a time to catch someone sober and tell them about the pain they've caused. Who knows? If I had stayed, it might have worked. It might've shocked me enough to break through my steel cocoon I had erected for protection.

But I ran, the same thing I had been doing most of my life. I moved to Hood River, Oregon, where I lived in a trailer. A guy from the garage where I worked in Bingen had told me about this place. Unfortunately, I was laid off from my job.

I picked up odd jobs here and there to earn a little drinking money. I found a job at another service station in Hood River.

In 1987, I was drinking one night at the Bungalow Tavern near Carson, Washington. I was sitting with friends from work, including a couple of Vietnam veterans. We were loaded, testy, and hot, sitting around a table, pounding down beers and cracking jokes.

Then someone spilled some beer on me. I jumped up, incensed, and started pounding on a Vietnam Army veteran, a big lumberjack named Jerry. We were buddies, but that night we both threw punches. I wore a Marine Corps ring on my finger and one of my punches ripped open his face. Blood poured from the wound, squirting like a foot in the air. He fell to the floor. I panicked. Seeing that spurting blood, I figured I was headed back to jail. I fled to Hood River. I later heard that a bunch of guys, including Jerry, armed themselves with guns and followed, looking for me. They set an ambush in the neighborhood where I lived.

Fortunately for me, I never returned home that night. They missed me, but I left anyway. I had broken my hand pretty badly too so I stopped at a hospital where doctors found I had broken three or four bones; they put my hand in a cast. I was really sorry about that fight. I don't think Jerry ever filed charges. Barroom brawls erupt over stupid things. I didn't run into those guys again but I sent several large payments of $300.00 each to Jerry, trying to make things right between us.

A man in Hood River hired me to clean his house that he had rented to people who trashed it when they left. My employer had heard about me from the pastor of the local church I was attending. Both the pastor and the employer were trying to help me out, give me a hand up instead of a hand out.

When the job was finished, I waited for my wages. But the man told me the pastor offered my services free. What? I was so angry at the guy, at the pastor, at everyone. This guy owed me money for my work! I thought so, anyway.

I confronted the guy.

"Look, I did all this work. I made all these dump runs. You owe me this amount of money."

He said, "Well, see your pastor."

I knew seeing the pastor would accomplish nothing. I think the pastor figured I could do the work as a trade-off for living rent-free in this trailer. I thought I was paying rent, but I might have been mistaken. I was drinking heavily.

I knew where this man lived, so I waited until he was gone one day. I broke into his house by smashing a small window and unlocking the door. Nobody was home. I found his checkbook and wrote myself a check for the amount I felt I was owed. I forged his signature at the bottom of the check. I didn't take anything else.

I packed all my belongings and boogied out of there. I cashed the check in Portland. But I was speeding and when the police stopped me, they arrested me on a warrant for burglary and forgery. I was booked into the Hood River County Jail. That was the absolute worst jail in which I had ever been incarcerated in my life.

The jailers and twenty-five or thirty inmates at that dungeon of a jail where I spent four months feared me. I was a hardened criminal, a San Quentin con, a big guy with a bad attitude and a long record. I'd had plenty of experience in jails and prisons, but nothing was as bad as the Hood River Jail. The food wasn't fit to eat. It was delivered in sack lunches from a nearby restaurant and bar.

I kind of took over the jail cell area, acting like the big cheese, working out and showing off my karate, judo, and shadow boxing. I huffed and puffed, behaving like an animal. Inmates could smoke cigarettes in jail, so we lit our mattresses on fire. We tried to run everyone out of the jail complex with smoke.

We plugged all the toilets, stuffing clothing, whole rolls of toilet paper, and everything we could find into them, then flushed them over and over till they overflowed, flooding the jail cells. We caused havoc and damage whenever and wherever we could. We even managed to flood the offices and caused real problems.

We ordered one guy who was about to be released to change the nearby restaurant's name on its sign by adding an "s" and an "h" to the words "This Is -- It."

"If you don't go rename that place, we're going to fix you when we get out,' I threatened him. 'We're going to find you and we're going to hurt you. Get a can of spray paint and go down there and rename it."

We could see the sign through our window so he knew we would know if he did it. He spray-painted in white an *sh* before the word *it* in the name.

We also smuggled out a letter to the editor of the newspaper complaining about conditions in the jail, the horrible food, the lack of fresh air. We had no television, no recreation, no books to read. We felt like victims. Yes, we definitely deserved to be in jail because we'd been rotten, but we didn't need to be treated as if we were subhuman. We were treated worse than dogs.

Three inmates even filed a lawsuit against the county. Reporter Joan Laatz wrote an article about the lawsuit published in *The Oregonian*.

"Three inmates of the Hood River County Jail are suing the county and its sheriff over what the inmates say are 'abysmal, unconstitutional conditions' at the jail," she wrote.

"The plaintiffs—James Patereau, Rodney Behee and Arthur Gibson—said inmates were physically abused by jailers for complaining about conditions. They said inmates in crowded conditions were forced to sleep on the floor without mattresses, given only cold water in the cells, and prevented from any privacy while using toilets. Improper plumbing, they said, let raw sewage in the drunk tank's toilets flood the floor. Showers were allowed only once a week. Their attorney, Portland lawyer Spencer M. Neal, described the jail's conditions as the worst he had seen at any jail in Oregon." The publicity led to reforms and better food.

I became the ringleader. Oh, I was nasty. I was not a good character. I was one ugly child to put it mildly. Finally, after we threw feces and urine at the jailers, they'd had enough of my trouble-making. They brought in about twenty cops with guns and escorted me out and threw me in isolation, where I stayed for a few weeks until I left to go to the big house—the Oregon State Penitentiary in Salem.

When I appeared before the judge for sentencing, the prosecutor described me as a troublemaker at the jail with a long criminal history.

The judge looked me in the eye.

"Mr. Brandon, I understand you don't like our accommodations here too much."

"Judge, that's putting it mildly,' I responded. 'Accommodations? What do you mean? You've got us in a doghouse pen down there. It ain't fit for lizards to live in."

Jail house conditions were exposed for how bad they were. Within a short time, the jail was torn down and completely rebuilt, providing decent, humane treatment for future offenders.

I was sent to Oregon's State Penitentiary to finish my sentence of five years. This is the main prison where Oregon's death row inmates stay. Conditions were much better than at Hood River County Jail. My reputation followed me, so they stuck me on a special unit—the California convict unit—for inmates who had done time in Soledad, Folsom, San Quentin or other evil big-name prisons. I fit right in. We all respected one another. We didn't take crap from anybody. We were the bad boys and nobody messed with us. We pretty much got along. The guys who had a really hard time were the child molesters, rapists, and sex-crime inmates. Prisoners did evil things to them.

I tried to keep out of it and just did my time, worked out in the iron pile, and attended school when I could. I took classes offered through Chemeketa Community College.

I was sentenced to five years, but I wrote a letter to the judge. I told him I was a changed man. I didn't really burglarize the home; I just went there to pay myself what was owed me."

The judge wrote back.

"Mr. Brandon. Next time you have a disagreement with someone, you can take it to the court. I advise you to get a lawyer and sue next time. You don't have to take it into your own hands." I think the judge may have asked the parole board to shorten my prison sentence.

The parole board released me early, after serving only eighteen months. It was another case of the grace of God.

I lived in Salem, Oregon for a while and then found a job working as a janitor at the Bonneville Dam. I contacted Bonnie and we patched things up, so she let me move in with her again in Stevenson. I had quit drinking again, so she saw hope for our relationship. Bonnie should've gotten a medal for hanging in there. She saw potential in me, I guess. She loved me, and I loved her, in my own weird way.

I didn't really understand the concept of love. I feared my dad, and I feared God. I didn't love anyone really. Not even myself. Especially not myself.

But Bonnie loved me through all the ups and downs, and she took me back again. We lived in a rental house. By that time, Ronda had graduated from high school. I attended her graduation and, shortly afterward, walked her down the aisle when she married Steve. (Years

Ron and Bonnie at Ronda's wedding

later I also attended both of my sons' weddings.) Ronnie Jr. was nearing graduation from high school and joining the Marines, like his old man. Danny was still in junior high.

We did well for a while. I was cutting wood, selling firewood, building up a pretty good business. I stayed busy working six days a week for nearly two years.

Then, my dad became sick in California so I moved south. I arrived in time for my dad's last days. When I first arrived at the hospital where my father was, I went to his room, looked down at him in that bed, then leaned over and gave him a kiss on his cheek. I took him by the shoulder and arm and embraced him.

My brother, Ferral, who arrived before Forrest and me, told us that as each one of us had come in, separate from each other, we had all performed the identical ritual, leaning over, giving Dad the brief kiss on the cheek, and a short embrace. Curious. We loved and respected our father very deeply. I read a book to my father aloud, *Heaven, My Father's House*; Dad went there thirty days later. Forrest D. Brandon died December 17, 1987 at the age of sixty-three. He and Mom had been married more than forty years. He was buried at Cypress Hill Memorial Park in Petaluma.

After returning from California back to Washington, I found a union job which paid well with good benefits. Thompson Metal Fab hired me as a welder helper in Vancouver.

Though we were paid well, we worked in a rough environment: an open bay in which we froze in winter and boiled in the summer. I liked the work operating overhead cranes, using other machinery and tools, and building various structures like a huge catamaran. It was going to be used in Hawaii as an island-to-island ferry boat.

With 22 degrees registered as the temperature one wintry day, my hands were cold and I started belly-aching. I whined and sniveled and complained. During our break, I lit a smoke and up walks one of the welders whose name was Luke. He got in my face and said, "Are you a man or a mouse?"

He was about five feet eight inches tall, 180 pounds at most. I was six foot three inches and 230 pounds of steel-like muscle. I glared at him. He was fearless. He told me he heard all my bitchin' and that I ought to be grateful for a job. He didn't like listening to my complaining. So he said, "Either shape up or ship out!"

I could have jerked him up off the ground and thrown him ten feet through the air! I was stunned, in shock at his audacity. Other guys were watching and listening. Suddenly, I burst out laughing! It just hit me that he was right! Within five seconds, I knew I was acting like a 'pantywaist.'

I laughed, "Why Luke, you're dead right! Thanks for tuning me up!"

They all left. I never complained again, ever, about anything! Luke and I became good friends.

A couple years later, again I had to leave Bonnie and the kids so I could take care of my mom. It was only a temporary move. We didn't want to take the kids out of school, and Bonnie wanted to stay in Stevenson.

Mom and Dad had lived in Mill Valley but after Dad received the settlement from his work-related accident, they bought a four-bedroom ranch-style house at Rohnert Park which was where she still lived alone. I moved in with Mom and found a job as a mechanic at a service station again. She missed my dad a lot. They really did love each other. After Dad finally quit drinking, Mom softened. She became the woman she was when we were little, before something hardened her heart.

My parents had a lot of friends who cared about them. They helped out when my Mom was diagnosed with cancer and I ignorantly refused to believe it would kill her.

Forrest visited Mom for the last two years of her life almost every week and they finally put the past to rest. By then Forrest had given his heart to the Lord. He sat in the kitchen, while his mother rested on the couch. He asked her forgiveness for mistreating her and speaking ill of her. She thanked him for being honest with her, when he sent that letter from Vietnam. He told her he forgave her for everything he felt she had ever done wrong to him. He asked her to forgive him for the pain his letter caused her.

"Forrest, I forgave you the day after I read it,' she said. 'I know your heart. That was no problem."

Mom and Forrest had a lot of good conversations. He learned that she always wanted to be baptized in the Holy Spirit. Forrest had done it in high school, and again in 1973 when he recommitted his life to the Lord.

She told Forrest that she knelt down and prayed sometimes for an hour for my safety when I was in Vietnam, especially after hearing horrible reports of Marines dying in combat. She prayed for Forrest too, even though he was in a pretty secure area most of the time. They never were overrun and he never had cause to fire his weapon at the enemy.

I never had a heart-to-heart like that with Mom or Dad. I was not in the frame of mind to do that at all.

Ron in 1986

Both Forrest and I grew up in the same middle class home, with parents who stayed married forty years despite alcoholism, violence, and coldness. We attended the same schools, the same church, and the same youth group. We were close. We both served overseas in Vietnam as Marines. We both drank too much, blacking out. But he became a cop. I was a con.

Forrest was medically retired from the San Rafael Police Department, after more than a dozen years on the job. He crushed discs in his back while helping paramedics move a more than 300 pound man out of a building where he had suffered a heart attack. Without a doubt, Forrest helped save the man's life.

He underwent low back surgery but couldn't return to work within a year so they retired him medically in 1983. He worked in the San Francisco Bay area as a security officer, and he even hired me to work with him sometimes. I earned twenty-five dollars an hour as his assistant. Our job included moving vagrants along from the front of the Golden Gate, Curran, and Orpheum Theaters during their off-Broadway performances. I kept a low-profile, off the record, because, given my felony convictions, they probably never would have hired me.

After Ronnie Jr. joined the Marines, Bonnie moved down to California with Daniel and we moved into a two-bedroom apartment. I was working full time, drinking, buying and selling weed, and still watching after Mom. I didn't get caught, but I didn't want Danny, who was only fifteen, almost sixteen, following in my errant footsteps. I set down two rules—don't ever do drugs and don't bring in girlfriends when we're not home. He had his own room.

I worked for this company out of Sausalito and I drove all over the whole Bay area delivering high-priced, exotic imported food items, mostly seafood.

It was about this time that we sent Daniel back to Washington to live with his sister and her husband, Steve, at the Naval Base at Bangor. He graduated from high school. I didn't attend his graduation. I missed both boys' graduations because I was again incarcerated.

None of my kids ever did time. I prayed they wouldn't. God answered my request.

One night while I was driving down Highway 101 in California, I fell asleep at the wheel of the car. I woke up feeling like someone, or something, grabbed the steering wheel hard and jerked it back to the left, onto the road. I slammed on the breaks and gazed over the cliff toward the ocean below, where the car had been headed. I looked around the car, trying to see who or what jerked the steering wheel. I believe it had to be an angel protecting me from sure death if I had gone over that cliff.

After Mom was diagnosed with lung cancer in 1989. I took her to medical appointments, lived in the house with her, and made sure her needs were met. The doctor told Forrest, Ferral and me that she was about to die. He said she would probably live at most six more months. They didn't want to tell her though. That responsibility rested on my shoulders.

"You get six months to live," I said. I didn't break it to her easily or gently. I just bombed her with it. I was blunt.

She burst into tears. My abrupt news really hurt her. I didn't even try to comfort her. Forrest and Ferral did though. I didn't feel anything. I had not yet forgiven my mother.

My brother Forrest was sitting next to my mom one day, as she lay in the hospital bed, near death. Suddenly he was overhearing a very real clear conversation going on between my mom and Someone who turned out to be Jesus. He could not hear Jesus' words but he definitely heard our mother's words.

"Jesus, I would really like you to heal me so I can testify about my healing and my life story."

"Daughter, you are going to be in heaven soon. Do not fear."

Whatever He told my mom, she seemed to accept it just fine, because she had a big smile on her face as she passed away peacefully shortly thereafter."

When Comoretta Brandon died September 16, 1989, twenty-two months after my dad passed away, Forrest and his wife, Pep, were with her. Forrest entered the hospital's dining room to tell Kelly, Ferral and me the news. It didn't bother me. I never shed a tear when she died. Like my dad, Mom was sixty-three also.

One day while living in California, Bonnie and I hiked up Mount Tam in the Mount Tamalpais State Park.

"We were talking and I mentioned it had been almost twenty-five years,' Bonnie recalled, considering the years they had been married. 'I started crying and said if the second twenty-five were as bad as the first I could not go on."

After Mom died, we helped clear out the house and prepare it for sale. Then Bonnie and I moved back to Washington. By then my in-laws had moved to Vancouver. Bonnie's mother was suffering from dementia.

"Ron and I both moved back, much to my family's dismay,' Bonnie recalled. 'That Thanksgiving I was not invited to any family celebration as they were upset that Ron came back."

One day, I'd been drinking when I returned to the house where we were staying temporarily with Bonnie's parents. I found Rev. Walton down in the basement on his knees, praying for me. He stood to his full five-foot-five height and pointed his bony finger in my face.

"I've been praying for you, Ron, and one of these days I'm going to see you in heaven!' He said it with determination, as if he knew it was true. 'You're going to change your life one of these days," he prophesied.

After Bonnie's mother died, her father moved into an apartment, where people could visit for only a week at a time. Bonnie and I spent a little time in a homeless shelter before we found an apartment we could afford. I wasn't working, but Bonnie had transferred from her job in Petaluma to one in Portland.

"Ron started drinking and acting crazy again,' Bonnie recalled. 'I needed a car. I'm sure my dad helped me then to get another one. I parked it close to his house and Dad pulled his car real close behind because I was afraid Ron would come take it. Sure enough, in the morning, the car was gone!"

Meanwhile, Forrest, who was executor of my mother's estate, sold the big house at Rohnert Park and other property she owned in northern California, which sold for the same amount she paid for it.

I received a check for $26,000 as my inheritance, a lot less than we thought we'd have after the lawyer finished taking a huge cut. I almost had a murder charge on me because I wanted to kill him. My brother Forrest talked me out of that one after I called that shark every curse word I knew.

We used the inheritance money to pay off bills. I repaid all outstanding court debts too. I wanted to buy a house. Bonnie wanted to save it. I couldn't save anything. We stuck about seven thousand in banks, but before long, I took it out to cover my drinking and gambling. Bonnie worked full time for a company in Portland and I squandered my inheritance. It was pretty much gone.

Then one day while Bonnie was at work, I had a company clean out the apartment and pay me for our furniture. I sold it right out from under her. Then I took the $400.00 or $500.00 and left on another of my drunken runs. I just didn't care. I figured she could always find help from her parents.

Talk about a rotten dog. That's how rotten I was. Bonnie went through hell.

"I came home one day and found it had been emptied,' Bonnie recalled. 'Ron had called an auction place and sold all I had left. I threw a huge fit. And it was just like God asking me what I was waiting for now."

She moved into an apartment with her father for a year. A small church they attended helped them find a home.

A nice surprise occurred in 1988, when Steve and Ronda were stationed in Scotland and invited me to visit for a month. (Steve was a career Navy man specializing in nuclear submarines. After retiring from the Navy, he went to work as a police officer for several years. He now volunteers for Samaritan's Purse and does mission work. He's also a pilot.) But life was tough for Bonnie.

About that time, Bonnie recalled, "Ronda got married, Ronnie joined the Marines, my parent's house burned down, Danny moved to work with his 'Aunt Elaine Solheim' and he lived with Steve and Ronda. I had to sign custody of Danny over to Steve because he was living on a naval base. Danny had a hard time forgiving me for that.'

'That was a hard year for me as their dad ended up in prison again and I lost everyone. My nest was empty," said Bonnie.

But during a visit to a small church with her dad, Bonnie heard a woman give a prophetic word: "Someone in the audience needs to be released from bondage."

"I knew that was for me, and it had something to do with Ron,' Bonnie said. 'I went forward for prayer and told the pastor 'I don't understand' but this has something to do with Ron and me." Before that service, I still loved Ron, but the Lord released me from him. I think it was before Easter and I always look at that time as a healing for me."

Bonnie filed for divorce a second time in 1990. By then I was back in an Oregon jail on drunken driving charges, first in Clackamas County and later in Wasco County.

Then, while working in Vancouver, I found a contractor's pile of business account checks that he'd actually left somewhere on a job. I forged his signature on a few—up to five thousand dollars on one. The banks cashed the checks, I pocketed the money, and then I drank and gambled it away. I didn't really feel bad about it; I knew he had insurance. He wasn't going to lose a dime. I figured *He's wealthy enough he wouldn't miss it.* I was taking care of me—my needs, my booze, my drugs, my gambling money. Nothing else mattered.

Addicts don't care. They'll hurt anyone. They'll even take money from their own kids—food money, rent money, whatever—to spend it on themselves. That's the way I was.

It took getting busted, locked down, and sobered up to realize what I had done and how terrible it really was. I would feel remorseful and, at the same time, I felt sorry for myself, so I would cut off all emotion. I'd bury my brain in a book.

I was arrested, booked into Clark County Jail, and charged with forgery again. It was late 1990. I was sentenced to five years in prison.

12
Last Time in Prison

The last time I was in prison, everything changed.

They sent me to the Washington Corrections Center at Shelton, the receiving center where prisoners are evaluated, and from there to Larch Corrections Center near Yacolt, Washington. The 500 men honor camp didn't have fences or armed guards. The inmates helped the State Department of Natural Resources rebuild trails and bridges as well as fight fires.

One day we were working in the mountains in below-freezing weather. I was carrying a chainsaw in one hand, a gas can in the other, when I stepped on a rock and my foot flew out from under me. I landed on top of the rock, smashing my back between the shoulder blades. I was given Tylenol and put on light duty.

Inmates there didn't have an incentive to fake injuries because they were paid for working. If they didn't work, they didn't earn any money. If you didn't work, they'd ship you out of the work camps back to the big house. We liked working in the honor camp, even though the guards tried to make our life hell at that time. I was still pumping iron, lifting weights, to keep in shape and to burn off tension. I wore my hair and beard long, and looked like a wild man. I was not friendly to anyone. But when I sat in the visitors' room where chapel services were held, I tried to show all my teeth, smiling, acting friendly, flirting a little with the single ladies from a visiting church, Crossroads Community Church in Vancouver, Washington.

I started out pretending to listen as a guy and a gal stepped forward to share their testimony. They talked about how they used to be so messed up, but then Christ changed their hearts and minds. One guy was a violent drug addict who broke the law, but he'd never been caught. He said, "You know, if I was caught for all the stuff I did, I'd have been in prison."

They did prison ministry, they said, because Christ had done so much for them and they wanted to share His love with us inmates. They were people truly full of the grace of God! I could tell there was something really different about them. They seemed to love us.

As I sat listening to their testimonies, God started speaking to me. Their stories sank in deeply. God broke through my hard shell and pierced my heart. These people shared how God had delivered them, hauled them from hell, freed them from drugs and alcohol, jail and prison.

I felt so alone, hopeless, looking at my wasted life. I thought of all the people I had hurt—Bonnie, my kids, my folks, my siblings (especially Forrest), Bonnie's folks, and the people I had robbed and terrorized.

I was right where I should be. I deserved punishment. I felt I was rotten, inside and out. I thought of all those guys I knew in Vietnam—the ones who died right next to me. They never lived. I did, but I lived a mean, rotten, wild life, hurting everyone I knew. I was always running, running, running. From what? From God? From myself? From my nightmares?

When I left prison, I would have nowhere to go. No car. No clothes. No nothing. It was scary. "I've got to do something. I've got to change. I'm forty-four years old. I can't deal with this."

I couldn't sleep most of the night. I pulled a blanket over my head, muffled my words with my pillow, and prayed to God.

I asked God to save me, to deliver me, to set me free. I begged him to remove the murder from my heart, the bitterness, anger, and violence. I wanted him to clean me from top to bottom, remove my filthy mouth, my nasty jokes, and my lustful mind. I confessed all my sins, spewing all the garbage I'd built up inside my heart.

"Lord, take it all out of me. Take it away. Deliver me from this stuff. I don't want to live like this anymore. Change my life. Make something useful out of me."

The dam broke; tears flowed from my eyes, snot dripped from my nose. I surrendered it all at the foot of the cross. I pulled the blanket tighter. I didn't want any inmates to know I was sniveling and whining to the Lord.

The next day, I felt tremendous peace. For the first time in my life, I trusted somebody. I knew He could succeed where I had failed. Something had broken inside me. Pain poured from every follicle of my body, and Jesus wiped away the tears, soothed the wounds, and covered my pain with His loving arms.

"I don't want to continue down this road of misery and criminal behavior and insanity," I prayed fervently. He really heard my prayer and He began to do a work. He began to change me and He put a desire in my heart to go to chapel and start reading the Bible.

I started hanging with guys that were going to chapel. I had a new crowd of friends, but I still wasn't an ideal inmate.

After I broke my back, I couldn't do the work at the conservation camp, so they sent me back to Shelton as a medium-security inmate. At first I was in R Units, but eventually they assigned me to mainline. I remained there until my release. I worked and went to school. I also spent a lot of time on the yard running laps and in the weight-pile. I was surprised to run into a former Marine, an African-American, who was into 'driving iron' also.

He and I had known each other a couple of years. We hit it off well. One day my two-man cell had an opening, so I invited 'Reggie' to join me, if he could handle the heat. Blacks and whites never mixed usually. Getting together was one thing, but living together was another.

He said, "Sure, why not?"

Sure enough, one day another black man got in Reggie's face about living with me, a white boy.

Suddenly, Reggie just reached out with one arm, caught the guy by the throat, lifted him off the floor, choking him. He warned him to keep his mouth shut and mind his own business. Then he dropped him on the floor. Reggie was like me. He was big, ugly, mean and was bench-pressing 540 pounds! I was benching about 400 pounds. Nobody messed with us again. We had some serious respect.

Ron, 1993, Free at Last from His Prison Days

I ended up serving two-and-a-half years' total time this last stretch. I was given work release in January 1992. But I left this time with hope for the future. I had put some twelve years behind bars during the past twenty-three years.

13
Introducing Donna, My Future Wife

Pearl Donita Mscichowski, who has always been called Donna, was born in Vancouver, Washington, at St. Joseph Hospital, which is now Southwest Washington Medical Center. Her father, Boleslaus Mscichowski, emigrated from Poland to the United States when he was eighteen, in the early 1900s, and became a United States citizen in 1918.

After serving sixteen of his thirty-five years in the U.S. Army, and eventually earning the rank of Master Sergeant, he traveled back to Poland in search of a wife with whom he could share his life. Since dating was not customary in Poland, twenty-four-year-old Pelagia Rogowski met thirty-seven-year-old Boleslaus only twice before she married him in her home town in her local Catholic Church. Her most vivid memory of her wedding day was how much she cried, saddened that she would be leaving her warm and happy home to move to an unknown America with a man she barely knew.

Donna's father was fifty-five and her mother forty-three when she was born. Her three older brothers, Joe, Dick, and Pete, were eighteen, seventeen, and fifteen years older than her.

Because of her unhappy marriage, Pelagia returned to Poland three times, once with Peter when he was very young, once with Donna when she was a preschooler, and then again when Donna was in grade school. On all occasions they stayed at her grandparents' home.

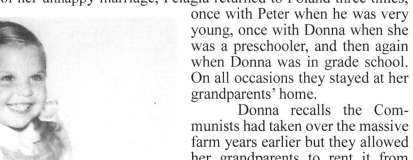
Donna Mscichowski 1946

Donna recalls the Communists had taken over the massive farm years earlier but they allowed her grandparents to rent it from them. Her grandparents were one of the wealthiest families in this little village and Communists had taken everything from them. A couple of her relatives on her mother's side died in concentration camps in Siberia.

Pelagia planned on staying in her home land permanently with Donna, but decided to return to the United States so Donna could take advantage of a better education.

Donna, who couldn't speak English when she started kindergarten in a parochial school, felt incredibly lonely as a child, since her older brothers, who no longer lived at home, were more like uncles and there was such an atmosphere of disconnect in the home. All the children attended Catholic grade schools; Donna went to Providence Academy in downtown

Vancouver, where she graduated in 1962. Her brothers graduated from Fort Vancouver High School.

Surrounded daily with sounds of hostility, Donna's fingers blistered from hands that constantly sweated, and she suffered eating problems because of the tension she always felt.

Donna states "I walked through my childhood on 'tiptoes', trying never to make waves."

But unlike the displays of daily rage and hostility that she experienced, she never expressed anger. Her nickname in school was 'Smiley'.

Her mother, strangled by her own loneliness and bitterness, frequently poured out seething hatred toward her husband to her sensitive young daughter. Pelagia traumatized Donna with her recitation of the abuse she suffered from Boleslaus. Her parents screamed daily, often cursing each other loudly in Polish. Donna felt psychological stress and constantly sought acceptance from others. Her family never spoke about their feelings; she plastered a smile on her face so people would like her. Most weekends found her in the confessional reciting her perceived sins and failings.

Some of Donna's happiest childhood memories evolved around dance lessons. After her mother enrolled her in tap dance, she recalled standing in the front recital row, leading the rest of the young girls in their step, step, shuffle, shuffle routines. Her mother provided piano lessons and sewed her clothes, as this was her way of expressing care. Donna also participated in Girl Scouts, attending summer camp each year which brought her great joy.

Donna picked berries and babysat often to earn money, and later worked at Vick's burgers on Fourth Plain Boulevard in Vancouver. These were legitimate ways to escape the war zone in her home. She loved to socialize, attended school dances and dated fairly frequently as a teenager. One summer, when she was fifteen, she met a man on the tennis courts; she was flattered to receive attention from Robert Schafte, a handsome athletic jock and a big hero who had just graduated from Hudson's Bay High School. He picked her up in a large car with fins that seemed as large as a shark's. Her parents didn't like her dating such an older boy, especially since he wasn't Catholic.

Bob's family, which seemed so "peaceful," drew Donna into its circle of four, parents Leonard and Ida, Bob, and his sister, Eileen. They never argued. They enjoyed meals together and went bowling as a family. She loved the idea of spending time with people who seemed to genuinely care for one another.

Bob gave her an engagement ring for her high school graduation. Donna left college, where she majored in drama and psychology, to marry Bob, who had converted to Catholicism, on January 5, 1963.

Bob worked as a longshoreman, earning a good salary to support their growing family. Early on in their marriage, Donna worked as a bookkeeper. She later attended parent participation classes at Clark College with each of her children and earned her degree in Early Childhood Education.

She and Bob had three children—one girl, Denise, and two boys, Damon and Derek. Donna's love for children bloomed as she poured her life into theirs. She later became an instructor in the Family Life/Parent Education Program at Clark College, putting to good use her training in Early Childhood. She believes God used her fractured childhood to lead her to a career in guiding families.

On a fall evening, when Bob was thirty-five years old, he staggered down the hallway, bumping into the walls. His eyes were dilated and his speech was slurred. He was rushed to the hospital and after intensive testing, was diagnosed with encephalitis, a swelling of the brain which he most likely contracted on the water front. He lost all ability to talk and was having severe seizures.

During the testing the doctors also discovered bone cancer. A priest was called to administer the last rites, as there was concern Bob was going to die. Later, he spoke of going down a tunnel toward a brilliant light, and then turned directions to find himself back in his hospital bed.

Donna's mother had moved into their home just before Bob's hospitalization, suffering from brittle diabetes and needing frequent care. Before her death thirteen years later, Pelagia told Donna that one evening, as she was lying in her bed, she saw Jesus standing near her, bringing her great comfort. She saw sandals on His feet and a crown dazzling with beautiful jewels on His head!

Donna faithfully attended the Catholic Church Mass every Sunday with her children. She felt such a void, especially after the death of her father. He had changed dramatically after the birth of Donna's children and they would spend hours talking on the phone. She experienced the sought-after relationship with her dad that she had longed for her whole life.

She thought faith must hold more. An announcement in the church bulletin kept catching her eye concerning a "prayer meeting" that took place on Tuesday nights. In her search for finding that 'something more' she attended a charismatic, Spirit-filled meeting and realized Jesus died on the cross for her personally. She need do nothing to earn it; she simply must accept His gift. He loved her unconditionally, enough to die for her. In what seemed to be just minutes, yet an eternity, her life was transformed. She surrendered her life to Him and moved from a fear-based religion to a life-changing relationship with Jesus.

The leader of this meeting queried, "Would you like to receive the baptism of the Holy Spirit?"

"Yes, I would."

And so she prayed to receive the Holy Spirit. The foundation of her life was solidified. She was given a greater compassionate heart for the downtrodden, the throw a-ways that society rejected.

Donna continued attending the Catholic Church with her mother, but sought out a Spirit filled church that could feed her hunger for the intimacy with the Lord that she so desired. So on Saturday nights, she attended the Catholic Church with her mother, and on Sundays she visited Crossroads Community Church. She was on fire for the Lord. Donna remembered crying through the worship time for several years at Crossroads, as if God was releasing the dam of a fractured life, rebuilding it with His refreshing, living water.

Bob did not join Donna on her faith journey, but many prayers went up for him over the years that he lived, and their son Damon led him to the Lord on his death bed. He had lost several inches in height and would break a bone just turning his neck. Multiple myeloma is one of the most painful cancers that exist.

She and Bob had been married for twenty-eight years when he died in 1991 at the age of 50.

Donna was employed for over thirty years as a parent educator in the Clark College Family Life/Parent Education program, where she facilitated many classes in a program where parents participated with their children in a pre-school setting to earn college credit. One of her most rewarding efforts was working with adults and children that were court referred to attend. She received an award as Outstanding Adjunct Faculty of the Year from the Social Science Department at Clark College.

DONNA SCHAFTE, Parent teacher educator from Clark College, reads to Roxane Manesh at the Co-Pep Preschool. The preschool, which has been housed in Battle Ground High School's Central Building, will be looking for a new home at the end of this month.

Donna and preschooler, 2000
Photo from The Reflector, *a Battleground, WA newspaper.*

14
New Beginnings

Ron and Donna's wedding 2000

Donna, who was forty-six with three adult children, joined her new church on a mission trip to Mexico, where a dozen people helped build a hospital. Donna recalled "plastering walls and being sent out into high foliage to cut it back with a weed whacker, being given the instructions that if I ran into snakes, to just cut them in half!"

Upon their return to the US, the twelve travelers talked about doing something of significance in the community, something that would reach others with the good news of the gospel. They chose to go into Larch Corrections Center, a minimum security prison about 45 minutes east of Vancouver, WA, for their mission field. Inspired to reach others for Christ, they began ministering to the inmates at Larch, where I was incarcerated.

More folks from Crossroads became involved at Larch and some led in worship, while others shared their testimony. They brought homemade desserts each week and that was a huge hit with the men. I joked that "It was the women and the food that drew me to the meetings."

I remember that during prison visits, Donna went by a pseudonym, Donna Pearl, in keeping with regulations to never give out her last name at the prison. She had felt drawn to prison ministry, feeling certain that Christ could change convicts' hearts and lives if only they knew and loved Him. Scripture has encouraged Christians to visit prisoners and share the Good News with them. Donna, who has possessed unbounded mercy, felt that call on her life. She has always fought for the underdog.

> *"See, I am doing a new thing! Now it springs up; do you not perceive it? I am making a way in the wilderness and streams in the wasteland."* (Isaiah 43:19 NIV)

Donna was among the group that visited Larch the night my life changed. She has recalled, "I vaguely remembered him from the meetings as a man with shaggy hair and a bushy beard."

After discontinuing prison visits for a season, Donna felt led in the direction of opening her home for meetings for those that wanted to support folks in prison and for the families and the ex-offenders upon their release.

"I remembered a vivid dream,' Donna recalled, 'where ex-offenders and their families were gathered in my front room, focusing on strengthening their walk with the Lord. I felt prompted to make that dream a reality."

She commented that "I started corresponding with several inmates as well, encouraging them in their faith during that time. I felt God was leading me to do this and I never had fear."

Soon the Full Gospel Business Men's Fellowship joined the group of fervent folks whose focus was on providing support to those that had been incarcerated, as well as some ex-offenders and their families that lived in the Vancouver area.

Donna said, "I had to set up chairs running down my hallway and kitchen because there were so many that attended those first meetings in my home."

Donna when she first met Ron

Outgrowing her home, the meetings were moved to Turning Point Church where *Breaking Free Ministries* was officially born. Donna and a network of volunteers provided housing, aftercare, and counseling for hurting ex-offenders and veterans.

I wrote to a Donna Pearl, in care of Crossroads Church, thanking them for their visit and sharing how God broke me that night, changing my life.

"The church office tracked me down and gave me the letter, as they knew I was involved in prison ministry there and went by my first and middle name. I answered it along with several others from prisoners in the state of Washington," Donna recalled.

Donna and I continued to write while I was at Larch, and then I was transferred to a work release program in Longview, WA, about thirty minutes north of Donna's home. She began visiting me on occasion.

Donna recalled, "On one visit, I attended a church service with Ron. When I went forward for prayer, I remember sensing someone standing next to me. It was Ron; a warmth flooded me as I appreciated being with someone that shared my faith."

After leaving Longview, I relocated to Vancouver and became a part of *Breaking Free Ministries*. A new chapter in our lives was birthed.

Our Friday night services at Turning Point Church grew rapidly, and we provided housing for ex-offenders and veterans, assisting them with help in finding jobs and other needed resources to function in society. After a board of directors was formed, I became the first manager of the housing program.

Donna stated, "I also became a student at Warner Pacific College after Bob's death, and earned a second degree in Human Development."

She completed that degree while helping found *Breaking Free Ministries*. God was bringing support for those that were released from prison as others from Crossroads went into Larch. Donna continued teaching at Clark College.

"I used to think that the only people who cared about prisoners were their immediate family and friends,' former prisoner Ed Parke wrote in his book, *Jailhouse Religion*. 'Then you meet people like Donna. God spoke to her and she became one of the principal founders of *Breaking Free Ministries*, which was not only to be a prison ministry, but one that included veterans as well."

One sunny afternoon, Donna and I enjoyed a picnic lunch and each other's company in a local park. We were at peace as we gazed at the lake and the beauty of God's creation. As we talked, we felt sparks charge between us, as if a camera flash burst over a current filled with electricity. Friendship began flowering into fondness.

We felt bonded and wanted to spend as much time as possible with each other, but Donna was cautious. Although I had made dramatic changes in turning my life around, familiar spirits intruded at times, rearing their ugly heads. The adage that old habits die hard is true.

Donna became like a teacher to me. Her non-judgmental attitude gave me hope and I respected her greatly. She's an excellent communicator, and this helped me feel safe and more open.

After completion of work release, I was living in a trailer on the property of someone from Crossroads. I was employed as a manager at a gas station in Woodland. Those familiar spirits were suffocating me again, crying out for release. I caved in and went to drink and gamble in La Center. Addictions were my way of escape, numbing pain I had experienced for many years. I desperately wanted to be set free but they still had a grip on me.

When I ran out of gambling money, I decided to 'borrow' some money from my boss's safe. I fully intended to return it in the morning, as soon as I won more.

However, continued drinking and smoking weed destroyed any sense of doing the right thing. I again lost all that 'borrowed' money so ashamed of myself, I took off drunk in my car. I was stopped by a Clark County Deputy Sheriff who hauled me off to jail.

I made bail the next day and hired a good attorney to represent me, rather than using another 'public pretender.'

Over the next few months I found another job, paid the money I had stolen back in full, and wrote a letter of apology to the owner. I then got a 'plea deal' worked out between the prosecuting attorney in Cowlitz County and my attorney, in exchange for a guilty plea to a reduced misdemeanor charge, full restitution (which I had already made), and two years of probation, with no jail time.

However, when I went to court for sentencing, the judge blew up. He told the court that he was not going to let this criminal, with a long record, go without doing jail time! He threw out the plea bargain, and gave me one year in jail immediately. I was cuffed and hauled off once again into custody.

While in jail I was given a book to read called *From Prison to Praise* by Merlin Carothers. It really spoke to me about my need to forgive instead, start praising God! I also attended many Bible studies while at that jail. They really helped me with making the necessary changes to becoming a lawful citizen, rather than continuing to do illegal activities.

After serving nine months, I was released early for good behavior. I had worked in the kitchen as a trustee for six of those months. Reverend Don Kennedy picked me up and took me to find housing in Vancouver. Don became a good friend over the years, meeting with me in Bible studies and Full Gospel Business Men's meetings. This incident took place during 1993-1994.

While I was in jail, Donna began once again dating other men, and attended Christian single dances regularly. I also began dating others upon my release.

I was plagued with bone spurs growing from my spine, where I had broken my back while I was an inmate at Larch. They were pressing in on nerves and organs, causing unbearable pain when triggered by excessive exertion, cold weather, and stress.

This medical condition, along with my need for primary support for my PTSD, qualified me for an inpatient program at the VA after my release from jail, which required me to remain clean and sober. While working on the hospital campus, I trained through the Portland VA's rehabilitation program that helped me purchase mechanic's tools. That was when I received the 30 percent disability.

Next I worked at a popular hotel near the Portland Airport. Jim Dotson, their general manager, was a Christian man who hired me. I never betrayed his trust and became a dependable, full-time worker. Along with a Marine and a former cop named Max Rusk, I worked the graveyard shift and we forged lifelong friendships.

After a year, I quit that job to work for Jim Cottrell at Teen Challenge as a client supervisor, offering guidance to recovering drug addicts, grown men anywhere from eighteen to forty-eight who voluntarily entered the Christian treatment program. My slips became further and further apart.

Even though I had committed my life to the Lord and was trying to surrender my life to Him, I continued to have slips, sometimes after three years of sobriety. Strongholds in my life that couldn't be overcome by sheer will power became more evident. I told Donna about the curses that were placed on the Vietnam Vets by the Buddhist Monks. I needed deeper healing.

Ron Receiving his Master of Divinity Degree

I continued dealing with my issues, and started taking more responsibility for my actions. The Salvation Army's Rescue mission in downtown Portland hired me to help out. Continuing school, I earned my bachelor's degree from Beacon University's ex-

Celebrating Ron's Master Degree are daughter Ronda, granddaughter Abigail, Donna, and deans.

tension campus in Vancouver, WA, taught by Dr. Mark Pelletier, and pursued a master of divinity at Warner Pacific. After transferring to Triune Bible University, I obtained my master's degree.

The VA paid for my education, which was unheard of since religious credits were not normally covered. God opened doors that man could not.

I interned as a chaplain in 1999 in the very prison I served time! Chaplain Bill Cardin was my supervisor at Larch Corrections, and New Heights Church was my covering as I worked under Pastor Terry Barrett. I was also taking chaplaincy classes at Portland Community College. God swung open doors that seemed impenetrable. I completed my pastoral training while again working as hotel security and airport shuttle driver, building a good reputation for stability.

Donna is not one to be pushed around and she said that if we had any future together, I needed to seek further treatment. I received help again from a program at Kaiser. Through a conversation Donna had with a nurse there, Donna learned that the nurse's son who had struggled with mental health issues was greatly helped by building the serotonin and dopamine levels in his brain. Donna began investigating this natural avenue of healing.

My brain was very depleted from lifelong trauma. I started taking megadoses of fish oil as prescribed, as well as vitamin D and the B's, along with other supplements that nourished my starved brain and body. Staying on the supplements was the challenge.

Donna has recalled, "I had tested the waters by dating others over the years. Some had sought my hand in marriage, but my heart was with Ron. I had hope for him and for our relationship. I saw his deep faith and desire to serve God." We started dating again.

I pursued Donna for eight long years in our roller coaster relationship. I loved her deeply, but knew she was wise in her caution, because I needed more time to seek the help I required for my many years of trauma and poor decision making.

In June, 2000, I was living in an Oxford House in Portland, Oregon, attending AA meetings, and working grave yard at a popular hotel. Returning home from work one morning, I spoke to the Lord. *I'm tired of being alone. I need a wife and I want to marry Donna. I understand why she is cautious. Would you speak to her, Lord?"*

Shortly thereafter, Donna was walking on her usual trail with her two dogs, and she almost heard an audible voice. She felt a warmth flow from her head to her toes. *This is the time to marry Ron.*

She had never experienced anything like that in her life and uttered, "God, is this you? Is this really you?"

Two days later Donna called me, "Ron, the Lord spoke to me and said it's time for us to get married."

That's the first time that she has felt a total peace about marrying me, I thought. *What an answer to prayer!*

She explained that I had been stable for several years and that gave her hope for our relationship. We had been counseling for several months with a gifted Christian therapist. He too thought we were ready to marry.

My friend, Chaplain Roger Wolff performed the ceremony on a pleasant sunny afternoon and the Southwest Veteran Honor Guard provided military honors.

Forrest is praying over Ron and Donna at their wedding. Chaplain Roger Wolff is at left; the Honor Guard is in the background.

We were married August 24, 2000, in a large outdoor wedding held at her niece's beautiful estate in Battle Ground, WA. Our wedding announcement proclaimed the scripture:

"For I know the thoughts that I think toward you, says the Lord, thoughts of peace and not of evil, to give you a future and a hope." (Jeremiah 29:11 NKJV)

The severity of my PTSD was brought to full light when I again fought the powers that be at the VA to upgrade me from 30 percent to 100 percent disability. The psychiatrist who was brought in from Lake Oswego, OR to assist the VA, performed my evaluation.

"If you're not granted 100 percent disability status, I'll go to court with you on your behalf," the doctor promised. He said that in all his years of assessing cases, I had the lowest score that he had ever seen. The psychiatrist explained that the lower the score, the more severe case of PTSD. Donna accompanied me to the assessment.

Although it hasn't been completely smooth sailing, Donna said, "My love for him has never failed. I love that man so much."

All this time, God pounded on me, chiseling away through Donna, my brother, the pastors He'd put in my life, and many more wonderful people as mentioned in Chapter 16. I also served on the Southwest Washington Veterans Honor Guard for twelve years.

My new wife, our church, and the veteran organizations that supported me gave me a sense of value. I always felt worthless, ashamed, and guilty. But my involvement in these organizations restored a sense of pride in my service. I came back from Vietnam a nutcase; twelve years in prison, seeing all that death and slaughter, affected me greatly.

I patterned my life after these good people, trying to emulate them. The more I hung with them, the more I realized I couldn't go on doing some of the things I had been doing. I couldn't continue with a life of drunkenness, wildness, gambling and total irresponsibility. These men and my wife and what they stood for helped change me. I did not want to do anything whatsoever to bring any kind of discredit or shame on them.

Donna and Ron with their two dogs.

Ron and Donna have also presented Veteran's Day programs in schools such as the Washington State School for the Blind.

Veterans Honor Guard of Southwest Washington was honored in July 2001 and *The Columbian* newspaper featured an article about our work.

Ron, Jinx, and Skip in Honor Guard

1992 Vietnam Vets Color Guard L-R: Ron B., Jack Q., Greg W., Lloyd W., "Sarge"

Ron cares about veterans in White Salmon Cemetery, Memorial Day 2013

3rd Battalion, 3rd Marine Division, Hilton Hotel, Seattle, Reunion

Ron interviewed by Channel 6 News at Veteran's event

15
Together in Ministry

"Brethren, I do not regard myself as having laid hold of it yet; but one thing I do: forgetting what lies behind and reaching forward to what lies ahead, I press on toward the goal for the prize of the upward call of God in Christ Jesus." (Philippians 3:13-14 New American Standard Version)

In September 2000, Donna started working for the Children's Home Society in downtown Vancouver. But within three years, she became extremely ill. She had been blessed with remarkable health and very seldom used her sick leave in all the years she taught at Clark College. She was doubling over as the pain shifted from one part of her body to another. She began wheezing and coughing constantly, while feeling an exhaustion that never left. It became more and more difficult for her to concentrate in her position as an instructor of family life classes.

I had hired a friend to come in and replace the faucets in the tub of one of the bathrooms of our home. I was not aware that every time I showered, the hot water faucet dripped behind the walls, causing black mold to grow where it couldn't be seen. We grieved as we lost our gentle black Lab Lucy to the mold poisoning. The insurance company tested the home and found extremely high toxicity levels and moved us out within three days of receiving the test results. Donna contracted asthma, brain fog, fibromyalgia, and leaky gut syndrome, forcing her into disability. She had never heard of a case where disability was granted for fibromyalgia on the first try. She felt that she, like Lucy, was close to death. The focus of our life became recovery from our health issues. By this time, we had started attending City Harvest Church in 2005, which was located very close to our home. It was an incubator of healing for us. We were surrounded by an undergirding of prayer covering and support from parishioners like we had never experienced. The head pastor, Bob MacGregor, exuded compassion and generosity. He helped us step out of the pressures of a growing ministry called *Eutychus*.

In April 2003, *The Columbian* wrote an article about *Eutychus Ministries*[26] and the dedication of our housing center in Fruit Valley both for homeless veterans fighting alcoholism and drugs, and for criminals transitioning into life as productive civilians. Community leaders attended the opening ceremony. I became the first executive director of our new board of directors. Eutychus is the Greek name for a young man in the Book of Acts, who fell asleep and plummeted to his death from a third-story window during Paul's teaching. He's resurrected by Paul; thus our use of *Eutychus* for our transitional housing ministry, which means 'Good Fortune' in the Greek. *Eutychus* provided lodging for as many as twenty-two ex-offenders and vets.

---

[26] Appendix IV

The stressors were more than we could carry, as it triggered my PTSD, as well as it exacerbated the other health issues we had. The many responsibilities of running the Eutychus housing program as well as continuing to go into Larch Cor-

This duplex and a similar one housed Eutychus' guests

Eutychus Housing Unit Dedication L-R Keith Fitch, Tim Boone, Wayne Benson, Gail S., The Honorable Brian Baird, Ron, Donna, Mayor Royce Pollard, Lt. Col. Bill Cardin, Chaplain Roger Wolff

rections were a crushing burden. Donna was still working at Children's Home Society. Pastor Bob clearly saw our overload directed by fervor. We were listening and open to his guidance as our pastor. He counseled us to step out of *Eutychus*.

Eutychus was closed in 2005, and the two Eutychus duplexes, which Donna had inherited from her brother Richard in Fruit Valley, were sold, and then men who lived in the rental house in Orchards also vacated. (By the way, we were blessed to be able to buy a cabin cruiser in which we shared many good times together.)

Donna recalls that even their previous pastor from New Heights Church, Matt Hannah, whom we greatly respected, told me that my call was to go into the prisons and to drop the housing.

Ron and Donna's cabin cruiser

The cabin cruiser with Donna's brother, Richard Mcischowski, in back

My desire to help those incarcerated was birthed from my own awareness of the tremendous need for support upon release from prison. I have volunteered at Larch for years, driving up the unfinished roads full of chuck-holes in pitch black on Friday nights, and creeping through the dead of winter, snow everywhere, often times in fog so thick that I had to crawl along at five miles an hour in some spots trying to stay on the road, determined to meet with a group of inmates. The time I spent with them forged a deep connection with their struggles. It wasn't easy to release this draining labor of love to assist them with after-care support upon their release.

I traveled again down the slippery slope on the crossroads of gambling and drinking. There was so much that was better in my life than had been for many years, yet the screams of the demons that haunted me still surfaced. Donna received a life line of support from the Robinson house church (a small weekly study group which offers more individualized support and prayer for City Harvest Church members) that she had joined.

I entered into an in-depth PTSD program at White City, Oregon, near Medford where I stayed for five months. Before that, I had been in six other treatment programs.

I received disability from Social Security after my first application, and shortly following, I was awarded my 100 percent service-connected disability from the VA.

Upon my return from White City, I became involved in a deliverance ministry at City Harvest Church. With the encouragement of Rod Robinson (my house church pastor), I started meeting with two dedicated pastors on staff at City Harvest Church: Larry Knox, a Vietnam combat vet himself, and Dave Schaaf. These men devoted many hours over an eight-week period to meet with me, walking me through the trauma in my life from childhood to my current situation. They addressed the curses placed on the Vietnam vets by the Buddhist Monks. A deeper

Away with the motorcycle; freed for ministry

level of spiritual surgery was necessary for me. Donna saw the most dramatic change in me because of those focused hours addressing soul work spent with these concerned, knowledgeable pastors.

Another pastor who worked with me was Dave Minor, an ex-police officer, pastor, and author who counseled me for two solid years. I flourished more during this time than any other that Donna can remember. City Harvest Church reached out with a daunting commitment that broke many spiritual shackles that had gripped me tightly.

Another passion in my life was riding my motorcycle. It was a process to let go of my strong zeal for it. Donna fearlessly rode with me on the back of my Harley, and I have many enjoyable memories tied to it. After undergoing deliverance ministry, and on the advice of Pastor Minor, who rode a motorcycle himself for many years, I sold my last one, a big Harley Road King. That freed me up to focus on prison ministry and the veteran community.

Occasionally visits to maximum-security prisons brought back painful memories, but we have gone where ever God called us. In 2004, I was honored to receive the Volunteer of the Year award for my work at Larch. Donna and I attended my award ceremony in Olympia with Governor Gary Locke.

Donna became well enough to return to teaching for an organization called *Pathfinders,* as a family life educator, bringing her years of expertise in this field to the inmates in Columbia River Corrections. She was greatly fulfilled and grateful to God for leading her to a time of restoration in her health where she could combine the two passions in her life: bringing support to those incarcerated in the area of parenting classes. Donna believes God brought closure to the previous chapter in her life so she could focus on returning to the prisons on a more consistent basis with me.

"I really do believe that Ron is called to go into the prisons and jails,' Donna said. 'Together we bring balance. It's like Chaplain Bill Cardin, from Larch, has commented 'It's so good to have a couple come in because you role-model a Christ-centered marriage for the inmates.'"

Ron honored as Volunteer of the Year 2004

Donna was honored in 2015 as a volunteer of the year[27] at Larch Corrections.[28] She felt that several dear friends Cris Hamilton, Mily Boone, and Teresa Ropa deserved that honor, too. They poured the same fervor of commitment to the inmates at Larch over many years as convicts looked to them as positive role models that radiated God's compassion under my covering and that of City Harvest Church. Their undergirding of prayer and true friendship strengthened and enriched our mission.

L-R: Volunteers at Larch: Mily Boone, Milt Alvarez, Mel Novak, Donna and Ron Brandon, Robert Keller

---

[27] See APPENDIX V for nomination form.
[28] See APPENDIX VIII for tribute to both Donna and Ron by Larch inmate

Dr. Leroy Micals, president of Triune Biblical University headquartered in North Bend, Washington, ordained me as a minister in 1997. Donna and I started working in prison ministry at New Heights Baptist Church, and then later at City Harvest Church where we now attend. In a formal ceremony at City Harvest Church in 2012, Dr. Lawrence Day, the current director of Triune, reordained me. Since Pastors Matt Hannah and Bob MacGregor from their respective churches confirmed we were to drop *Eutychus Ministries,* we have gone into prisons most every week, usually Larch Corrections Center and South Fork Prison Camp in Tillamook, Oregon. We've also visited Stafford Creek Corrections Center and the Washington State Corrections Center at Shelton, Washington.

Ron with Donna who was honored as Volunteer of the Year 2015

We have facilitated Bible studies, sitting in a circle with a group of men, reading the Bible and discussing what we've learned. We've held church services at least once a month with usually about fifty to sixty or more men in attendance. Inmates have provided the worship music and they're quite talented. We pray for people, with details of miraculous healings in Chapter 19. Sometimes we have invited guest speakers such as former Pittsburg Pirate's baseball player turned Hollywood actor Mel Novak, to share their testimonies. Kate White's Band (pictured next page) often has entertained the men.

Donna and I have also been involved in a prison transition team headed by Scott Newman. Called *Men on the Outside*, we have been meeting regularly to develop aftercare programs and curtail recidivism

Mel Novak sharing at Larch

among prisoners by providing support during the first six months after a prisoner's release.

The group has been bringing together people from several churches—pastors, volunteers, ministers, staff from Larch Corrections Center including humble and compassionate Chaplain Jakstas, dedicated Nancy Simmons, and others. We represent *Unchained Prison Ministry* at City Harvest Church. Ed Parke of *Breaking Free Ministries* and *Lord's Gym* also participates. We pray for the men and women transitioning into society. The group brings in speakers and trainers who share information about resources available as well as mentors for those fresh out of prison. *Unchained Prison Ministry* also provides lists of felon-friendly churches and employers.

Kate White's Band and friends at Larch. Kate is a recording artist, violinist, worship leader, speaker and developer of other artists. She tours regionally with her band and nationally as a solo artist and speaker. She is the founder of Music That Matters, an organization dedicated to using the arts to bring hope to the hurting.

Our goal is to share the love of Christ with inmates. He can make all things new, no matter how much guilt each person carries. They're hungry for the Word. Accepting Christ brings peace and salvation. We give Him all the glory. God is the anchor. We need to hold on to Him and never let go.

I also became involved in the *Full Gospel Business Men's Fellowship* (FGBMFA) about 1993. The local chapter of *Full Gospel Business Men's Fellowship* in Vancouver, Washington, represented by Mr. Bill Robertson and Mr. John McGraw solidified their support for Donna's vision of providing a hand up for ex-offenders and veterans.

I went to FGBMFA for many years off and on since I had been a business owner from the 1980's. My first business had been simply "Brandon Wood-Heat" in Stevenson, Washington. My four employees and I sold tons of firewood, delivering two to three cords at a time anywhere between The Dalles, Oregon to Portland, Oregon, and White Salmon and Bingin, Washington to Vancouver, WA. We also sold any and all kinds of wood burning equipment and tools from ash removal tools to wood stoves.

After I stopped selling wood products, I opened up a small two-man auto repair shop in Oregon. Located right off a major highway, I kept very busy towing disabled vehicles and did quite well. I had also managed businesses for a lot of years, including serving as vice president and co-owner of a non-profit corporation called *Eutychus* Ministries, a 501(c)(3) business, offering support to ex-offenders and veterans so I joined FGBMFA in the 90's.

At first, I didn't attend many meetings, nor did I make it to very many men's conferences or camp outs. But by 2005, I started attending frequently and got to know Stewart Kent, President of the Local Clark County chapter. He encouraged me to be more involved and I came to really like him, as a brother and mentor. Stewart was a passionate, dedicated and hard-working man. I respected him greatly. I thought he did a great job and it was an honor for me to serve as chaplain.

When Stewart moved away one year, we elected a new president, Arnold Rekate, an accountant. Arnold and I have become good friends. I have served two years as chaplain and after two more years as vice president, I was just re-elected to serve as V.P for 2016. Working with Arnold has been a real joy for me and it's an honor to serve in such a great ministry, reaching out to businessmen and business owners in our local area as well as other speakers.

I've also served on the committee to put on the annual 'Prayer Breakfast' held at the local Hilton Hotel downtown. This used to be the 'Mayor's Prayer Breakfast' but no longer. It seems that was not 'politically correct' so we are now a 'community gathering.' We look forward to this fellowship of Christians, who sponsor nationally recognized speakers and care about and pray for our city, county, state and federal leaders. We want them to be safe and to be blessed as they serve the people who elected them to lead us.

Mr. Robert Bignall, National President of FGBMFA, has been an inspiration to me for many years. He does an excellent job and I thank God for dedicated, faithful men like him, who lead this ministry on to greater heights!

Our Family: In Gratitude for Their Love and Support Throughout our Journey

Ron Jr., Donna, Ron, Daniel, and Ronda

Children, their spouses, and grandchildren on Donna's side

Children, their spouses, and grandchildren on Ron's side

Ron and daughter Ronda

L – R:Sister Kelly, Brother Ferral, Aunt Willadean, Ron, Aunt Billie Jean, Brother Forrest

Forrest's wife Pep, Forrest, Ron, Aunt Tina

Cousin Ginger Madison, Ron, Aunt Bertina (Tina) in 2014. Aunt Bertina, a devout Christian woman, had prayed for me all through the years. She just passed away at 88 years of age!

16
Serving Others; Give to Grow

Ron in Veteran's Honor Guard

After *Eutychus Housing* closed, I continued serving on Clark County's Veteran's Resource Board, and in early 2011, we talked about forming a new nonprofit—the Clark County Veteran's Assistance Center—to open and operate a drop-in center for veterans at 1305 Columbia Street in downtown Vancouver. The center opened in April and still operates today, helping veterans find housing, obtain federal benefits, apply for jobs, and seek health care and counseling. Several trained veteran volunteers are there at any given time, Monday through Friday, assisting veterans with their needs.

While involved in the Veteran's Honor Guard of Southwest Washington, I felt privileged to participate in more than 500 funerals over a twelve-year period. One of the faithful partners who served with me over the years was Gary Porter. He and his wife Gloria opened their home for our first house church adventure.

My commitment to the veteran community is my way of saying thank you for their service to a country I staunchly support. I also served both as chaplain for the local Marine Corps League detachment and also as vice president of the Vietnam Veterans of Clark County. The welfare of the veteran community flows deeply in my veins.

Men That Mentored Ron

God never intended us to walk alone in this world. He made us a community of believers and invited us all to join the 'family' of God. Men need other men in their lives. Believers need other 'living stones' to rub against, to polish them, to smooth out their rough features. Another scripture refers to 'iron sharpening iron'. In the process of this rubbing and banging together, Christians begin to shine, to be rounded out, to mature and to grow into the image of Christ.

Men like Chaplain Lloyd Ward, a Navy veteran of Vietnam, persuaded me to get involved with Vietnam Veterans of America in 1993, something I had never done in the twenty years since I had left the military. Lloyd was a brother to me, forgiving, and a mentor of what it meant to be a man of God. Lloyd even opened his home for me to stay with him for a time.

Jerry Keen, chairman of Clark County Veterans Assistance Center with Ron listening. Picture taken from The Columbian newspaper

Chaplain Jerry Keen, former command master chief with nearly thirty years in the Navy, and Director of the Vancouver, WA chapter of Point Man Ministries, also became a mentor for me. I have really looked up to him. Jerry had been in prayer for me on many occasions and visited me in various hospitals where I was recovering from one ailment or the other. *Pointman Ministries* is a Christian organization that supports combat vets. He is also very active in the 40 et 8 service organization which is the honor society of the American Legion.

Having completed three tours in Vietnam, former Staff Sergeant Richard Jenkins, Green Beret, US Army, was my commander while I served in the Veteran's Honor Guard for nearly twelve years. Richard prayed for me on many occasions and we worked together forming *Breaking Free Ministries*. He was a great inspiration for me. During one of the many funerals that we performed, we stood side by side in below freezing temperatures, icicles running down our chins as we provided a rifle squad for a fallen hero.

Ron, Donna, and Marine John Russell, good friend and fellow biker

John Russell, a former Marine and Vietnam veteran, befriended me; we have gone on many bike rides together and served together in the Patriot Guard Riders organization. I also worked with John forming the Clark County Veterans Assistance Center(CCVAC). He has been a mentor and big brother to me for many years. After two years of involvement with the CCVAC, including a short time as Chairman, and two plus years volunteering as Chaplain, the center now administers a $425,000 contract with Clark County. During this time, I worked with Jerry Keen, Morris Geisler, John Russell (the real workhorse and engineer of our startup), Jerry Kccsee, and others, and later worked with Joe Fettig, Bob Nichols, Judy Russell, Frank Hyatt, and Otis Warren among other valuable people.

A lot of great folks volunteered their time and money helping put together the Veteran's center. It was truly a team-effort!

Many times I served in the capacity of counselor; at other times I hauled donated supplies, clothes, food, and performed wherever needed. I also helped to raise funds in many different venues. I continued performing Chaplain duties for those two years. The Center also handles and manages the yearly "Stand Down" which has been a big success. Serving on the CCVRC (or Clark County Veterans Resource Committee) was an honor for me, as a representative of the Marine Corps League, of which I have been a member for the past 12 years. We were able to work with the County Commissioners to take care of our veterans. What an accomplishment!

Well over 500 men and women have been helped per month by coming to the center and receiving benefits such as help with housing, car repairs, work tools, food, clothing, and legal assistance. Mike Langsdorf has served with the Vet Center and done an outstanding job volunteering legal advice, and for a time serving as Chairman. It has been an extreme honor for me to have been involved in helping to start and maintain this wonderful Clark County Center to assist our deserving veterans! Mr. Bob Nichols (former Lt. Col. U.S. Army) and Mr. Odis Warren (U.S. Army) as well as Joe Fettig (U.S. Air Force vet.) and Judy Russell, have gone far and above the call of duty to give sacrificially of their time, effort, energy and money to make the Center what it is today.! Semper Fi! OoooRaaaah!

Several other men have had a big influence on my life. Starting with Chaplain Roger Wolff, an Air Force veteran, he served as the chaplain at the VA Hospital where I was in transitional housing. Pastors Larry Knox, Dave Minor, Dave Schaaf, Bob MacGregor, and Randy Zeigler, who was a combat vet himself, all spent many hours working with me in making the transition from hard-core bad guy to 'saint of God'. If it were not for these men and so many others, including their prayers, in my life, I would most likely not be here today.

I was also greatly impacted by David Gilford, a former house church pastor and one of the most encouraging and non-judgmental men I've ever met. Scott Newman, Larry Meyers, and Pastor Randy Warnecke have all contributed mightily to my growth and maturity in Christ.

The Marines of the local Clark County detachment of the Marine Corps League have also made an indelible impression upon me since I joined that distinguished organization twelve years ago. Marine Phil Rumschottel spent nearly four years trying to talk me into joining them; I was reluctant due to my criminal past.

Former Gunnery Sergeant John Stofiel, Former Colonel Mike Wilson, commander of the Young Marines Program, and Marines George Pobi, Keith Fitch, former Gunnery Sergeant John Hudson, Marine Rex Hopper, Commandant Bill Hauser and many others set such a high standard for me, a high bar of conduct and community involvement. I was awe-struck by such an honorable, humble, yet proud group of men, who put honor and faithfulness higher than life itself. They worked a powerful change in me over the years. I went from not feeling worthy of being accepted into such an esteemed body of warriors to total acceptance into their brotherhood. They voted me to serve as both chaplain and briefly as judge advocate until my illness and resignation. I was nominated and accepted into the distinguished order of the Marine Honor Unit, 'Devil Dogs!' Semper Fidelis Marines! Thank you for a second chance.

There are several other men who must be mentioned here. Mel Novak, former pro-baseball player turned Hollywood actor followed by his role as a prison ministry chaplain, came into my life at a Full Gospel Business Men's Fellowship meeting many years ago. We became friends and brothers in Christ, ministering together at Larch prison. He has made a lasting impact on my life as a helper and mentor. I have tried to duplicate his ministry in which thousands of convicts have come to Christ because of Mel's devotion in jails, prisons, and skid row.

Another brother in Christ, Captain Milt Alvarez, has modeled effective ministry when we were together many times at various prisons in several states. Milt has prayed for me many times and set a great example for me of the love of Christ. He is my 'Barnabus'. Milt travels the world so often that we can hardly keep up with him.

Reverend Jim Cottrell has run *Freedom House* in Vancouver, Washington. When I first worked for him, he ran Teen Challenge in Portland Oregon. He has been a loving, forgiving man of God and so dedicated to helping the drug addicts, alcoholics, and street people.

There is one more man who probably influenced my life more than anyone else besides my brother Forrest. He devoted more than fifty years to active ministry. He once climbed out of his basement where he was down praying for me, stuck his bony finger in my face, and said, "Ron, one day, I'm going to see you in heaven." Saying it like he meant it, he was my former father-in-law, Bonnie's dad, Reverend Jim Walton. What a great man of God he was. Thank you, Dad.

Ron's mentor and close friend, Chaplain Roger Wolff

Men That I Mentored

Without mentioning their names to protect their privacy, I will use the first initial of some men I have helped or in some way influenced toward serving the Lord more fully.

- L, the electrician, for whom I officiated at his wedding ceremony. He went into missions and ministers at Larch Corrections with *Prison Fellowship*.
- D, the bus driver, who was Eutychus's trusted house manager at one time. He has become a dear friend and his skills as a landscaper and handyman have assisted us greatly. D is a man of great integrity.
- S, a business manager who supervises others, for whom I performed his wedding ceremony. He and his wife head up *Families on the Outside*, which provides support to the families of those incarcerated. They both also teach a class at Larch Corrections called *Preparing for Release*. They have three children and a happy home of their own.
- D, the talented musician who was the chaplain's clerk at Larch for four years and never missed a Sunday meeting that Donna and I led. After prison, he formed a worship band called *The Forgiven Four* with other inmates. He now holds down a permanent job at Medical Lake in the VA Hospital and leads worship in his church every week.
- C is a devoted father with a stable job. One of the highlights for his four children is attending church weekly with their dad.
- P recently retired from a successful business that he started. He paid off his home and operates a nonprofit organization. He's well-known and respected in the community.
- K is now on disability but is a valued member of a local church and happily married. He works with a Christian motorcycle group giving back to the community.

There are many others and Donna and I are thankful for each of them. The common denominator in all their lives is Christ. They have all accepted Christ and have followed hard after Him. They're all involved in their local churches and giving back to the community.

Many other men we've assisted are working their way toward ownership of homes and businesses, serving as productive members of society.

When I see some of the guys we've helped, men who have left their criminal pasts behind to become business owners and upstanding citizens, I know we're making a difference, one life at a time. They are success stories and we played a small part in their transition to a better life. We shared God's love and light with them and they've carried it forth to others. Many, like Ed Parke, work in ministry today, giving back to others the assistance they had received upon leaving prison.

After serving twenty years in Florida's prison system, another man has become a church leader and operates a successful business. He makes a point of hiring people with criminal records, giving them a second chance to improve their lives. Having just purchased a new home, he is a living example of hope for the future.

"Ron has the most tender heart,' Donna said. 'The way he prays—he cares about people. These guys come back and say, 'You saved my life, Ron.' I don't know how many men he has helped come out of the dredges and given them the hope of a better life."

The letter below was written upon former inmate Larry's release, and it confirms the support given him:

> *Dear Ron and Donna,*
> *I would like to take this time and thank you so much for all you have done for me. You both were such a blessing to me when I was at Larch Corrections and continue to be a huge blessing to me to this very day. You have poured out so much love, care, and support and I would really just like to give a heartfelt thank you. All the books, cards, and going way out of your way to get me to church is greatly appreciated.*
> *Making the transition from prison to the free world is not an easy one. It's one filled with emotional highs and lows and lots of uncertainties. I am certain that I have a lot of care and support in my corner. So many times you both have showed me this love and care. Every time I bow my head in prayer you are there. May the God we serve pour out the floodgates of blessings upon you. I thank the Lord for bringing you into my life.*
> *Sincerely, with love,*
> *Larry*

17
Prophetic Words Bringing Confirmation of God's Call

"As the heavens are higher than the earth, so are My ways higher than your ways, and My thoughts than your thoughts." (Isaiah 5:59 NASV)

Several times in my life, I've had people with a gift of prophesy pray over me. While working at the Springs of Living Water, we had visiting missionaries and prophets. In retrospect, I firmly believe in the gift of prophesy because each prophesy has turned out to be true for both myself and Donna. God spoke to His prophets in the Old and New Testaments. He has revealed things then and now.

Earnest B. Gentile, considered to be one of the most mature and experienced men in all of the prophetic ministries, defines the gift of prophecy in his book *Your Sons and Daughters Shall Prophecy*. He explained the gift of prophecy as "occurring when a prophetically inspired person extends his or her faith like a spiritual antenna, receiving some divine thoughts of God for that given moment and then speaks them forth by the power of the Holy Spirit to an individual or group for the glory of God."

In other words, a prophecy gives the hearer hope, encouragement, and possibly direction for his life. This is what happened to Donna and me.

In 1978, while I was living at Springs of Living Water in California, Reverend Dick Mills, a famous prophet of God, came to speak along with other preachers. I was sitting in the audience of about 500 and they didn't know me from Adam. They stopped in the middle of the service and pointed into the audience.

"You!" one of them said.

Everybody looked around, trying to figure out if they were the ones being singled out.

Finally, I stood. "Me?"

"Yes, it's you." The preacher started prophesizing, the gist of it being that God has a call on my life and someday I'll be ministering and preaching to thousands of people in both large and small groups. I would be like a bull dozer, a great threshing machine, plowing up human hearts, planting the word of God. My words would hit like an earthquake.

It would be years before that prophesy was fulfilled.

The next year, Iverna Thompson, a lady prophetess, visited Richardson Springs and confirmed the previous message given by Dick Mills. Neither of these people had ever seen me before.

A Christian brother by the name of Harold Bredesen arrived at the Springs where we climbed the surrounding hills together. I asked for, and received, prayers from him.

Some twenty years later, the same Rev. Dick Mills traveled to Vancouver, WA where he picked Donna and me from the back row of church, called us to the front, and prophesied: "God is going to restore all the money that has been stolen from you by the enemy, man of God. You will preach the Word of God to thousands of people." He also added words almost identical to the ones in the third paragraph preceding this. Rev. Mills remembered nothing of his previous encounter with me in California. Could this again be God speaking to me?

After Donna and I became members of City Harvest Church in Vancouver, WA, we were encouraged to be a part of the prophetic assembly which took place every year. Our house church pastors sponsored us and the message that my wife received by one prophet in particular was hair-raising. Because I knew it to be true, I became a total believer in God's prophetic word through men and women who were gifted in prophesy.

As I've already explained, Donna became extremely ill when the black mold infiltrated our home. Besides debilitating asthma, severe fibromyalgia, and leaky gut syndrome, blinding cataracts formed over her eyes from the heavy steroids that were prescribed to her.

At the prophetic assembly of 2007, God gave Donna hope! She was told that God had a plan for her life and wanted her to know it in the midst of her great despair. In her weakness she would be made strong and God would bring order out of chaos.

The prophet, Pastor Brian Daehn, declared to Donna, "You will live a long and productive life. You should live with the expectation to see many years and good days. Your smile will break oppression and you and your husband will get families back together again."

Pastor Brian also spoke out that we would have many kids in the spiritual realm and that we would pray prayers that would break open doors!

I marched in my last of many parades in the Veteran's Day celebration in November 2013 in Vancouver, WA. I was joined by Keith Fitch, Wendy Baker, Fiorin Zeviar, and Don Cheney, all loyal members of the Marine Corps league. As I tried to keep in step, my eyes blurred and my hands became tingly. I somehow managed to complete the arduous route. My wife was watching the parade, along with our special little friend and daughter of our renters, four-year-old Giovanna. When I explained my symptoms, Donna insisted we go immediately to the hospital, as she believed I may have suffered a possible stroke. I spent three days there and many tests were run. I was diagnosed with a mini-stroke.

Ron holding the American flag in Veteran's Day Parade 2014 where he had a mini-stroke

During my hospitalization, Donna received an encouraging e-mail message from one of the pillars of City Harvest Church named Harry Oldenburger. Harry was in his eighties and has been greatly respected for his wisdom and dedication to supporting others in their faith walk. The subject column read: *He is able*. The body of the e-mail said: *Just got word about you, Your assignment: Listen to the Lord; Listen to your wife; Meditate on His promises; Keep praising; II Cor. 12:9; Harry Oldenburger*

Donna looked at this e-mail as a powerful prophetic word giving me great encouragement and direction. She especially liked the part about *listen to your wife*. But I really took to heart what I felt the Lord was saying in a still small voice,

> *"My grace is sufficient for you, for my power is made perfect in weakness.* (II Corinthians 12:9 NIV)

More encouragement came from Shawn Ferguson on February 22, 2015 who was president of a Full Gospel Business Men's Fellowship in Battle Ground, WA. First he spoke to Donna, "The enemy has caused you great affliction, but it has backfired, and it has made you stronger. You are a warrior for God's kingdom." Donna had recently been extremely ill with two bouts of MRSA, a drug resistant staph infection, which had kept her bedridden for close to three months. Shawn knew nothing of this.

To me, he confirmed, "You have debris inside you that has no value and is being removed…. Your words will become like an earthquake."

About a month and a half later, in March, 2015, Donna and I experienced another prophetic confirmation at our City Harvest Church, when Pastor Charlie Sweet from New York, 2800 miles away, called us forward from the audience, having never seen us before this occasion. At a special service the night before, he had called for a man named Ron who was involved in prison ministry. I wasn't there because Donna and I were attending a wedding, but Kevin Gipp, a faithful and greatly anointed prison ministry volunteer, was present and told me about this as soon as church was over. I made sure we were there the next morning.

The first words Pastor Charlie spoke to us[29] were a quote from Psalm 34 Verse 17:

> *"The righteous cry and the Lord hears and delivers them out of their troubles. The Lord is near to the brokenhearted and saves those who are crushed in the spirit."*

In the Spirit, Pastor Charlie said he saw me with a big key ring, which the Lord told him opened jail cells.

"I believe that God uses the two of you in a mighty way where people are crushed and broken and where society has given up on them," he said, noting that the Lord said, "I'll take the ministry into the world, surrounding both Donna and Ron with men in uniforms.'

'I saw the brokenhearted and the crushed and I believe that God is using the two of you to bring a light where no one else will bring a light, where no one else

---

[29] See APPENDIX VI for the complete text from Pastors Charlie, Erik, and Bob.

wants to go,' he prophesied, 'where society has said, 'It's over with. It's finished. There's no second chance for them.'"

Pastor Charlie said he felt the Spirit of God anointing me, giving us greater favor in what we're doing. "I believe what the two of you do gets tiring at times and God is saying, 'I'm going to increase your army. I'm going to give you more recruits,' says the Lord your God. 'And know this,' says the Lord your God, 'favor is coming. Favor is coming.'"

He said more doors would open for us, which we'll enter humbly but with the spirit of God's truth, and, "I see you getting in people's faces."

"I believe that God is going to win them over,' Pastor Charlie said. 'And God says, 'Get ready, Ron, I'm about to bust the jail cell doors open,' says the Lord your God, 'and a wave of my spirit is about to blow in. It's never going to be the same again. It's a new day and it's a new hour.'"

He noted, "You know the ending of this book."

Pastor Erik Butler, the other prophet from New Jersey, added his prophetic vision, seeing me surrounded by military men in uniform, chanting, "Get it right. Get it right." They lined up and marched in order as I helped resurrect their love of the Lord.

"Father we bless this word over them,' Pastor Bob MacGregor concluded. 'We just thank you for Ron and Donna. We thank you Lord God for their heart for people, for the broken, for those in prison. You said, 'When I was in prison, you came to me.' Thank you that they reflect the heart of Jesus."

A few months later Shawn Ferguson prophesied to us again saying, "God will use you through signs and wonders. You will be ushering healings into the prisons." Donna recalls feeling inadequate and almost fearful when she heard this. But miraculous results did indeed occur as described in Chapter 19.

Donna and Ron, Christmas, 2015

18
Worms and Redemption

No longer a worm but a fisher of men.

I have heeded God's call to share with a wider audience by writing this book. But to tell the truth, it's been tough to revisit the past. Reexamining the years spent in Vietnam, my lowlife criminality upon my return, and the sins I committed overseas and here at home triggered my PTSD again. Guilt and shame given to God resurfaced as I recounted the stories, the pain I caused, and the bloody brutality of war in Vietnam.

"I so believe that this is God's will,' Donna explains. 'I believe that Ron has been compelled to write this for many years and he can't procrastinate any longer. I support him 100 percent in what God is calling him to do. This is part of his healing, as painful as it is for him."

Unfortunately, we've had guys who returned to their former lives. Ed Parke in his book, *Jailhouse Religion: One Man's True Story*, does a good job discussing recidivism and how a lot of guys come to Christ in prison. It's real, but they're like Lazarus coming out of the tomb, still wrapped like a mummy in their old habits and thinking patterns. They're like children, baby Christians who need guidance and help, just as Lazarus needed assistance from other believers in removing his grave clothes when Jesus called him from the tomb.

We need more people helping these guys. Just like other babies, their diapers can get stinky. They need to be fed milk and babysat. They need help and hand holding in a spiritual sense. That's why we work so hard on aftercare programs in the prison transition ministry, *Men on the Outside*, working with churches where these men are welcome, where believers will come alongside them and help them as they transition to a new life as Christians in a society unrestrained by steel bars.

They need to feel wanted, loved, and accepted. We have at least seven local churches helping with their transitions to life on the outside of prison.

Even when they backslide, these guys need anchors and role models who see potential in their lives that they can't see in themselves. They need people who will walk with them, hand in hand, through the pain of the past into a brighter future.

Although I have stumbled since leaving prison in 1992, I will never return to the man I was. The Lord is too important; He means everything to me.

I remember the occasion where God started erasing my shame. While home alone one day in 1987, I picked up the Bible and focused on the story of God calling Jacob a 'worm.' Jacob was such a deceiver, a con artist, and seemed to not have much of a backbone at all. Those words seemed to jump off the pages as I read them. At one point the words in Isaiah 41:14 jumped off the page at me—*"You worm!"* I felt like I heard God speak those words directly to me, calling me a worm. It was so profound that I convulsed with laughter. The concept struck me as extremely hilarious. God had pegged me all right. My life was all screwed up and I had been living as though I had no spine, no strength, no ability, and no hope.

Then suddenly it hit me: "Wait a minute. This isn't good. Was God calling me a worm? Was I a spineless, slimy, mud-sucking worm?"

I broke down and wept bitterly for hours, knowing I failed the only One who mattered. What I didn't do was read the rest of that verse:

> *"'Do not be afraid, you worm Jacob, little Israel, do not fear, for I myself will help you,' declares the Lord, your Redeemer, the Holy One of Israel."* (Isaiah 41:14 New International Version)

God was trying to tell me that He would assist me! He was trying to tell me that He would comfort me, defend me, that He knew I was weak and afraid and did not know what to do with my current situation, or with my life, for that matter. I wiped my face and then rose and left, headed for the nearest bar for a drink. Again I sabotaged myself with my inability to understand God's nature and message. Self-destruct was my middle name.

Years later, I was recounting this story at a house church meeting in the home of a devoted Messianic believer named George Golden. George is a learned Jewish man who knew the Torah, which is the first five books in the Old Testament. He approached me after I had shared this story during a presentation.

"Ron, I've got good news for you,' he said. 'That's not a bad thing, to be called a worm by God. God called Jacob a worm, but then He turned his name into Israel. Israel means *Prince of God* or *One Triumphant with God.*"

George further explained that he had once raised millions of worms for a living, operating a huge worm farm.

"Worms are extremely vital,' he explained. 'They take manure and waste products, and they turn it into something that causes trees, plants, vegetables, and everything else to grow at an amazing rate. As a matter of fact, this substance they create is so potent that it has to be measured very carefully. If the plant or tree received too much, it would explode in growth and die prematurely."

George compared my prison ministry to that of a 'worm farmer' or one who goes into the garbage cans of society, where the inmates both men and women were thrown and locked away as if they were refuse. Instead of taking manure, I was taking the Word of God to these so called 'worms' and seeing them transform into powerful, awesome men of God. They were being trained and equipped for service to the Master. Many of these men who have left prisons have become a dynamo for Christ today!

The apostle Paul is probably one of my favorite characters in the Bible, next to Joseph. Paul persecuted and imprisoned Christian men, women, and children, yet God loved and saved him. Granted, God had to knock him off his horse and blind him, but in a very real sense that's kind of what God did to me, only He had

Jack (Murf the Surf) Murphy (far left), a reformed prolific jewel thief and prisoner for 20 years, was a guest speaker at Larch Corrections in 2013. L-R Chaplain and Mrs. Alvarez, Donna, Ron

to knock me off the horse about five times because I had an extra thick skull. But He got my attention finally. The Lord is good. He's merciful and He doesn't give up on us.

Today, my weapons of choice are the Sword of the Spirit, the Word of God. I believe our nation needs to turn back to the Bible and repent. He wants us to turn from our wicked ways.

God has blessed me with the privilege to go into these prisons and to reach these guys. I've won quite a few different awards from the state, county, and the mayor for the work I've been doing as a volunteer in the community. I've tried to earn an honest reputation and have a good name. I've served in a lot of different positions. All that stuff doesn't mean anything to me though compared to winning the hearts of prisoners and veterans to Jesus.

Donna and I were invited by Chaplain Milt Alvarez, River Church pastor, to go with him to a Bill Glass *Beyond the Walls* Prison Ministry outreach in central California in 2014. This ministry goes into all the prisons in America on a regular basis.

After driving to Fresno, California, where we stayed a week, we went with the Bill Glass team into three penal institutions. Their team actually visited seven other prisons as well in that area.

Thousands of men came to Christ during the events. Included in the hundreds of volunteers that joined us in the prisons were Hollywood actors, professional sports stars, and even motorcycle riders with their Harleys.

We saw our friend Chaplain Jack Murphy (Murf the Surf) once again. He is a master violinist, author, and genius, who was known as *Murf the Surf Murphy,* the most prolific jewel thief of all time who turned prison chaplain, after serving twenty some years himself in a Florida state prison.

We also met Mr. Bill Glass himself, who is a former football Hall of Fame member as an all-pro defensive end) and twelve-year veteran of the Detroit Lions and Cleveland Browns. It was his ministry that worked so effectively within the prison walls.

We found that Mr. James (Hollywood) Henderson also had a heart of ministering to the prisoners. He is the World Champion heavy weight bench press athlete who holds the Guinness World Record of a 714-pound bench press. (Unofficially he managed a 740-pound lift on one occasion) I felt very small next to Henderson, who stood about six foot six inches, 300 plus pounds, and is as wide as two men. We watched as he tore some telephone books in half and many other stunts. We were blessed to minister with Mr. Henderson on two different days in three prisons. He is a gentle giant, full of the love of Christ! We hope to be able to work with the Bill Glass ministry team again in the near future!

I also find it amazing that God has also arranged for me to meet Sterling Hayden, Rod Taylor (an Australian Actor), famous fighters Floyd Patterson and Mohammed Ali, football players Joe Montana and John Brody (with whom I played golf), and Jesse Owens, the fastest man on earth during the 1936 Olympics in Germany. Forrest and I met him at a football game.

God really did take a hold of me. He changed me from being a low-life criminal to something better.[30] I have a good reputation now because I put off that life of madness and put on a new life with Christ.

He provided me great opportunities for education and I'm really, really grateful. You're not truly educated unless you know the Bible.

After reading a devotional on Habakkuk 2:2, I felt compelled to write this book. Another scripture in Isaiah advises that we write down our story and share what God has done for us.

---

[30] See Appendix IX for my thoughts on the ***Three Strikes You're Out*** law.

Jesus is my hero. He's the one that saved me because I was one lost, miserable wretch. I was blind, deaf, and dumb all rolled into one. I'm very thankful today that my name is no longer *worm*; instead, the Bible calls me a *saint, soldier of Christ, mighty man of God,* and *minister of reconciliation.* The Lord is certainly doing a work in my life.

19
Miraculous Healings

The first time that God used me and my prayers to heal someone was in a hospital in Santa Rosa, California. Entering a darkened room, I observed a young woman lying on the hospital bed alone. She had a white sheet draped over her. She appeared to be grey in color, cold to the touch. The doctors had stated that she was in a coma, terminal with a nasty cancer and would die by the end of the week. Her relatives had been summoned from Germany and Brazil. It was a long way to travel but the doctors were sure of her passing away very soon.

I leaned over her, anointed her with oil and prayed, "Death, I command you to leave now. I speak life into this body, this young lady. May the Lord rebuke you, spirit of death. Get out of here and get out now. Do not come back. You will live and not die. You will now begin to recover and you will rise up out of this bed of infirmity, affliction, and disease. I speak total healing to every part of this body, from head to toe. I curse this cancer and command it to die even now. I speak total recovery to her now, in the Name above all names, in the name of Jesus Christ of Nazareth. Amen!

I left for home. That young woman fully recovered and went home two days later totally healed.

The next time God used me to pray for a miracle was when my nephew Dimmie John had been in a horrible wreck. Asleep in the passenger seat of a truck driven by his friend, they crashed head-on into another truck on a highway in Bremerton, Washington. Dimmie had been thrown through the front windshield, landing on the hard pavement of the roadway. Life flighted to Seattle, he was lying near death and was not expected to make it. The doctors had sent for his mother in Colorado, since his life was in the balance. His body had gone through horrendous trauma; many of his bones were broken. Also, his heart had suffered a torn aorta, and he had emergency open heart surgery to repair the damage. He was not expected to live, but the doctors had done the best they could to save his life.

Dimmie was in bad shape. I first saw him in his hospital bed, with a hose stuck down his throat so he could breathe since he wasn't able to on his own. I cried when I saw him. *What a shame. So young, so handsome, so strong looking and in the prime of life. Now very possibly he was about to die. So broken and scarred. So helpless and alone.*

I began to pray. Suddenly I spoke loudly, angry that this had happened. I took out my anointing oil, placed it on his forehead, and prayed, "Dimmie, you will live and not die. I rebuke death right now in the name of Jesus, I speak life into this body. You will live; you will fully recover. Father God, I ask you to have mercy on Dimmie. I ask you to allow him to fully recover. I ask you to have mercy on this young man's life. Be healed in the name of Jesus! I speak total healing to this heart. I speak healing to this torn and busted body, in the name of Jesus, Amen!"

I left the hospital and went back home. Two or three days later, Dimmie fully recovered and got up and went home.

On another occasion, Donna and I went into Larch Corrections one Sunday evening expecting God to move in a might way. After our service, we invited men to come up to the front for prayer for healing. Robert Lightfoot came forward. He was sixty years old.

"I've had Hepatitis C for some forty years, not from using drugs, but from a blood transfusion when I was a teen. The doctor recently told me that I have only a short time to live."

From top left to bottom right: Dimmie, his daughter, his wife Heidi, my brother in-law Dave, my sister Kelly, and their daughter Shanna

He was obviously very ill and weak. We prayed for him, anointing him with oil. We also prayed for several other men for various healings including Hepatitis C.

The following month, on August 28th, 2015, Chaplain Jakstas from Larch Corrections approached Donna and me at a meeting of *Men on the Outside*.

"Hi Ron and Donna. You will be most interested in what Robert Lightfoot said to me the other day. He told me he came forward for prayer for healing of his Hepatitis C at one of your *Unchained Prison Ministry* services over at Larch. He told me he was in the later stages of the disease and felt he had a very short time to live. Tests were run twice after he was anointed with oil and prayed for and there were no signs of Hepatitis C! In fact, he declared that results indicated he had the enzyme levels of a thirty-year-old even though he is sixty years of age."[31]

A month later the Sunday evening *Unchained Prison Ministry* service at Larch was electrifying. Robert shared, "I asked for prayer a few months ago because two other men that Ron and Donna had prayed for here were also healed of Hepatitis C!"

---

[31] See APPENDIX VII for Robert Lightfoot Smith's handwritten testimony.

God healed Robert Lightfoot Smith from Hepatitis. C

Robert definitely looked and acted stronger than before. We praise God for His healing touch. We healed no one. Jesus healed these men, using us and our prayer of faith. Praise the Lord God Almighty!

I was approached by another inmate that said, "When you prayed for me, I was healed of a serious kidney condition!"

The prophecy which indicated we would be used by God to heal other people was coming true! We attribute this new depth in our ministry taking place at Larch and South Fork to the fervent effectual prayers that are being sent heavenward by our house church, now called a community group, led by a devoted couple, Gene and Peggy Beardsley, and others who have committed to cover the ministry. The faithful people in our group are like family to us, covering the prison ministry and the prayers of the inmates on a regular basis. We share life together.

I myself have been healed of some of my ailments. When I was in terrible pain from three peptic ulcers, I called my brother Forrest. I couldn't touch anything that had milk or cheese in it or it would put me on the floor in agony. Forrest prayed for me over the phone. Suddenly I felt a warmth, and I felt just fine. I was healed totally at that time, and later the doctor informed me that all three ulcers could not be found.

Frequently we have experienced healing ourselves, and have seen the power of God come down upon many men in prison who have been healed from all kinds of afflictions, pains, and diseases. We can only praise God for His kindness and great love!

Former chaplain Roger Wolff, Pastor Bill Courtney from the Rock Church, and many other saints of God have also been praying for *Unchained Ministries*, as well as the prayer team from *Families on the Outside,* headed up by Sid and Sheri Carter, two dynamic people who have dedicated their lives to supporting felons, ex-felons, and their families. Pastors Jan Stahl and Dave Schaaf met with us and Chris Hamilton in the early hours once a month for several years to cover this ministry. The Staff of City Harvest Church and the Board of Elders have sent up prayers faithfully as well. May God richly bless each one of them! A praying church and a

Our City Harvest Church Community Group has often prayed for us and the inmates.

healing church are the two primary characteristics of this body of believers and we are so grateful to have been drawn there by the Lord!

Often during our marriage, Donna has heard me scream in terror and gasp for breath many panic-filled nights. My nightmares were affected by Vietnam and prison life. But lately, she has also heard me talking with the Lord in my sleep, laughing and conversing as if he was my best friend, right in the bedroom with me, which let us both know that I was getting better.

What a blessing has been mine, focusing on what society may consider its refuse, its human gar-

Michael Hines, Correctional Program Manager; Diana Hoiberg, CPM Secretary; Donna and Ron at Veteran's Day program, 2015 where Ron addressed those staff who were former military.

bage, its throw-away convicts, and with God's help redeeming their lives into something worthwhile that helps to grow His kingdom.

My story is really God's story. Jesus is the real hero. He's *my* hero. He's the one that saved me. I'm very thankful today that the Lord is doing a work in my life. He's not finished with me yet nor will He be until I have drawn my last breath.

One day, loud and clear, I heard the question voiced in Isaiah 6:8: "Whom shall I send?" And I gave the same response: "Here I am, Lord. Use me. Send me."

He's been doing just that ever since.

Above: Chaplain Jakstas; faithful volunteer Mily Boone who has been going into Larch for about 12 years with us; Robert Keller; Milt Alvarez that ministers in prisons all over the world; Ron and Donna; and Mel Novak, who is currently a movie star, skid row and prison chaplain for 29 years all over the USA. He is a favorite speaker at Larch and lives in LA. These inmates are some of our most faithful serious attendees.

I would love to hear from you, especially if anything I have said has helped you in any way. You may reach either Donna or me at donnaronb@comcast.net.

If you enjoyed this book, I would also appreciate it if you would take a moment and leave your comments at createspace.com as well as amazon.com. Thank you very much

Sincerely in Christ,

P.S. Be on the lookout for Donna's memoir in 2017.

Ron and Donna Brandon

BIBLIOGRAPHY

- "Anniversaries: The Waltons," *The Oregonian*, Sept. 1, 1984.w
- "Arcata woman arraigned for embezzlement, theft," The (Eureka) Times Standard, July 17, 1975.
- "Arrest Made in Burglary," *Marin Independent-Journal*, Sept. 13, 1973.
- Brandon, Donna Schafte, Oral history interview, Vancouver, Wash., May 26, 2015.
- Brandon, Forrest, written recollections, 2015.
- Brandon, Forrest, Oral history interview, Vancouver, Wash., April 26, 2015.
- Brandon, Ronnie Fayell, Oral history interview, Vancouver, Wash., March 26, 2015; April 1, 2015; April 2, 2015; April 10, 2015; April 13, 2015.
- Brandon, Ronnie Fayell, Testimony before Clark County Full Gospel Business Men's Fellowship, March 30, 2015.
- "Clark County Veterans Assistance Center reaches out to those who served," *The Columbian*, May 6, 2011.
- Fulkerson, Norman J. *An American Knight: The Life of Colonel John W. Ripley, USMC*. The American Society for the Defense of Tradition, Family and Property; 1 edition (October 25, 2009)
- "Guilty Plea Made to Reduced Charge," *Marin Independent-Journal*, Oct. 12, 1973.
- Hodge, Lt. G. Gustave "Gus" and Cpl. David Schwirian, *Navy Medicine*, March-April 2006. "Tiger in the Night," Oral history. http://www.gruntfixer.net/Guide/Ripley's%20Raiders/Purple%20Heart%20Log/Tiger%20in%20the%20Night.htm
- Hoppy, Doc, assembler. *Lima 3/3 Unit Diary, 12/29/1966-01/26/1968, 3/3 Unit Diary Pages, Specific to: PFC Ronnie F. Brandon USMC.*

- "Innocent Plea to Burglary Charge," *Marin Independent-Journal*, Sept. 22, 1973.
- Jewett, Russell J., assembler, *Ripley's Raiders Vietnam Chronicles*. Xlibris. Kindle Edition. 2013.
- Jones, Tricia, Special event will honor veterans honor guard," *The Columbian*, July 2, 2001.
- Laatz, Joan, "Inmates sue over conditions," *The Oregonian*, Aug. 13, 1986.
- "Man Arrested in Robbery of Gas Station," *Van Nuys (Calif.) News*, Dec. 25, 1969.
- Middlewood, Erin, "Spending process for veterans fund sparks a dispute," *The Columbian*, Oct. 16, 2003.
- Parke, Ed, *Jailhouse Religion: One Man's True Story*, Breaking Free Ministries, Vancouver, Wash., 2013.
- "Probation Given in Burglary," *Marin Independent-Journal*, Dec. 11, 1973.
- Prophetic Commission over Ron and Donna Brandon, City Harvest Church, 2014?
- Rice, Stephanie, "Veterans organization raising funds to open drop-in center in March," *The Columbian*, Feb. 22, 2011.
- Ripley, USMC Col. John W. "Tiger Bite Tale," http://l33namvets.com/Vietnam_tiger_bite_tale.htm
- "Sentences on Burglary Given Out," *Marin Independent-Journal,* Sept. 24, 1973.
- "Three Sentenced in Burglaries," *Marin Independent-Journal*, Dec. 17, 1973.
- Vogt, Tom, "Ministry lends a hand to veterans," *The Columbian*, April 27, 2003.

- "Washington County honors Vietnam War veterans in ceremony," *The Oregonian*, Nov. 11, 2014.
- Court records
    - Clark County Superior Court, Washington
    - Cowlitz County Superior Court, Washington
    - Hood River County District Court, Oregon
    - Humboldt County Superior Court, California
    - Skamania County Superior Court, Washington
    - Sonoma County Superior Court, California
    - Los Angeles County Superior Court, California
    - Santa Rosa County Superior Court, California
- Department of Corrections records, California
- Hood River News articles from 1984 to 1987
- Holy Bible, New International Version®, NIV® Copyright ©1973, 1978, 1984, 2011 by Biblica, Inc.® All rights reserved worldwide.

Ron and Donna –Valentines!

APPENDIX I

Interesting Thoughts and Facts About Vietnam Vets

For over twenty-five years, I, like many Vietnam veterans, seldom spoke of Vietnam, except with other veterans, when training soldiers, and in public speeches. These past sixteen years have found me joining the hundreds of thousands who believe it is high time the truth be told about the Vietnam War and the people who served there. It's time the American people learn that the United States military did not lose the war, and that a surprisingly high number of people who claim to have served there, in fact, DID NOT.

As Americans support the men and women involved in the War on Terrorism, the mainstream media are once again working tirelessly to undermine their efforts and force a psychological loss or stalemate for the United States. We cannot stand by and let the media do to today's warriors what they did to us forty years ago.

Below are some assembled facts most readers will find interesting. It isn't a long read, but it will (I guarantee) teach you some things you did not know about the Vietnam War and those who served, fought, or died there. Please share it with those with whom you communicate.

Vietnam War Facts assembled by Captain Marshal Hanson, U.S.N.R. (Retired) and Captain Scott Beaton, Statistical Source (Facts, Statistics, Fake Warrior Numbers, and Myths Dispelled):

- 2,709,918 Americans served in uniform in Vietnam
- 58,148 were killed in Vietnam
- Average age of men killed: 23.1 years
- 97% of Vietnam Veterans were honorably discharged
- 91% of Vietnam Veterans say they are glad they served.
- 87% of Americans hold Vietnam Veterans in high esteem.
- Over half of the Vietnam vets have died since the war. 1,250,000 are still here as of 2015.
- An average of 123 Vietnam Vets died daily in 2015.
- Isolated atrocities committed by American Soldiers produced torrents of outrage from anti-war critics and the news media while Communist atrocities were so common that they received hardly any media mention at all. The US sought to minimize and prevent attacks on civilians while North Vietnam made attacks on civilians a centerpiece of its strategy. Americans who deliberately killed civilians received prison sentences while Communists who did so received commendations. From 1957 to 1973, the National Liberation Front from North Vietnam assassinated 36,725 Vietnamese and abducted another 58,499. The death squads focused on leaders at

the village level and on anyone who improved the lives of the peasants such as medical personnel, social workers, and school teachers.

- Myth: The common belief is that the domino theory was proved false. Fact: The domino theory was accurate. The ASEAN (Association of Southeast Asian Nations) countries (Philippines, Indonesia, Malaysia, Singapore, and Thailand) stayed free of Communism because of the U.S. commitment to Vietnam. The Indonesians threw the Soviets out in 1966 because of America's commitment in Vietnam. Without that commitment, Communism would have swept all the way to the Malacca Straits that is south of Singapore and of great strategic importance to the free world. If you ask people who live in these countries who won the war in Vietnam, they have a different opinion from the American news media. The Vietnam War was the turning point against Communism.

- Myth: The common belief is that the fighting in Vietnam was not as intense as in World War II. Fact: The average infantryman in the South Pacific during World War II saw about 40 days of combat within four years. The average infantryman in Vietnam saw about 240 days of combat in one year thanks to the mobility of the helicopter.

- Myth: The United States lost the war in Vietnam. Fact: The American military was not defeated in Vietnam. The American military did not lose a battle of any consequence. From a military standpoint, it was almost an unprecedented performance according to General Westmoreland quoting Douglas Pike, a professor at the University of California, Berkley, "A major defeat for the VC and NVA."

- The United States did not lose the war in Vietnam, the South Vietnamese did. The fall of Saigon happened 30 April 1975, two years AFTER the American military left Vietnam. The last American troops departed in their entirety 29 March 1973. How could we lose a war we had already stopped fighting? We fought to an agreed stalemate. The peace settlement was signed in Paris on 27 January 1973. Thanks for the perceived loss and the countless assassinations and torture visited upon Vietnamese, Laotians, and Cambodians goes mainly to the American media and their undying support by misrepresentation of the anti-war movement in the United States.

- As with much of the Vietnam War, the news media misreported and misinterpreted the 1968 Tet Offensive. In actuality, the Tet Offensive resulted in a major defeat for the Communist forces on all fronts. 45,000 NVA troops died and the Tet Offensive accomplished a complete destruction of the Viet Cong elements in South Vietnam. But according to the news media and the political arena, the Tet offensive was a disaster.

APPENDIX II
Post-Traumatic Stress Disorder

It was hard to avoid the nightmares as I recalled the vivid details of combat service and prison. They were always present but exhibited different PTSD symptoms like anxiety, anger or irritability as in the chart below:

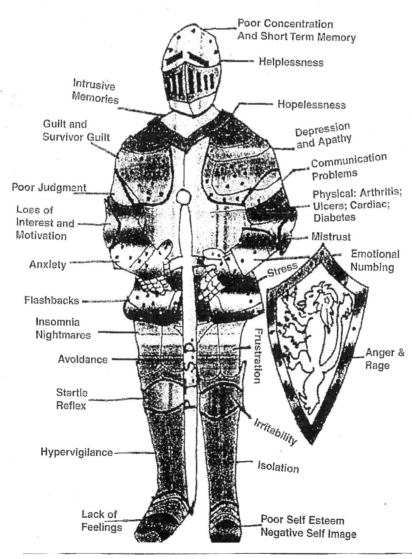

APPENDIX III
More on PTSD with Audie Murphy

Audie Murphy, one of America's most decorated war heroes (World War II) and Medal of Honor recipient, had severe PTSD or Post-Traumatic Stress Disorder. This condition lasted all of his life. He would sleep with a loaded gun under his pillow wherever he was.

Audie was an actor for over 20 years, making mostly good westerns. He made various commercials, appeared on TV, and spoke at many public events all through his life. However, he would not make any alcohol or cigarette commercials, not wanting to be a bad example to youth.

His PTSD brought on his abuse of sleeping pills and alcohol, and he was addicted to gambling, high stakes gambling, the adrenalin rush…and died in a 1971 airplane crash in terrible weather.

When Audie died, he was practically destitute, having gone through nearly all of his funds from all the movies and celebrity work. Fortunately, his wife won a law suit over the plane crash and received 2.5 million. She worked for the VA for over 35 years, earning a living, and as a volunteer, who really cared for the veterans.

PTSD is very real, and can be very devastating. Many men who have gone to war, such as Audie Murphy and Ron Brandon, have had to deal with the destructive symptoms and driving forces of this affliction. So do not be so quick to say 'it's just a weakness' because it is not! Some of the bravest, most heroic men who ever lived, have suffered in one form or the other from PTSD, including Captain John Ripley, Ron's commander during his tour of duty in Vietnam. Alexander the Great, valiant warrior King, and Greek General, who conquered the known world, died of alcoholism (self-medication) and other illnesses as well as from old battle wounds. Drugs and alcohol were used, and still are used to attempt to ease the pain and symptoms of PTSD. However, there is deliverance without having to use or abuse. There is a way out! Do not harm yourself! Contact Ron if you need help! He will gladly talk to you about how to get free!

donnaronb@comcast.net or www.asmolderingwick.com

APPENDIX IV

The Whole Armor of God

Memorizing relevant scriptures helped me put on my armor quickly.

Helmet Of Salvation
Put on the mind of Christ
(Phil. 2:5; I Peter 4:1; I Thess. 5:8)

Breastplate of Righteousness
The Righteousness of Christ
(II Cor. 5:21; I Thess. 5:8)

Belt / Gospel of Truth
Putting on the Truth, Integrity and Holiness of Christ Jesus
(Luke 12:35; Isaiah 11:5)

Shield of Faith
ABOVE ALL means paramount
(I John 5:4; Romans 13:12)

Sword of the Spirit
Offensive and defensive weapon
(Hebrews 4:12)

Sandals / Gospel of Peace
(Isaiah 52:7, Ephesians 6:15)

THEREFORE TAKE THE WHOLE ARMOR OF GOD, THAT YOU MAY BE ABLE TO WITHSTAND IN THE EVIL DAY, AND HAVING DONE ALL, TO STAND.
EPHESIANS 6:13 (RSV)

APPENDIX V

Eutychus Housing Article from The Columbian

Religion and military rules are tools used to rebuild shattered lives

By TOM VOGT
Columbian staff writer

They are no longer in uniform, but they still have a fight ahead of them. This time the enemy is homelessness, a bottle or a criminal record.

And they have an ally. A Vancouver group, Eutychus Ministries, is opening up a housing center in the Fruit Valley area to help troubled veterans make the transition to civilian life. Fourteen or 15 veterans eventually will occupy the pair of duplexes at West 31st and Thompson streets.

The center was dedicated Saturday. Special guests included Rep. Brian Baird, D-Vancouver, Mayor Royce Pollard and Lance Cpl. Ty Shaw, a Longview Marine who was wounded in Iraq. Shaw's left leg took shrapnel from a mortar burst on March 26. He is in a wheelchair after surgery, but it could have been worse, the 20-year-old Marine said: "Another guy in the same fire fight lost his hand."

There are other perils for those who have served their country, said Ron Brandon, executive director and chaplain of Eutychus Ministries.

"People go through things in their lives," said Brandon, a former U.S. Marine.

Some of the veterans they work with have been released from prison or jail. Some are unemployed, and most are broke, Brandon said.

In addition to providing transitional housing, Brandon said the group also will offer job-placement and family-support services for veterans, as well as something else: structure.

The rear bumper of Brandon's Dodge pickup, parked in front of one of the duplexes recently, hinted at the ministry's joint mission. One bumper sticker read: "Real Men Pray." Another sticker proclaimed: "Semper Fi!"

Christian values and military organization will be the guiding principals of the center, Brandon said. Drugs, alcohol, weapons, theft, violence or threats mean automatic expulsion; regular church attendance, 12-step meetings, group fellowship and house Bible study are mandatory.

All residents are expected to find full-time employment or schooling, or find so-

EUTYCHUS, page C5

EUTYCHUS MINISTRIES

■ **MISSION:**
Veterans helping veterans

■ **NAME:**
Greek for "good fortune"

■ **CONTACT:**
360-721-4310

Continued on next page

Eutychus:

From page C1

cial-service support. Housing fee is $290 a month.

Dan Hoober will provide supervision as the center's on-site manager.

The ministry sought the approval of the Fruit Valley Neighborhood Association before opening the center.

"I was torn in two directions," said Lee McCallister, chairman of the neighborhood association. "I'm a vet myself, and I want to help my brother veterans, wholeheartedly. But I must protect my neighborhood."

McCallister said he thinks the veterans' center can do some good in Fruit Valley.

"They cleaned up the property and promised to be a part of the neighborhood," McCallister said.

Not all of Fruit Valley's current residents would be willing to abide by the ministry's guidelines. So 14 or 15 men who agree to follow a strict code of conduct would be a good influence.

"We're hoping these guys will see what's going on and help us out," McCallister said. "We help them, and they help us."

A turnaround is possible, say both Brandon and Hoober.

After serving 10 years in the Army, "I was partying hard," Hoober said.

Brandon said he was "seriously messed up" after his Marine hitch. He walks a bit stiffly after a series of motorcycle crashes, but he was able to get his life straight in 1992 after accepting Christ, he said.

And they're not the only veterans who can attest to the possibility of a turnaround.

"I'm a recovering alcoholic; I have been for 22 years," said McCallister, chairman of the neighborhood association. "You can build credibility back. I don't hide the fact I've done these things. But we can overcome it."

APPENDIX VI
Newspaper Article on U.S. Rep. Brian Baird regarding Eutychus Ministries.

Baird to speak at dedication for veterans housing

Brian Baird

The Columbian

U.S. Rep. Brian Baird and Vancouver Mayor Royce Pollard will speak at the dedication of a transitional housing development for veterans Saturday at West 31st and Thompson Streets.

During the event, Baird, D-Vancouver, will present Blue Star Service Banners to the families of local men and women currently stationed abroad in the armed forces.

Representatives from more than a dozen local veteran service organizations will attend.

The veterans housing complex will be administered by Eutychus Ministries Incorporated, a faith-based nonprofit organization that began operation in 2000 to help veterans with their transition into the community.

Vets admitted may be recovering from illness, may have been homeless or may have had difficulty finding employment, said Matthew Beck, a spokesman for Baird.

The services include housing, counseling, education, job training and religious workshops.

This is the third property in the Vancouver-Portland area that EMI has acquired and refurbished to house local veterans.

APPENDIX VII
Volunteer of the Year Nomination

VOLUNTEER OF THE YEAR NOMINATI

Nominee Name	Work Site
Rev. Ron Brandon and Donna Schafte-Brandon	Larch Corrections Center

Please provide first name, middle initial, and last name. Print legibly and ensure correct spelling.

PLEASE SELECT ONLY **ONE** CATEGORY PER NOMINATION FORM – See below for criteria.

 Community Corrections Division   Prisons Division

JUSTIFICATION NARRATIVE:
(Describe in detail the accomplishments during the previous year which qualify the nominee for the award category indicated above. One additional sheet may be attached).

To Whom It May Concern;

I would like to nominate two LCC Volunteers Rev. Ron Brandon and Donna Schafte-Brandon (husband & wife) with Unchained Prison Ministries.

I'm new with DOC and I only met Ron and Donna on a few occasions, but what I saw and how I felt about them is more tha enough to nominate them as Volunteers of the year. They are truly loving, caring people, committed to God and to their ministry with indisputable believe for the second chance.

I am proud that we have Ron and Donna on-board and I don't know what we would do without them.
I have never seen a volunteers work so tirelessly and for so long for a cause, and I encourage you to recognize Ron Brandon and Donna Schafte-Brandon with this great honor of Volunteers of the Year.

Please contact me with any follow up questions.

Sincerely,
Chaplain Zilvinas Jakstas

APPENDIX VIII
Prophetic Assembly 2015

PROPHETIC ASSEMBLY 2015
Ron and Donna Brandon

Charlie Sweet
Hallelujah. Hallelujah. Hi Ron. I'm the real Charlie. Donna. Hi. Glad to meet you. In Psalm...34 verse 17, it says, "The righteous cry and the Lord hears, and delivers them out of their troubles. The Lord is near the brokenhearted, and saves those who are crushed in the spirit." And when the Lord gave me your names—actually, Ron, I saw this big key ring on the side of your belt, and there's all kinds of keys, and I said what are those keys, and He says they open up jail cells. So... I believe that God uses the two of you in a mighty way where people are crushed and broken, and where society has given up on them, and, you know, I see—I'm gonna take it out of the world, and I'm gonna take it to the world of—you know, I went to Argentina once and they took us to this prison. And it was horrible, and all the time I was there I just wept and cried, and, you know, and it just broke my heart. And I believe that God has put—I saw you in uniforms. I saw the two of you around people with uniforms, but there was uniforms of authority, and there was uniforms of submission. And those uniforms are submission is where I saw the broken hearted and the crushed. And I believe that God is using the two of you to bring a light where no one else will bring a light. Where no one else wants to go, where society has said, "It's over with. It's finished. There's no second chance for them," but we know that we serve a God of more than a second chance. And I felt as I was praying over the two of you, I felt the Spirit of God all over you. I felt like, there is an anointing of the Holy Spirit upon you Ron, and I believe that God is gonna even give you greater favor in whatever you're doing. And I believe that, you know, sometimes I believe what the two of you do, it's tiring at times, and God is saying I'm gonna increase your army. I'm gonna give you more recruits, says the Lord your God. And know this, says the Lord your God, favor is coming. Favor is coming. I don't know who the governor of the state is, or what, but I'm telling you by the Spirit of God, I feel favor is coming your way that more doors are going to be opened—to you. Hallelujah. You're humble. You're meek-when it comes to what you are called to do in the Lord, but you are by no means bashful—when it comes to the things of the Lord. And man, I see you getting in people's faces. Now those people that are uniforms, I'm just gonna say it, I see you in jails and prisons, and all of these things, but I'm telling you that jailers are about to get set free, and they're gonna be set free, and who He sets free is free indeed. And I believe there's a particular couple of 'em that just—you just wanna lay hands on them and around their neck, it's not on their body. And I believe that God is gonna win them over. I believe, because of your steadfastness, because you have said, "I'm here because of you, Lord. I'm here because You have mandated me to be here. I am here because You have called me here, and if You don't do it, I can't do it." And God says get ready, Ron. I'm about to bust the jail cell doors open, says the Lord your God, and a wave of My Spirit is about to blow in, says the

Lord your God. It's never gonna be the same again. It's a new day, and it's a new hour. And I'm telling you, I feel favor's gonna come from the top-down into your life. And when that happens, you just keep plugging along. You're like the little engine that could, you know, chug-a chug-a chug-a chug-a chug-a chuga—because you know, sooner or later, you know the ending of this book. And because you know the ending, it doesn't bother you with the little steps in between. Don't worry. God's gonna make a way, and He's gonna make a way where there seems to be no way and where that real dry spot is right now that you're dealing with, God's gonna send a flood, and you're gonna laugh and step back and say, "This can only be my God."

Eric Butler
I just wanted to add this to, um, what pastor Charlie was saying. I see you as almost like a guy that, um, like a military person that served. And you have all these—I saw people in Naval outfits, that were around you, and you were like their general, and you were telling them you got to get this right. There a lot of young men. Get it right, get it right, and they were lining up and getting themselves into order. And God says even in your personal life, your family life, I saw God doing something with your children. And I saw each one of them, they were kind of sitting like this at first, and they were in different postures, and you did like this, "Let's go! Ten hut!" And they began to all step up like this, one, two, three, four, and they began to just step up and come into alignment because God says I'm gonna bring order and orchestration and right down the line, everything in your life, in the lineage is coming right into perfect alignment in this season, say the Lord. Says the Lord. You will resurrect, and what he was talking about, you will resurrect even people that are wayward. They're out there out to sea. They're out to sea, and you have an ability, you have a father's anointing and a mother's anointing to bring them together like bam. You clap your hands one time and you shake people up. You don't even realize it because you're so nice. You're so nice. And yet, when you look at people in their eyes, they feel the father, parental anointing upon you, and they start to line up and say, "Yes. I got it." God's getting ready to do it for you. It's gonna happen in your own family in a special way. It's gonna happen in the lives of all those you touch. Be blessed says the Lord.

Bob MacGregor
My only problem with your word, Eric, is she's nice. You don't call a Marine nice. You know, Ron's a—Ron's a Marine. You're never an ex-Marine, you're always a Marine. He wears Marine underwear, Marine socks—brushes his teeth with a Marine toothbrush. He has every Marine decal ever made on his car. You almost got me arrested—he gave me a Marine knife the other day. I put it in my backpack—forgot I put it in there. I went to the airport and I got caught in security. Big thing that could cut a lot of people's throats, you know. It was good—yah they kept it, Ron. Thank you. Thank you. I got it in my pocket—I will not put it in my backpack today. Amen, but you're prison ministry guys, they have restored a lot of people, and worked with prisoners when they come out,

and we just love 'em. Father, we bless this word over them. We just thank You for Ron and Donna. We thank You, Lord God, for their heart for people, for the broken, for those in prison. You said I was in prison and You came to me. Thank You that reflect the heart of Jesus. Just let this word continue to be fulfilled. Much fruit, Lord, in the days that lie ahead. In Jesus' name. Amen. Let's stand to our feet and worship.

Prophetic Assembly
March 2015
Ron and Donna Brandon

APPENDIX IX
Robert Lightfoot Smith's Testimony
Miraculously Healed of Hepatitis C

Dear Ron,

This is my testimony about my healing when you and Donna prayed for me on Sunday night. Not only my health has been restored but my faith as well. You see, I had a blood transfusion in my twenties. This is what led to Hepatitis C. I've had it for the past 35 years or so. I was given a short time to live by the doctors. I was very sick and looked like it too. I felt horrible, tired all the time.

Now I am healed! No trace of the disease! Blood tests have confirmed it is gone! I look better, and feel so much better and the doctors said I have the enzymes of a 30-year-old! I cannot thank you enough for praying for me. God is still in the miracle working business for sure. Your faithfulness is very evident and all of us inmates are so grateful for your love for us!

Thank you so much for 'anointing me with oil that night' according to the scriptures and laying your hands on me and praying such a prayer of faith. God used you to heal me; He healed me of course but He used you two. I will forever be thankful to you and to the Lord!

When I came back to prison I was a 'backslidden' Christian. I had accepted Christ before, but allowed my old life style to take me down again. Now my faith has been restored and I am determined to follow hard after the Lord who has healed me, who has given me another chance at life! Thank you and thank you City Harvest Church for Unchained Prison Ministry which has been coming in here for the past 16 years now. May God bless you! I love you all!

Robert Lightfoot Smith
DOC# 790200   Oct. 22, 2015

Robert Lightfoot Smith

APPENDIX X
Copy of Spoken Tribute to Ron and Donna by Larch Inmate

Hello to everyone, I'm Thomas Hill and even though I don't attend all the meetings, I would like to thank all the volunteers for being so faithful to us inmates. And due to your faithfulness most of us wont be called inmates any more. You all are making a difference in this world and changing lives! (Can we give them an hand.) I was blessed to speak on behalf of the guys here at LCC to acknowledge how thankful and blessed we are to have a group of people we call family. The winner's Circle and or unchained ministries. These individuals have a sincere love for us that continues beyond these confinements. Not only do they take time out of their busy lives in the community, to drive up this mountain in all weather conditions, but we are all in their daily prayers. That's genuine! They dont leave here and forget about us. These are the faithful people Jesus spoke of in Matthew 25:37-40. Thank You Kevin, Gleen, Milly, bob and all those that join this faithful group to bring the love of Christ to us by their example. And I, we, want to give a special thanks to the corner stone of this ministry, Ron & Donna. These two have put this team of believers together for us. Ron & Donna (You are my Spiritual Grandfather & Mother, full of wisdom. I've never left a meeting w.thout being filled with that wisdom knowledge and understanding that only comes from God's obedient children. Thank You Ron & Donna for being obedient through thick and thin. Because of You two I look forward to every Sunday afternoon. Always showing up with the intent to learn from role models I strive to be like.)

Continued next page.

There have been weeks I've been down or feeling condemned, and as faithful as always I could count on a healing coming every Sunday afternoon's. You two have been doing this ministry for over a decade and not only for us here at LCC but other prison's as well, even out of state. These thank You's from us at LCC are genuine and we love You all, for first loving us. But nothing will compare to when You all here, "Well done You good and faithful Servants." God Bless You all, Amen!

APPENDIX XI
Ron's Essay on the "Three Strikes You're Out" Law

Now, let's just imagine, for a moment, that the "Three Strikes You're Out" law was in effect in my time, which it wasn't, thank God!

I'd still be 'doing time' at taxpayer expense. I would have no new family like I do today. I wouldn't have the education I do today. Ordination as a minister would not have been possible. Twenty years of prison ministry would not have occurred. Thousands of men either introduced to Christ, or encouraged to return to Him, would have been left without hope. I would certainly not be a home owner, a business owner, nor would I have written this book. As a matter of fact, I'd have no life at all!

In my opinion, the "Three Strikes You're Out" law is pure lunacy, insanity. You cannot deal with men or women, human beings, like a silly baseball game! Statistics clearly demonstrate that the vast majority of 'criminals' stop doing crime at age fifty, and stop going to prison. Prisons are full of young people for the most part. Why pay the cost of continued incarceration, when it is clearly not necessary?

Do some criminals need to stay in prison forever? Yes! Do some criminals need to be executed? Yes. Some will never change. There are exceptions to the rules. But stripping judges and parole boards of the ability to judge, to evaluate, to make decisions about how to deal with human beings on an individual basis is total madness! Is it fair or rational that a starving homeless man who stole a twenty-dollar pizza for the third time be thrown into prison for the rest of his life?

Men can and do change! Most men can be taught, can be trained, can be helped. In many cases, healing is what is needed and when men are healed, they can change their behavior. So why on earth should we pay millions in tax money to keep them locked up? "Three Strikes You're Out" needs to be repealed, thrown out, like the garbage it is!